Contents

Introduction

This is a handbook of woodland management. It is intended to be used by conservation volunteers and others with an interest in maintaining or improving valuable habitats through manual work. By 'woodlands' is meant both the ancient woods – areas which have been under native tree cover at least since the year 1600 – and also the plantations, small coverts, scrubby thickets and other secondary woodlands which between them make up the majority of Britain's woods – both in number and total area. Also covered, though in less detail, are the trees of hedgerow and farm, suburb and city. In a country in which only about 8% of the land surface is wooded, these non-woodland trees have an amenity and often a wildlife importance out of all proportion to their numbers.

Once, much of Britain was forested. The history of man in this country is largely a story of woodland clearance. The few old woods that remain are hardly 'primeval', since they have been managed for many hundreds of years to provide coppice products or timber, or have been modified under centuries of grazing and browsing to become pasture-woodlands. Yet woods and trees retain a powerful hold on people's imaginations. Landscape design has for long been concerned with re-establishing woods and trees in patterns which seem 'right'. The outcry against hedgerow and woodland clearance and against the insensitive block-planting of conifers in the uplands, show the strong attachment many people have to the traditional landscape.

While people can if necessary adjust to landscape changes, wildlife, all too frequently, cannot. Much of Britain's wildlife is adapted to, and in some cases, dependent on, woodlands. Current changes in the type and distribution of woods are having important consequences for plants and animals. Planting of conifers and the regeneration of woodland on previously open areas have provided many new habitats, particularly for birds and small mammals – though often at the expense of valuable grassland, heathland and moorland habitat.

This is a time of great changes and great opportunities for woodlands in Britain. As detailed in the Forestry Commission's 'Policy for Broadleaves' (p18), there is increased importance being placed by the government on the planting and management of broadleaved woodland. Ancient semi-natural woodlands have been given protection, and the tax incentives which led to vast tracts of upland Britain being clothed in conifers have been removed. Agricultural surpluses have led to new thinking on uses for surplus farmland, of which one result is the Farm Woodland Scheme. This is being introduced in late 1988, with the aim of encouraging planting of 36,000 hectares of agricultural land in the following three years. To fulfill this aim presents a great challenge for suppliers of planting stock, contractors, volunteers, woodland managers and many others, as well as increased potential for the conversion and marketing of timber.

Nor are urban areas being left behind. Many towns and cities have their own organisations who are concerned with the 'greening' of urban areas, the 'Forest of London' project being one of many. The great storm of 1987 has been a reminder to people in the south east of the impermanence of mature trees and woods, and with it the great challenge of redesigning and replanting many wooded landscapes.

The ultimate success of these plans and opportunities will depend very much on those who do the practical work of planting, maintenance and management, which is where the voluntary movement, landowners and other individuals will play their part. The appeal of woodland work is immediate and long-lasting, from the nurturing of young trees through coppice management to the harvesting of mature trees. The aims are many – to create and maintain a diverse and interesting landscape, to learn and pass on traditional skills, to create and improve habitats for wildlife and havens for people.

1 A Look at Woodlands

The Original Forests

At the height of the Ice Age, most of Britain must have been bare of trees. Birch and willow scrub possibly persisted along the lower margins of the ice, with pine in places. It may even be that relics of the pre-glacial flora survived in sheltered bays along the western coasts of Great Britain and Ireland. But on the whole, ice swept the land clean as far as the south of England, where tundra conditions prevailed.

The development of Britain's post-glacial flora (Godwin, 1975) can be deduced from studies of pollen and seed deposits in peat and by means of radiocarbon dating. From about 8000 BC onwards, dwarf birch and willow spread slowly northward across the country, eventually followed by silver birch and hairy birch, Scots pine, hazel, and later, oak and elm. After the warming and drying trend of the Pre-Boreal and Boreal periods, the climate turned warm and wet in the Atlantic Period (5500–3000 BC), during which time alder became widespread and lime penetrated the English lowlands. Later, when the land bridges connecting Britain to the Continent and Ireland to Great Britain finally failed, and the sea level rose relative to the land, the natural immigration of trees into the country was restricted. After this time, it was man who was responsible for most further introductions, including such common European trees as spruce and sycamore, which readily became naturalised once they were brought to this country.

What was the natural woodland like, before man seriously interfered with its composition and structure? The map (based on Rackham, 1976, p42 and information from Dr Martin Ball) shows, as far as is known, the dominant species for around the time 3000 BC.

In the lowlands, small-leaved lime and oak flourished in combination with hazel and various other trees, such as pine in the East Anglian Breckland and ash in Somerset, to produce a number of regional woodland types which are still recognisable in the remaining fragments of ancient woods. Some species, such as yew and juniper, became widespread but remained very local in distribution. Others, such as beech, hornbeam, whitebeam, wild service tree, maple and a few broadleaved trees grew in the South, but made slow progress northward due to climatic restrictions or the fact that they were late arrivals into the country. Some of these, notably beech, plus ash, elm and holly were aided in their spread by human activity, whilst others, such as the wild service tree, never became common. The forests were dominated by shade-tolerant species, whilst others survived as initial colonisers in gaps in the forest, at the extremes of soil and climate, and at shores, lake edges and inland cliffs.

Man's impact may have begun as early as Mesolithic times (8000–4000 BC), when the higher parts of Dartmoor and the North York Moors were cleared, and some of the southern heaths were created. However, it was the Neolithic farmers, from around 4000 BC, who made widespread clearances of the limestone and chalk uplands of the south and midlands, the coastal lowlands of Pembrokeshire and Anglesey, and the southern Pennines.

Other factors were also altering the prehistoric forests. Elm experienced a widespread decline around 3000 BC, perhaps in part because of its use as fodder, but more probably due to climatic change or to an outbreak of disease. The cool, wet Sub-Atlantic Period, beginning about 700 BC, saw the encroachment of bog over great areas of pine and birch forest, remains of which may still be found buried in peat far above the present limits of tree growth. Those pine forests which still survive in Scotland probably originated prior to the Sub-Atlantic Period, and have maintained themselves on the more porous soils and in the less wet regions ever since (Tansley, 1939, p166).

From around 400 BC, Celtic peoples arrived with iron tools and stronger ploughs capable of tilling heavy clay soils. The population remained sparse

Dominant species 3000 BC

Oak and small-leaved lime

Oak and hazel

Hazel and elm

Birch and pine

Birch and willow

Ash

No information

6

right through Romano-British and Anglo–Saxon times, but forest settlement gradually progressed until the natural woodland, at least in England, became split into discrete blocks isolated by cultivated or grazed fields. By the time the Normans arrived, this process was far advanced. Oliver Rackham (pers. comm.) suggests that woodland covered perhaps 15% of England in 1086, or about twice the woodland area of England today.

Such further loss of woods as occurred in the late medieval period was mainly associated with lowland clearances made before 1350. Between the time of the Domesday Survey (1086) and the Black Death (1348–50) the population more than doubled. The remaining forested 'waste' – which was in fact more often than not a valuable manorial asset – was a tempting place to start new farms. This process of 'assarting' was cut short by the plague; whole villages were abandoned in the late 14th century, and there was some return of 'tumbled down' farmland to secondary woods, a process which has tended to occur ever since in times of agricultural depression.

From earliest times in Britain, woodland – as opposed to agricultural – needs were fulfilled not by the felling of new areas of forest but by the periodic harvesting of managed coppice plots (Rackham, 1976). Coppicing allowed the natural deciduous woodland to survive, in modified form, despite its exploitation for fuel, timber and other necessities of medieval and post-medieval growth. The wide–held belief that woodlands were cleared for charcoal, fuelwood for brick and lime kilns and for tanbark is erroneous. In fact, these demands sustained the coppice woodlands, and it was with their demise that clearance increased (Evans, 1984, p2).

Woods where grazing was important tended to evolve along different lines, into pasture woodlands. The English woods came into general coppice or pasture-woodland management by the 13th century, with the Welsh woods following a little later. In Scotland and Ireland, patches of virgin forest survived longer, and systematic coppicing was slow to be introduced. Part of the Speyside pinewoods apparently escaped felling, and perhaps grazing, until the 17th century, although most of the Highland forests had experienced at least one episode of felling by this time (Steven and Carlisle, 1959).

PRIMARY AND SECONDARY WOODLAND

The terms 'primary' and 'secondary' as applied to a piece of woodland describe the site, but not the type of woods nor the age of the trees. Primary woodland describes a site which as far as is known has been continuously wooded since primaeval times. In Britain, any such woods have been greatly altered by management, grazing and other factors. Secondary woodland describes a site which can be proved to have not been continuously wooded, but where woods have grown up or been planted at some stage. Secondary woodlands are not necessarily recent, and

may be woods that grew up following clearance by the Romans, and have been in existence ever since.

The distinction is not a clear one in practice, as primary sites may not be possible to identify for certain, although undisturbed soils may indicate this. Very old secondary woodlands may be indistinguishable from primary woodlands. In practice, an easier distinction is between ancient and recent woodlands. Ancient is taken to mean any woods that were in existence before 1600, which is about the time from which maps are available, allowing the history of any woodland site to be traced. Planting of woods did not really start until after 1600, so that woods from before that time are likely to be closely linked to the original forest cover. Thus, though not strictly synonymous, 'primary' and 'ancient' woodland can be used to describe existing woods that were in existence before 1600, and are the nearest descendants that we have of the original forest. Most ancient secondary woods, unless isolated geographically from any primary woods, are likely to be very similar to the original forest. 'Ancient semi-natural woodland' is the accepted term used to describe an ancient woodland site which supports indigenous broadleaved woodland flora and fauna.

What remains of the original forests? In an unaltered form, probably nothing. Even Wistman's Wood on Dartmoor 'has a chequered history and has much increased within living memory' (Rackham, 1976, p64). Other 'near-natural' remnants include the Birkrigg and Keskadale oakwoods of the Lake District, parts of the New Forest, the Black Wood of Rannoch, Rothiemurchus Forest, Glen Affric and other Caledonian Forest fragments. Some of these woods are inaccessible or on land not worth converting to pasture or agriculture, although casual grazing has often modified their structure and restricted their regeneration. Other woods of precipitous hillsides, such as Floodbrook Clough in Cheshire, have seen rather more felling, but retain a more natural structure because grazing and other pressures have been less extreme. These woods may teach us much about the persistence of vestigial forest under extreme conditions, but they can hardly reveal widespread or characteristic features of the ancient natural woodland.

The natural history of British woodlands is therefore closely linked to the history of their exploitation and management. Although woods can be classified by ecological type, an appreciation of the different types of management systems is vital for understanding how the present woodland cover developed. These different management systems are described below.

Coppice Woodlands

'Coppice' comes from the French word couper, to cut. Coppices or 'copses' are woodlands cut on a fairly short rotation of seven to twenty-five years. In most cases, one part of the wood, called a 'coupe', is harvested each year. The coppice trees and their produce are known as 'underwood'. Underwood species, all deciduous, respond to cutting by sending up multiple stems from the stools. Periodic cutting actually extends the life of most underwood trees, so that coppiced ash stools, for example, may be hundreds of years old and contain a record of a sizeable proportion of the wood's management in their annual rings.

The practice of coppicing can be traced back to Neolithic times (4000 BC). Archaeological evidence shows that coppice products were used for numerous rural needs throughout the Bronze, Roman and Saxon periods, and by the 13th century, documents begin to describe restrictions on common rights to the coppice woods and the fencing of woodlands against casual grazing. Coppicing was the most widespread method of woodland management until the mid 1800s.

One-year regrowth of hazel coppice

This long history of coppicing is the reason why ancient coppice woodlands can be seen as the direct descendants of the original forest. It is perhaps a paradox that a coppiced wood, with a structure which looks least like one's idea of the ancient natural forest, is the one that is biologically closest to it. Early man no doubt 'discovered' coppicing by experience – by cutting down a manageable size tree, and then finding that it sent up many stems which could be cut again a few years later. It is unlikely that trees were planted for this purpose, or that any particular selection of species was made. Even in the late 18th century, it is recorded that 'the underwood was not carefully selected and planted; the production of it, both in quantity and quality was, for the most part left to chance' (Peterken, 1981, p21). In some places coppices were 'improved' through encouraging the valuable species by layering, planting and natural regeneration, to fill any gaps where old stools died. Unwanted shrubs and invasive species such as birch were sometimes removed to favour the desirable species. However, the general pattern of species remained very close to the natural cover, as these practices only slightly altered the existing composition, and did not bring in new species from

elsewhere. Planting only became commonplace in the improvement era from the late 18th to the late 19th centuries.

The ecological classification of woodland by stand type (see p22) is based on observation of existing ancient coppice woodlands, being closest to the natural woodland cover. To quote Peterken; 'The significance of coppice management for ecologists can hardly be exaggerated. Most ancient woods have been managed as coppice for most of the last one thousand years, leaving a legacy of semi-natural woodlands upon which our knowledge of the natural climax vegetation of Britain is founded' (Peterken, 1981, p17).

The system of 'coppice with standards' is also ancient, with records of felling dating from the 1200s. Under this system, some trees are grown as standards, with the coppice beneath (see p35). During the reign of Henry VIII, there was a legal requirement that at least 30 standards per hectare (12 per acre) be grown, but at other times numbers varied greatly, according to the demand. Periods of felling occurred during time of war, as well as after the Dissolution and during the Commonwealth.

Oak was by far the most abundant standard tree, although other species such as ash were occasionally allowed free growth. Every soil type and region had characteristic combinations of coppice species, since the woodmen depended on the 'natural growth of the soil' for the supply of underwood. These included hazel and ash on the Midland clays, beech and sessile oak on western sandstone and lime in central Lincolnshire (Peterken, 1975, p4). Hornbeam and sweet chestnut (a Roman introduction) grew widely in the South East, while local or minor underwood species included whitebeam, wild cherry, crab apple, maple and elm. Some underwood trees were particularly suited to specialised uses, and as time went on there was a certain amount of selection in favour of these. But most coppice remained mixed, to serve a wide variety of needs.

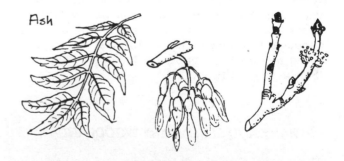

Ash

In the uplands, sessile oak was by far the most common species and dominated both the underwood and canopy of the coppiced woodland. Where conditions were difficult, standards grew too slowly and erratically to be worth fostering, so 'scrub oak' coppice without standards developed. Much of this was used for tanbark or charcoal.

The standards were generally felled when small, compared to modern practice, with few being left longer than three times the coppice rotation. Nothing was wasted in the traditional coppice system, with even the 'loppium et chippium' bundled or bagged and sold for firewood.

From the late 18th century, coppicing began to decline. One reason for this was the increased demand for larger timber (mainly for ship-building) and the consequent attractions of the plantation system. Many landowners greatly increased the density of oak in their coppice woods through supplementary planting, although much of this was never harvested. In the Chilterns, coppice working as well as pasture-woodland management declined through the encouragement of naturally regenerated beech for the furniture industry. From the mid 19th century, some of the most important traditional uses of coppice products diminished as coke and coal replaced charcoal and firewood for fuel, and artificial substitutes replaced tanbark in the leather industry. In addition, the general agricultural decline of the mid and late 19th century meant that less hazel was needed for sheep hurdles and other farm products.

Active commercial coppicing survives, mainly south of the Thames and in East Anglia, but the only really successful form is sweet chestnut coppice for fences and pulp. Being alien, this species is of less value for wildlife than other coppice trees, but even so supports a good bryophyte flora and is attractive to many bird species, including the nightjar. Ash and hazel are still worked commercially on a local scale, while a small amount of tanbark is harvested in Cornwall. Since the early 1970s, particularly with the increased use of wood-burning stoves, and demand for thatching spars, commercial coppicing has experienced a modest revival.

Pasture-Woodlands

Pasture-woodlands are woods in which grazing or browsing has played an important part in the use of the land. They include wooded commons, winter-grazed woods, Forests and chases, and parks (Rose and Harding, 1978). Some pasture-woodlands developed through centuries of use by domestic stock. Wherever cattle, sheep or, to a lesser extent, pigs, were allowed access, palatable tree species such as elm and ash were at a disadvantage. Only during periods of reduced grazing pressure, such as during agricultural depression, or where protected by thorn bushes or enclosures could new seedlings survive. Elsewhere, the woods were gradually reduced to grassland under a scattering of mature trees, with little or no natural regeneration. Such new growth as occurred was frequently of oak, a relatively unpalatable plant.

Trees intermixed with pasture had a number of advantages for traditional farming communities. They provided shade and shelter for livestock. Their branches could be pollarded at 2–3m (6–10′) above ground level, out of reach of grazing animals, to provide winter fodder or to produce many of the same woodland products as coppice underwood.

Sometimes the trees were left to grow up for timber, or even 'shredded' by repeatedly cutting off the side branches, leaving a tuft at the top, a practice still commonly seen in Brittany.

Pollarding, like coppicing, reinvigorates certain species of broadleaved tree and prolongs their lives. Even when pollarding ceases, these trees are likely to live on despite retrenchment, when branches die back to remain as 'stag's heads', or even partial decay. Many surviving pollards are 300 to 500 years old. These old trees, worthless and 'senile' from the point of view of timber production, are important for the habitats they provide for lichens, bryophytes, the specialised invertebrates of dead or dying wood, and for hole-nesting birds. This rich arboreal wildlife is in marked contrast to the generally impoverished ground flora beneath. Few woodland shrubs and herbs survive browsing and trampling. The only widespread 'understorey' shrubs tend to be plants such as holly, which is relatively inedible, or yew, which is poisonous and usually avoided.

Some trees of woodland-pasture were grown for timber rather than pollarded. These trees tended to develop relatively short, thick trunks, with widely radiating crowns above the reach of grazing animals. With such short lengths of clear timber in the stems, these trees are poorly suited to today's planking and milling technology, but in earlier times they were used in ship-building, and in roofing churches and other large buildings.

Wooded commons with pollards are a feature of lowland Britain, while winter-grazed woodlands are typical of parts of the hilly North and West. These are woods where domestic stock are enclosed, or where sheep and deer are allowed free access from the adjacent uplands during the winter months. The remaining fragments of native Highland pine and birchwoods are of this type (Peterken, 1977a, p230) and in some Highland areas the seasonal migration from open moor to sheltered wood is essential to the grazing economy.

Deer have a profound effect on pasture-woodland where they have been allowed to flourish, in particular in many of the 'Forests', which originated as hunting areas in Saxon times and were taken over and extended by the Norman kings. 'Forest' was a purely legal term that meant a tract of land where certain rules applied, regardless of the vegetation.

By the mid 13th century, when records of individual Forests become plentiful, they had become adapted to several important purposes in addition to the production of venison. These included grazing of farm animals, and the production of timber and underwood, for which the rights belonged either to commoners or to private individuals (Rackham, 1976, p155). Different Forests, even within the same locality, evolved very differently depending on the uses to which they were put.

The later history of the Forests was generally one of waning royal interest, with brief periods of attempted revival. Common rights and the old systems of verderers courts often survived into the 18th and 19th centuries, although now only the Forest of Dean, the New Forest and Epping Forest are much affected. More important today is the influence of the Forestry Commission on those Crown-owned areas which it has taken over, and the varying pressures of forestry and recreation on the management of each area.

'Parks', or 'policies' as they are known in Scotland, are enclosures for semi-wild animals. They came into vogue under the Normans to contain herds of fallow deer, an introduced species. There were, and still are, a few parks for red deer and semi-wild white cattle, and in medieval times there were also hare-parks for rabbits and swine-parks for wild boar (Rackham, 1976, p143). Medieval parks usually had a characteristic compact outline with rounded corners to save fencing costs. Often they contained both woods and pastures, but unless they were protected the former tended to evolve into the latter, from the effect of grazing and browsing. Because of the costs of fencing, small or irregularly shaped parks tended to disappear or revert to coppiced woodland. The larger parks were often better maintained and many were remodelled by the landscape designers of the 17th and 18th centuries to make our finest landscape parks.

Pasture-woodlands faced considerable pressures in the 18th and 19th centuries, especially from enclosure-hungry landowners who were often able to divest commoners of their remaining rights and convert the areas to arable or forestry plantations. Rackham (1976) traces the destruction of a number of commons and Forests which, unlike the relatively compact parks, tend to have straggling outlines which were readily fragmented. Most surviving examples of ancient wooded commons occur in the Weald, the Chilterns, Dorset and Wiltshire, and some of these are now protected under the Commons Registration Act of 1965. These are distinct in type and interest from the many newly wooded grass or heathland commons, where trees have grown up due to the ending of grazing and the post-myxomatosis decline of rabbit populations. Unlike the ancient wooded commons, the latter have little to offer in the way of specialised old-tree habitats (Rose and Harding, 1978, p6).

Among the surviving Forests, only the New Forest contains large areas of pasture-woodland, while on a smaller scale, Hatfield Forest in Essex still retains most of its medieval elements in working order.

On the whole, parks have fared rather better than commons and Forests. Good examples include Moccas in Herefordshire, Staverton in East Suffolk, and Sutton Coldfield, miraculously preserved in the midst of Birmingham. Few of the 16th and 17th century parks survive in anything like their original form.

Pasture-woodlands may be in for a revival under the modern name of 'agroforestry'. The aim of this system is to grow widely spaced trees in grazed pastureland, producing individual trees of high quality timber, whilst at the same time maintaining income from the grazed stock. This is one of many techniques for alternative land-use being investigated as food surpluses force changes in farming methods. Agroforestry is well-established in New Zealand, and research is now being undertaken by the Forestry Commission together with Long Ashton Research Station, as well as the Universities of Edinburgh and Bangor, to assess its potential for the UK.

Plantations

By the early 17th century, some landowners were beginning to look beyond traditional methods of woodland management for new ways to supply Britain's increasingly diverse and complex timber needs. It was at this time that the first English book on forestry appeared, and by 1664, when John Evelyn's influential work 'Silva' was published, the 'great plantation movement' was well underway.

The plantings of the 17th–19th centuries were marked by considerable experimentation as to the choice of species. Oak dominated most plantations, partly due to the rather misplaced emphasis given by Evelyn and later writers to the need to supply oak for shipping. Beech was also planted extensively, even though its use was limited to interior work, furniture, coachwork and handles. Ash was widely grown, as its tough elastic wood was needed for tool handles, oars, cart shafts and other special purposes. Elm, used for drainpipes, coffins and ships' keels, was seldom planted except in hedgerows where it soon spread by suckering to provide plenty of big trees. Spanish or sweet chestnut was grown as coppice for paling fences, props and poles or, with rather variable success, as a timber tree which produced edible nuts. Sycamore was particularly used for shelter belts, and often replaced beech as an amenity and forest tree in harsh and exposed conditions.

Aside from a few early introductions, including sweet chestnut and sycamore, exotic trees only became a feature of the British scene after about 1500, when each newly explored region of the world supplied its quota of species to add to the collections of wealthy fanciers with suitably sheltered estates. Their arboreta, pineta and landscaped gardens became the testing grounds for many exotics, as well as hybrids and sports of native trees and shrubs, some of which later found practical use in timber plantations. Many of the best timber trees came from the northwest coast of North America in the early and mid 1900s, but their comparatively late discovery meant that their timber qualities in response to British conditions could not be fully assessed until well into the 20th century. By this time the golden age of private plantations was long past, leaving the greatest use of the newest trees in state hands.

Most new planting was done in Scotland, where by the start of the 1700s afforestation had become a craze. In the north of Scotland, Sir Alexander Grant planted 50 million trees during the first half of the century. Prizes were sometimes offered to farmers who could plant the largest number of oak, ash and elm before a certain date. By the mid-1700s lords and lairds were competing keenly and by 1826 John, Duke of Atholl, had planted over 14 million larch at 5000 to the hectare (2000 to the acre) on the rocky ground of his estates (Tansley, 1939, p189). Scots pine, much of it from English seed-trees, was the most favoured species generally, although towards the end of the century European larch gained widely in popularity.

In England and Wales, the scope for afforesting new areas was more restricted, and landowners had to concentrate on increasing the density of timber trees in coppice woodlands through supplementary planting, or on marginally extending existing woods and parks. Oak and beech were very widely used, with Scots pine as a nurse. Before much of the oak reached marketable size, it was rendered virtually unsaleable by changes in the economy brought about by the Industrial Revolution and the flood of cheap imported timber from the expanding Empire. Many thousands of today's 'traditional woodlands' are in fact the derelict remains of the 19th century plantations, or of semi-natural woodlands abandoned after the collapse of traditional markets.

Private planting, in England and Wales as in Scotland, slowed toward the end of the 19th century. After the First World War it was restricted by economic uncertainty and lack of government support and by the breakup of many of the big family estates which had taken the lead a century before. The private sector, throughout Great Britain, seemed on the way out as a major force in forestry. But then in the 1950s, with increased government support, interest revived, and well organised syndicates entered the field and the private foresters became a major influence once more.

The plantation movement did little to offset Britain's growing dependence on overseas supplies. By the beginning of the 20th century about 90% of all timber and forest products were imported. The bulk of this trade was, and still is, softwoods from Scandinavia and North America, although tropical hardwoods also gained in importance. The strategic danger of this situation became obvious in the First World War. To meet demands and offset losses during war, the home timber trade was expanded to many times its normal size. Over four years, something like 180,000 hectares (450,000 acres) were clear-felled or otherwise depleted to meet demands (Edlin, 1970, p133).

The establishment of the Forestry Commission in 1919 aimed to ensure that the near-disastrous shortage of wartime timber would never occur again. By 1939 the Commission had established 230 new forests on about 265,000 hectares (655,000 acres) of land, with 145,000 hectares (359,000 acres) actually planted up (Edlin, 1970, p135). These forests were of fast-growing trees, mainly conifers, planted close together to get the maximum amount of timber per acre. Large even-aged blocks of single species or simple mixtures of straight-line plantings were often thrown across the landscape with little regard for variations in terrain or local features. As with many of the 19th century oak plantations, the new forests had a relatively uniform structure which provided comparatively poor habitats for wildlife, although some species, such as crossbills and siskins, benefitted from the widespread use of conifers.

When the Second World War came, the Commission forests were still so new that they could only supply a small proportion of the timber required. Once again, private woods had to meet the need. This time, 212,000 hectares (524,000 acres) were clear-felled or depleted. After the war, the Commission continued to concentrate on strategic conifers, mainly by afforesting areas of moorland, but also by suppressing old disused coppice. Gradually, under pressure from conservation and amenity interests and with a growing realisation of the multiple needs to be served by woodlands, the Commission broadened its policies and practices, so that by the mid-1960s – and especially after the Countryside Act, 1968 – it was devoting much more attention to the landscape and wildlife value of the areas under its control. Following the review of broadleaved woodlands policy, the Forestry Commission published in 1985 its 'Guidelines for the Management of Broadleaved Woodland', which outlines its committment to broadleaved woods.

HIGH FORESTS

The term 'high forest' is defined differently by different writers. Evans (1984, p12), writing from the point of view of timber production, defines it as woodland in which the main purpose is to grow utilizable timber, and in which at least half the species are marketable. This differentiates it from poor quality or scrub woodland which has little timber potential, and from coppice woodland which produces small–size roundwood, rather than timber trees. Peterken (1981, p74) uses the term to describe stands which are grown mainly from seedlings, rather than from coppice shoots. Both agree that in Britain, most high forest stands are plantations, and are not therefore either natural or semi-natural woods. The only exceptions are possibly the Chiltern beechwoods (which used to be coppiced) and some oak stands in southern Britain such as Alice Holt Forest in Hampshire. Although not qualifying under Evans' definition of productive woodland, the ancient pine-woods of northern Scotland and small areas of broadleaved woodlands on inaccessible upland sites could also be described as high forest. More recent non-planted high forest stands include some of the highland birchwoods of Scotland, and the secondary woodlands growing up on heaths and commons, mainly in southern England.

Woods were rarely managed as high forest during the Middle Ages, though many woods in the Scottish highlands had a high forest structure, due to the absence of management. In this century, high forest or plantation management has replaced coppice as the dominant management system in Britain. Former coppice woods have been changed to high forest management either by promotion of selected coppice shoots (called 'singling', see p36), or clearing the coppice stools and replanting with seedlings. Of these two methods, the latter has been the more common.

Coverts and Other Small Woods

Coverts are small woods, usually in the midst of farmland, which are managed primarily for game. Often the terms 'covert' and 'copse' are used interchangeably, and in fact old coppices were often adapted for gamekeeping purposes, with or without the maintenance of the traditional woodland rotation. Other small woods were planted mainly for amenity interest, especially in the 18th century, as were the beech groves crowning the heights of many southern downs, and pine and beech clumps of the southern uplands of Scotland.

Some coverts originated in the 19th century, when pasture-woodland 'scrub' was enclosed and left to regenerate. In exposed parts of the country, gorse clumps were sometimes started in much the same way. These had the additional purpose, according to Neville Havins (1976, p114), of discouraging poachers from stealing young fox cubs. More recently, the value of broadleaved woods for pheasants and foxes has meant their preservation in some cases, despite the attractions of economic forestry.

Coverts which have been adapted without change of boundary from existing, often ancient woodlands are often irregular in shape. Purpose-built coverts and landscape 'follies', on the other hand, are often geometrical: square, oblong, circular, triangular or even crescent, kidney or diamond-shaped according to the whim of the planter (Edlin, 1970, p123). Most of the planted coverts are between 0.4 and 2 hectares (1–5 acres) in extent, but there are also many smaller patches of woods and narrow shelterbelts which served to some extent to provide game habitat, and which increasingly are important as refuges for birds and small mammals.

Gamekeepers, until recently perhaps, have tended to regard woodlands purely as producers of their chosen animals. Coppiced woods provided good cover for game, so their retention could be argued on sporting grounds. Where no coppice existed, exotic undershrubs such as snowberry, leycesteria, rhododendron and cherry laurel were planted for food and cover. The value of the latter two shrubs was much over-rated, particularly as they are rampantly invasive and tend to choke out other underwood and herbaceous plants. These species are good indicators of woods which have been 'interfered with', most probably in the interests of game. Fortunately, the general need to preserve a mixture of species and a high proportion of woodland edge, especially for pheasants, means that most coverts retain much general wildlife value.

Scrub or 'Poor Quality Woodland'

The Forestry Commission Census of Woodlands and Trees 1979–82 recognises a category of woodland described as 'scrub'. This is defined as poor quality woodland which has a poor stocking of marketable species, other than for firewood, and where more than half the trees are of poor form or defective (Evans, 1984, p90). Poor quality only refers to timber production, and many such woods may have high wildlife, landscape or amenity interest.

This category can include recent semi-natural woods which have grown up on previously cleared land, or previously managed woods where management has been discontinued. Examples can include woods where fences are dilapidated and animals are allowed uncontrolled access to graze and browse, and where there is consequently no regeneration. Overgrown rides hinder management for timber production, and are also a loss of valuable habitat. Details on the improvement of scrub or poor quality woodland for timber production are given on page 44.

Scrub that has grown up on previously cleared land can be termed secondary succession. This can be traced back many centuries, and widespread scrub development certainly occurred during the Dark Ages, on ground that had been previously cleared by the Celts and the Romans. Such scrub is only temporary, and if left will usually succeed to wood-land, although the effect of cultivation in altering the soil or drainage may slow or halt the succession. On some sites, scrub can be the natural climax vegetation, due to limiting factors of site, soil or climate. Scrub as a part of natural succession is described further below.

Woodland Ecology

STRUCTURE AND HABITATS

The complex structure of semi-natural broadleaved woodland offers a great diversity of habitats in which plants and animals can live. Like other aspects of the woodland environment, structural features are impermanent and ever-changing. One of the main aims of woodland mangagement is to create, maintain or restore structural diversity where it has been lost or where, without management, it would decline.

Woodland structure can be seen both vertically and laterally. Often, three layers of vegetation can be seen beneath the tree canopy: a shrub layer, field layer and ground layer.

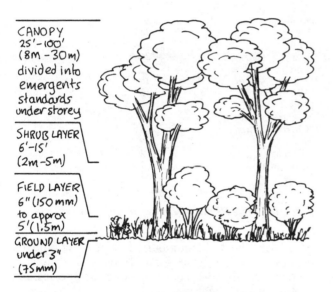

CANOPY
25'-100'
(8m -30m)
divided into
emergents
standards
understorey

SHRUB LAYER
6'-15'
(2m-5m)

FIELD LAYER
6" (150mm)
to approx
5' (1.5m)

GROUND LAYER
under 3"
(75mm)

Further layering may develop where the dominant canopy trees are overtopped by occasional emergent trees, or where they grow in the company of somewhat lower understorey trees. The field layer may develop two sub-divisions: a layer of tall herbs and undershrubs, and a layer of low herbs. Trees of the canopy and shrub layers may consist of plants of a single species, but of different ages and sizes, or they may be of different species which reach varying heights when mature. In a mixed wood, typical emergent species may include elm or beech, with oak or ash as dominants and crab apple, wild cherry, holly, rowan or field maple forming the understorey. The shrub layer may include hazel, hawthorn or blackthorn. Bracken (*Pteridium aqualinum*) , rosebay willow-herb (*Epilogium angustifolium*) and bramble (*Rubus spp*) may form a tall herb layer with bluebells (*Endymion non-scripta*), dog's mercury (*Mercuralis perennis*), ramsons (*Allium ursinum*) and smaller ferns among the low herbs. The ground layer would consist of mosses and liverworts, plus the seedlings of the plants of the taller layers. Where the woods are coppiced, the lower layers are likely to include coppiced shoots of the canopy species.

Not all woods have all these layers, and none would be likely to have them throughout. Some canopy species, such as ash, let in quite a lot of light so that full layering can develop. Others, such as beech, cast a heavy shade so that the shrub and field layers are largely absent except where there are breaks in the canopy. Plantations usually show little diversity within stands. A well-stocked oak plantation is unlikely to contain much besides sparse brambles and a ground layer of mosses. Spruce plantations are dense and dark and lack anything other than fungi from the time the canopy closes over until the first heavy thinning. Pasture-woodlands usually lack the shrub layer and higher field layer, due to grazing, while in scrublands the shrub layer forms a canopy in the absence of taller woodland trees.

Woodland plants are adapted to the structural conditions. For example, yew and holly are typical trees of the understorey, as being evergreen, they are able to compensate for the dense shade of summer by growing at other times of year. Dark leaves, such as holly and ivy, also contain a relatively large amount of chlorophyll, so they are able to use low light levels efficiently. Many of the species in the tree and shrub layers produce flowers before they come into leaf, as being wind-dispersed, the seeds need to ripen before the unfolding leaves shelter them from the wind. The plants of the field layer have to grow and flower early, before the canopy closes over them. Annual plants, that must germinate and complete their cycle within one growing season are at a disadvantage, and hence are poorly represented in woodlands. Most of the field layer plants are perennials, with bulbs, corms, tubers or rhizomes which get them off to a rapid early start in spring.

Lateral structure is also important for diversity. Where woods are allowed to develop unhindered, some canopy trees eventually die and create gaps, where seedlings of canopy, shrub or field layer can spring up. Coppiced woods are often especially diverse because at any given time they are likely to contain some coupes which have recently been cut over, some where the coppice has created a dense shrub layer, and others where the coppice has matured into an understorey with standards as canopy dominants.

For some forms of wildlife, these relatively short-lived openings in the canopy are less important than longer-lasting glades, margins, lawns and rides. Such sheltered, humid but well-lit areas are much richer in species of ephiphytes and invertebrates than either shaded woodland or open-ground habitats. It seems likely that they occurred frequently in the primaeval forest, perhaps maintained under natural conditions by heavy grazing and browsing (Rose and Harding, 1978). In this respect, relatively open pasture-woodlands may retain more similarity to the original forests than do dense plantations, ungrazed, unmanaged woods or even coppice woodland.

However, the maintenance of shelter within a woodland is of great importance, providing a microclimate that is moist, sheltered and shaded, with smaller temperature fluctuations than those that occur outside the wood. Many woodland species, including flowering plants, mosses, ferns, liverworts and invertebrates have limited ability to disperse, and can be lost by changes in the woodland cover that are too drastic.

Topography may also influence lateral structure. For example, in those Scottish pinewoods which grow on an irregular moraine topography, pines occur mainly on the moraine ridges with more open cover in the hollows between. Even small changes in topography and in soils can affect the distribution of tree species, with accompanying differences in layering.

Within a woodland, various associated features provide many additional habitats, especially for fungi and invertebrate animals which are often restricted to these situations. The most important of these from a management viewpoint include large and old trees, decaying wood, streams and ponds, and climbing plants. Important microhabitats include flowers and fruits, fungi, carrion, dung and nests.

Semi-natural broadleaved woods may contain many of the 60 or so native species of trees and shrubs, as well as a wide variety of flowering plants and ferns, with even small woods containing 20 or more species, and large diverse woods supporting over 200 species. A diversity of plant species in turn supports a variety of insects, birds and other fauna. Some tree species, notably oak, willow, birch and hawthorn are outstanding in the fauna they support, with blackthorn, aspen, elm, hazel, beech and Scots pine also being important.

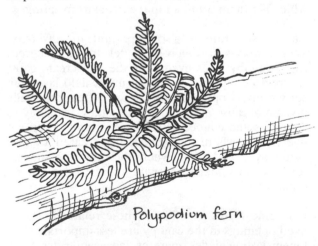

Polypodium fern

The bark of trees also provides a habitat for epiphytes, which are non-parasitic plants that grow on other plants. Epiphytes are normally only found on trees within woodland, where the shady, humid atmosphere allows sufficient moisture for them to survive. Mosses, liverworts, algae and lichens may all be found growing as epiphytes, with one higher plant, the fern (*Polypodium vulgare*) also occurring in Britain. Epiphytic growth tends to be much more lush in the moist and mild westerly areas, and lichens only survive in unpolluted air. Lichens and other ephiphytes grow slowly, with the richest communities found on the oldest trees of stable, undisturbed woodland, making an assemblage of great conserva-

tion interest. The tables below indicate the value of tree species for insects and lichens.

Table 1a   The Value of Trees for Insects

This table lists the number of insect species associated with common trees and shrubs in Britain. An asterisk indicates an introduced species.

TREE OR SHRUB	NUMBER OF INSECT SPECIES
Oak, pedunculate and sessile	284
Willow spp	266
Birch	229
Hawthorn	149
Blackthorn	109
Poplar spp (incl. aspen)	97
Crab apple	93
Pine, Scots	91
Alder	90
Elm	82
Hazel	73
Beech	64
Ash	41
*Spruce	37
Lime	31
Hornbeam	28
Rowan	28
Maple	26
Juniper	20
*Larch	17
*Fir	16
*Sycamore	15
Holly	7
*Chestnut, sweet	5
*Chestnut, horse	4
Yew	4
*Walnut	4
*Oak, holm	2
*Plane	1

Table 1b   The Value of Trees for Lichens

The table below, after Rose and Harding (1978, p12), lists the total number of taxa of ephiphytic lichens recorded from some trees and shrubs in Britain. By 'taxa' is meant species, sub-species and ecologically distinct varieties.

TREE OR SHRUB	NUMBER OF TAXA
Oak, pedunculate and sessile	324
Ash	255
Beech	206
Elm spp	187
Sycamore (introduced)	183
Hazel	160
Willow spp	160
Pine, Scots	132*
Birch, hairy and silver	126**
Rowan	125**
Alder, common	105
Holly	96
Maple, field	93
Lime spp	83
Hornbeam	44

 * In native Caledonian pinewoods
 ** Mainly in upland woodlands

SUCCESSION

Woodlands, like all communities of living things, are dynamic. Sometimes they change so slowly that little seems to happen in a human lifetime. At other times, as when a felled wood is left to regenerate or a grassy area is allowed to grow up to scrub, the changes are noticeable within a few years. It is important to take account of this dynamic aspect of woodland ecology when managing woodlands, since to ignore it may make management difficult, frustrating and ultimately unsuccessful. Where woodland succession is understood, it can be accounted for and if necessary, manipulated.

'Natural succession' is the process by which one community of organisms gives way to another, in a series from coloniser to climax. To give an idealised example, bare land is first colonised by annual 'weeds', then by grasses and mixed herbaceous meadow species, followed by shrubs and finally forest trees, which grow up through the scrub and largely suppress it. The weeds are the pioneer species, while the forest trees form a 'climax' community which tends to persist indefinitely.

In reality, succession seldom takes place uninterrupted by natural or man-induced agencies such as fire, grazing, felling or drainage. It is also usually much more complex than the picture given above. Certain trees and shrubs may come in immediately, depending on the proximity of parent or 'donor' plants, and on the feeding patterns of birds, which distribute the seeds of many of these species. Oak, for instance, is often present very early in the succession of grassland to scrub, and it appears that oak may often be an intermediate, rather than a 'climatic climax' species over much of the country as was once thought. The climax community may itself be more dynamic than theory may suggest. For instance, pinewoods regenerate best at their edges, where shading is reduced, and many Scottish pine and birch woods seem naturally to shift their positions over time, unless constrained by climatic and altitudinal limits. In some of these woods, pine also seems to alternate with birch in a relatively stable long-term cycle, depending on which species is better able to regenerate in a given area at a given time.

There are several situations where natural woodland succession may need to be managed to benefit wildlife diversity. For example if trees are encroaching on open-ground or marshy areas which are important habitats in their own right. A frequent example is where succession favours one species over others which are considered more valuable, such as rhododendron or sycamore over native trees and shrubs. Another type of problem may occur on wet upland sites where woods may gradually succumb to acid bog or grassland conditions, unless measures are taken to ensure regeneration.

WOODLAND ANIMALS

Although animals form 'species assemblages', which are often typical of definite habitat types, they interact with their environment in much more complex ways than plants. For many species the habitat requirements, and often the range, may vary considerably during different parts of the life cycle. This can make

it difficult to predict the effects of management on the animals of a given area.

'Take care of the habitats and the animals will look after themselves.' This is at present the best rule where the aim is general wildlife protection. The creation and maintenance of floristic diversity is usually the key to animal conservation since all animal food webs are based on plants, and because the greater the variety of plant life the better the chance of providing the necessary conditions for most animals.

Invertebrates

Diversity of habitat is the main requirement for invertebrates, as their complex life cycles require a range of conditions. Woodland edges, glades, rides and dead or dying trees are particularly important. The management of these features is dealt with below (see p51). Trees and shrubs vary widely in their importance for invertebrates, depending on the species, with native plants much more valuable on the whole than introduced species. Many adult insects depend on trees and shrubs for food in the form of nectar and pollen. Early and late-flowering species such as willows and ivy are especially useful at a time when other food is scarce. Some invertebrates have

Speckled Wood laying egg on grass

Table 1c   Some woodland butterflies and larval food plants

BUTTERFLY	LARVAL FOOD PLANT	HABITAT
Speckled wood	Grasses, esp couch	Woodland
Wall	Grasses	Woodland edges
Scotch argus	Grasses, esp couch, Molinia Grasses	Upland conifer woods
Ringlet	Grasses	Woodland rides
Pearl-bordered fritillary	Violets	Open woodland
High brown fritillary	Violets	Woodland clearings
Comma	Nettle, willow, elm	Woodland edge
White admiral	Honeysuckle	Woodland
Holly blue	Ivy, holly, buckthorn	Light woodland
Purple hairstreak	Oak	Woodland

very restricted distributions, specialised habitat requirements or poor rates of dispersal. Many species require specific food plants during the larval stage – some examples of woodland butterflies and their larval food plants are given above. Detailed studies are necessary before management can be planned to take these needs into account. For further information on woodland butterflies, see Robinson (1970). Additional references are listed in Rose and Harding (1970).

Reptiles and amphibians

Of Britain's six native species of reptile, three are at home in rough country including hedgerows and wood margins as well as heaths, commons and wastelands. These are the common lizard (*Lacerta vivipara*), the adder (*Vipera berus*) and the grass snake (*Natrix natrix*). The common lizard and adder are widespread in many types of country throughout Great Britain, while the grass snake is limited to England (rarely in the north) and Wales, where it is found mainly in woods and hedgerows near water at low elevations.

Woodland management for reptiles consists essentially of habitat protection and freedom from disturbance. The most important measure is to allow hedgerows, rides, glades and other edge habitats to develop a border of coarse grass and low shrubs. Where rides and glades are mown, it is worth leaving rough patches or sections for reptiles to bask. On sites where wood and hedge-banks are overgrown, it may be worth cutting them back in places on the south or west sides to let sun reach the ground. The creation of marshy areas and ponds can improve the conditions for grass snakes, and 'habitat piles' of branches, leaves and other woodland debris provide overwintering sites.

Undisturbed and uncleared woodland ponds, with plenty of weed growth and varying depths of water are important for amphibians, especially the great-crested newt.

Birds

The management of woodland and scrub for birds concentrates on providing suitable breeding habitat. One way to do this is to ensure a varied woodland and woodland-edge structure, with associated open and aquatic areas. At the same time, it's important to recognise that large blocks of woodland usually contain more species, although at a lower population density, than smaller woodland areas. Management work should be timed to avoid disturbance during the nesting season, which is April to July inclusive for most species. Other measures include providing nest boxes or bunches of branches tied to tree trunks, where it is necessary to supplement existing nest sites for certain hole and shrub-nesting species.

Trees such as oak, which support a large and diverse insect population, supply the most food for insect-eating birds such as tits and tree-creepers. Dense, thorny shrubs are good for nest sites, as are old or dying trees which have holes and loose bark. Ash is particularly good because although fairly short-lived the dead tree remains standing a long time. Shelter is most important for fledglings and for overwintering birds. Clumps or belts of evergreen trees and shrubs can significantly improve the value of broadleaved woods for birds in winter. Plantations can be improved for birds if brashings are piled up to rot rather than burnt after thinning (p137).

Where nest boxes are used, there are a few general points to keep in mind. It is best to put up nest boxes in autumn or winter, although in some cases they may be used even if put up in the breeding season. Boxes which are in place during the winter are often used as roosting sites prior to the breeding season. Boxes should be fitted level (if they have overhanging tops) or tilting downward, sheltered from direct sun and driving rain, and positioned so that rain trickling down the tree does not run into the box. Place boxes at least 1.2m (4') from ground level for small birds, and preferably over 3.6m (12') for large birds or where disturbance from people is likely. To protect nests from predators, position boxes so that the flight path to the box must be indirect, and so that there are no perches immediately next to the box. Nest boxes should never be nailed to trees. They are best fixed to tree stems using nylon string, which can be replaced as necessary when boxes are removed for repair and cleaning in the winter. It is a good idea to remove old nests, as these may harbour parasites which will infect next year's brood.

For nest box design, see Flegg and Glue (1971), and for a full discussion of the conservation of birds in broadleaved woodland, see Smart and Andrews (RSPB, 1985).

Mammals

The most important mammals from a management viewpoint are those which may cause damage to new plantings and coppice regrowth. These include deer and rabbits and, to a lesser extent, hares, mice and voles as well as domestic livestock which may have access to woods. Where these animals are present in some density it is important to protect trees by fencing or individual guards until they are well established. Grey squirrels can cause serious problems in broadleaved plantations, due to their habit of stripping the bark from pole-stage trees. Mammals as pests are discussed on page 101.

Roe and red deer, together with sheep, cause the greatest damage to woodland regeneration in Scotland. Lowe (1977) argues that it is impossible to reconcile large herds of red deer with conservation in Highland pinewoods. In England, red deer populations are much smaller and more local, and pressure from poachers and general habitat restriction makes it important to provide woodland sanctuaries such as Hay Bridge Nature Reserve in Cumbria. In the

English lowlands, it is mainly fallow deer which cause problems, especially in coppiced woods. Detailed information on the recognition, management and control of animals that affect woodland crops is given in the 'Wildlife Rangers Handbook' (Forestry Commission, 1985).

Among the smaller woodland mammals, a number of bat species are of management interest because they roost in hollow trees during at least part of the year. The best way to maintain roost sites is to preserve these trees and, where appropriate, to pollard new trees which may then become the hollow trees of the future. Simple roost boxes fastened to trees may attract five or more species of bats.

Boxes should be about 100mm (4″) x 150mm (6″) x 150mm (6″) square internally, with an entrance slit of about 20mm (¾″) width. The height may be increased to 200–300mm (8–12″), especially for noctules. Use rough sawn timber to give a good surface for clinging to, inside and out. Thick wood is best, and it must be untreated, as preservatives are toxic to bats.

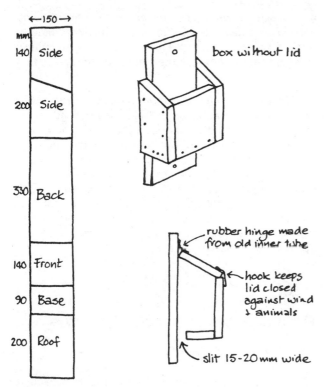

Plank 1·100 x 150 x 25mm

Boxes high above ground are attractive to more species than boxes lower down. Noctules require boxes at least 5m (16′) above ground, while long-eared bats and a few other species will use boxes as low as 1.5m (5′) above ground. Normally fix the boxes as high as possible, and either south-east facing for summer sun, or north facing for winter use. Boxes high up are also less likely to be vandalised. For further information see Stebbings and Walsh (1985).

Dormice favour middle-aged to mature coppice or coppice with standards, in which their density may be as high as 12 to the hectare. Young or senescent coppice are not suitable habitats, as they lack the variety of food sources and nesting sites. A 15–20 year cycle is most favourable, with adjacent coupes cut at different times so there is always some suitable habitat.

Dormice occur in the south of England, including Gloucestershire, Herefordshire, Hertfordshire and Essex, and in parts of Cumbria. They thrive in warm summers, but numbers can be reduced during mild winters interrupted by cold spells.

Botanical diversity is important, to provide a succession of food sources through the seasons. For example in May, oak flowers and various types of pollen may be eaten, followed by caterpillars and aphids in June, ash keys in July, and nuts and berries through the late summer and autumn.

Dormice nest in tree holes up to 10m high in the canopy, and amongst honeysuckle and bramble. They normally breed early in July and again in August, and individuals may have more than one nest. In suitable habitats, nest boxes can be very successful, with perhaps 60–70% of boxes being used, often by more than one individual at the same time. The boxes are similar to tit boxes, but with the hole facing the trunk. The only predators are human, so boxes should be put out of easy reach in inconspicuous places. Dormice may still be present on the margins of otherwise unsuitable woods, so it may be worth putting up nest boxes along woodland edges.

Among the predatory mammals, foxes, badgers and pine martens are strongly associated with woodlands, although by no means dependent on them. The best way to conserve these animals is to disturb them as little as possible.

Woodland adjacent to river margins can be important habitat for otters, and where they are thought to be present, disturbance should be avoided.

2 Woodland Management Planning

Woodland management is never a 'once and for all' task. Even the simplest amenity tree planting scheme needs consideration of suitable species, size at planting, positioning and spacing, protection and weeding, as well as maintenance in future years. The planting of a sizeable plot or a new woodland will require careful thought about the objectives of the scheme, establishment costs, maintenance, thinning and other work which future generations will have to undertake.

As has been shown in chapter one, the history of British woodlands is the history of their management and exploitation. Some woods need no interference to remain valuable ecological havens and features in the landscape, but many do need management if their value is not to diminish. Management for wood production and recreation can go hand in hand with management for conservation, and it is increasingly important not only that conservation should 'pay for itself' by selling woodland produce and so on, but that woodlands, like other habitats, should be managed with multiple objectives in mind. A basis of sound ecological principles is one on which other uses will thrive.

This chapter looks at management objectives, techniques of survey and assessment, and the drawing up of management plans. There is no single 'correct' method to suit all situations, but the various procedures given should be adapted to suit the needs of any particular project.

THE POLICY FOR BROADLEAVES

In 1984–85 there was a Government review of broadleaved woodlands policy, and the following management principles were issued by the Forestry Commission as guidelines for woodland owners and managers. They are not mandatory, but are followed by the Forestry Commission in management of their own woods, and establish the framework within which applications for woodland management grants and felling permissions from the Forestry Commission will be considered. For further details, see the free booklet 'Guidelines for the Management of Broadleaved Woodland' (Forestry Commission, 1985). For details of grants, see page 154.

The general policy is to encourage effective and sympathetic management of broadleaved woods, which are recognised as a vital and cherished part of the countryside. The aim is to achieve a balance between the various objectives of woodland management, including timber production, the maintenance of fine landscapes, wildlife conservation, recreation and sport, and provision of shelter for farm stock, property and people.

The management principles are as follows:

a *Woodland which is now broadleaved is expected to remain so.* This means that any areas felled in broadleaved woods will be replaced with crops which are either broadleaved, or which will develop into broadleaved woodland.

b *There is a presumption against clearance of broadleaved woodland for agricultural purposes.* There will have to be very strong reasons for this to be allowed.

c *The present area of broadleaved woodland is expected to increase* by new broadleaved planting on what is now agricultural land, by the natural colonisation of broadleaves on open or waste ground, and by some planting of broadleaves on ground now carrying conifers.

d *Special attention will be given to ancient semi-natural broadleaved woodlands to ensure continuance of their special features.* These woods are irreplaceable and should not lose their natural characteristics.

e *Managed woodland is more likely to survive than unmanaged woodland.* For this purpose adequate income from woodland is essential. With good management this can be obtained without detriment to landscape, wildlife or recreational interests, all of which can be better met by healthy, valuable trees than by neglected and moribund growing stock. This is obviously in both the growers' and the national interest, in view of the importance of continuity of supply of the major broadleaved species to the hardwood timber industry.

Management Plans

GENERAL PROCEDURES

The diagram below shows the outline approach to the preparation and development of a management plan for a woodland site. This same approach can be followed whatever the scale of the scheme under consideration, and also for other types of habitat management apart from woodlands.

The amount of time and energy involved in the preparation of a management plan will vary according to the size of the site, its ecological or economic value and many other factors. Some plans may take several years and a large amount of paperwork to complete; others will be completed in a couple of visits. Whatever the scale involved, a procedure of the type shown below should be followed to ensure that the work is properly thought through.

SURVEY Administrative details, species and habitat information, site and situation. May include survey of woodland structure, stand groups, stand condition, timber value, plus woodland history and archaeological interest.
↓
ANALYSIS Analysis of the above information and the options they present for management of the site.
↓
OBJECTIVES From the above analysis, management objectives are formed. These may be divided into general, long–term and short–term objectives.
↓
PROPOSALS The proposals for what you intend to do in order to carry out the objectives.
↓
IMPLEMENTATION The details of how you will implement the proposals. This will include work plans, planting plans, and estimates of costs.
↓
MONITORING AND REVIEW To monitor and review the progress of the plan's implementation.

The section below gives an example of the procedure outlined above. The details are based on the management plan for a 17 hectare (42 acre) wood leased by the Woodland Trust. Further details are given in 'Management Plans' (Countryside Commission, 1986).

SURVEY

The following information was gathered:

Administrative details
– name, area, location, access and map references
– landscape and nature conservation status, details of acquisition
– county, district and parish council addresses and contacts
– Countryside Commission, Nature Conservancy Council and Forestry Commission officers

Survey information
– literature references and previous surveys
– survey and management work carried out prior to plan preparation
– species lists with details of vegetation, lichen, birds, insects, mammals, molluscs etc

Site and situation
– altitude and aspect
– geology, soils, relief and drainage
– archaeological features
  public rights of way
– pedestrian and vehicular access
– services and public utilities
– buildings
– location in relation to settlements and roads

– other nearby woodland, and Sites of Special Scientific Interest
– surrounding land use, and recreational facilities

ANALYSIS

From the survey information, the following analysis was made:

Site structure
Managed as coppice-with-standards in previous centuries. No coppicing has been carried out since early this century and the wood has been neglected. The oak standards are of good form and the hazel coppice still vigorous but many of the ash stools are beginning to decay.

Fauna and avifauna
No rarities have been identified and the species lists are restricted by the lack of diversity in the wood.

Landscape importance
Visible from a distance but of main value as a local feature. The woodland edge is particularly valuable as a backdrop to the adjacent housing.

Recreational importance
The wood is well used by local residents and school children, and is valuable as a site for peaceful walks. Also provides the opportunity for local people to become involved in practical conservation work.

Nature conservation importance
Good example of intact coppice-with-standards woodland. Considerable potential for enhancing the number and range of species by reintroducing coppice management and opening up rides.

OBJECTIVES

From the above analysis, the following objectives were formed:

General
– to maintain the site as a broadleaved woodland
– to enhance the wildlife value of the woodland
– to improve the recreational value of the woodland
– to maintain the landscape value of the woodland
– to involve local people in the care and management of the woodland
– to produce good quality wood and timber, primarily for local markets

Long term and short term objectives were then given under the headings of woodland management, estate work, paths and rides, other habitats, fauna and avifauna, recreation, wardening, publicity, surveys and community involvement.

PROPOSALS

The following proposals were agreed on:

Woodland management
– ten hectares (25 acres) to be managed as coppice-with-standards, on a ten year rotation. One hectare

(2. acres) of coppice to be cut each winter, between October and March.
- the strip around the edge of the coppice area to be left to ensure that the woodland provides an undisturbed backdrop to adjacent development.
- the southern end of the wood to be managed as high forest on a selective system.

Proposals were then listed for the other headings given above under 'objectives'.

IMPLEMENTATION

Work plans were drawn up for years 1–5 for each of the headings given above. The work plans include details of operations, estimated costs, income, and who will do the work, eg volunteers or contractors. (Further details on work plans are given later in this chapter.)

MONITORING AND REVIEW

Records to be kept for each of the work plans given above, showing actual costs and income, whether the work was completed and other relevant details.

Surveys of vegetation, fauna, avifauna, insects etc to be used to monitor the success of ecological objectives.

SMALL-SCALE PROJECTS

The section below shows how this same procedure can be applied when drawing up the management plan for a small woodland. In this case, all the stages are completed over the course of a couple of visits, and although not necessarily in the formal order given above, all the elements are there. This information is based on procedures adopted by the BTCV South Glamorgan Woodland Scheme.

Preparation for site visit

Take the following items:
Map and directions of how to reach site
Map of site if obtainable, at 1:25000, 1:2500 or 1:1250 (the latter only available for urban areas)
Advisory leaflets and grant information
Spade Girth tape
Calculator

Discussion with landowner

This will normally take place whilst walking around the wood, or immediately after visiting it . Discuss the following:

a What does the owner want from the wood? Discuss objectives. These may include timber production, amenity, conservation, shelter, shooting, grazing etc (OBJECTIVES).

b Who can do the work? This might be the land-owner, contractors, BTCV volunteers, MSC labour if available, or other such as County Council team.

c How much can the landowner afford to spend? How much income might be generated from timber sales, or would the owner keep the timber for their own use?

d Is grant aid required? Give details of current schemes (see p154).

Concentrate on listening carefully to what the landowner has to say, rather than imposing your opinions at this stage. Discuss various proposals, but leave any firm decisions until after you have completed the survey and had time to think it over (ANALYSIS).

Site survey (SURVEY)

a Using the OS map as a basis, map the site and ownership boundaries, access points and access routes.

b Note the type and state of any fencing.

c Divide the site into management compartments (p22). Map the stand groups if appropriate. Map the type and location of features or species of special interest which must be protected.

d Estimate the volume of timber for felling if this operation is proposed.

Other research

Check with the NCC whether the site is an SSSI or ancient woodland, and with the District Council for Tree Preservation Order or other order.

From the information so far gathered, draw up your proposals for the site. (PROPOSALS). If necessary phone the owner to discuss these before making out work plans and estimates.

Consult the relevant authorities concerning grants, and with the Forestry Commission for any felling licence required (p56).

Work plans and estimates (IMPLEMENTATION)

Points include:

a Areas in which to work in the next 12 months, and during the rest of the scheme.

b Access routes to be used for management, including routes and methods of timber extraction. Provision for public access such as stiles or gates.

c Trees to be felled.

d Ground preparation for replanting or natural regeneration.

e Species and size of stock for replanting, and type of protection.

f Type and lengths of fencing.

g Maintenance for any of the above.

Estimates should include:

a Trees and materials required.

b Fencing required.

c Labour costs.

The rest of the chapter looks in greater detail at some of the procedures and techniques used in drawing up a management plan. Not all plans will require this sort of detail; others will require more. References for further information are included. The topics covered are surveys, stand groups, stand condition, timber measurement, management objectives, work plans, planting plans and estimates.

Surveys

Surveys establish a baseline against which future changes can be measured, and provide information from which management decisions can be made. Some survey techniques require specialised knowledge or equipment, but much can be learned from informed inspection of the site. Surveys of flora and fauna are best done in summer. Surveys of drainage ditches, boundary banks and other features, as well as the marking of individual trees, coppice plots and plantation blocks, are best done in winter when visibility is greater and mobility easier.

Ideally, woodland surveys should proceed for several years before you initiate a major management programme. It is always important to produce a clear description of the area, preferably based on a standardised approach. You should also gather as much historical information as possible. Vegetation, soils and features such as rides and boundaries are best noted on maps, ideally produced in an overlay system so that various factors can be superimposed as necessary to give a composite picture. The 'Wildlife Rangers Handbook' (Forestry Commission, 1985) includes details of a useful system of coloured symbols for drawing up a wildlife map of a woodland.

Sources of information

Seek out existing records and historical information. The owner may have some information on earlier surveys or previous management. Check with the local office of the NCC for SSSI or ancient woodland status. Woods without any special designation, but nevertheless of some ecological interest, may well have been surveyed in the past. The owner may have records, or local enquiries may unearth some information. Most areas have local naturalists and historians who may be the source of all sorts of interesting and valuable details. Contact the county Trust for Nature Conservation and Biological Records Centre who may be able to supply information or suggest contacts.

Vegetation surveys

Vegetation surveys can be recorded on standard cards such as those used by the Biological Records Centre or the Nature Conservancy Council. These require a good knowledge of woodland trees and shrubs, and vascular plants. Vegetation surveys form the basis of woodland classification, of which there are several different systems including the National Vegetation Classification, the 'Merlewood' system by R.G.H.Bunce, and the Peterken system of stand groups. This latter system is outlined on page 22.

Habitat survey

For many small farm or urban woods a habitat survey of the type outlined below (Bunce and Shaw, Institute of Terrestrial Ecology) gives sufficient information on which to base management decisions. If this indicates some particularly interesting habitats or species, specialist advice can be sought.

SITE DETAILS

Name	Grid reference	Area
Ownership	Altitude	Aspect
Geology	Soils	Drainage
Recorder	Date	

For habitats present indicate: a=abundant, f=frequent, o=occasional

A HABITATS ON TREES

Mosses on base of trunk	Lichens on trunk
Mosses on trunk	Lichens on branches
Mosses on branches	Ferns
Large fungi	Ivy

B DEADWOOD HABITATS

Fallen trees – not uprooted	Hollow tree
Fallen trees – uprooted	Rot hole in tree
Fallen large branch (10cm diam)	Stump (less than 10cm diam)
Rotten log	Stump (greater than 10cm diam)

C ROCK

Stones – less than 5cm diam	Rock ledges
Rocks – 5 to 50cm diam	Moss covered rocks
Boulders – greater than 50cm diam	Gulley
Scree	Rock piles
Rock outcrop – less than 5 metres	Exposed sand and gravel

Cliff – more than 5 metres	Exposed mineral soil

D FRESH WATER

Small pond – less than 1 metre across	Water vegetation
Pond – 1 to 20 metres across	Spring
Pond – greater than 20 metres across	Marsh or bog
Slowly flowing stream or river	Ditch or drain – dry
Fast flowing stream or river	Ditch or drain – wet

E OPEN HABITATS

Glade – 5 to 12 metres across	Track less than 5 metres wide
Glade – greater than 12 metres across	Track greater than 5 metres wide
Rocky outcrop greater than 12 metres	Metalled road

F HUMAN ACTIVITY

Drystone wall	Soil excavated
Mortared wall	Quarry or mine
Ruined wall	Rubbish – domestic
Embankment	Rubbish – other

G VEGETATION

Blackthorn thicket	Dense bracken
Hawthorn thicket	Mossy bank
Rhododendron thicket	Fern bank
Bramble clump	Grass bank
Nettle clump	Leaf drift
Wild rose clump	Tall herbs
Willowherb clump	Large fungi – on soil
Umbellifer clump	Large fungi – on wood

H ANIMAL SIGNS

Sheep	Badger
Cattle	Fox
Horses	Mole
Pigs	Squirrel
Red deer	Anthill
Other deer	Corpse/bones
Rabbit	Spent cartridges

Compartments

Woodlands can be divided into 'compartments' for ease of management. Divisions are made as far as possible along natural or existing boundaries, such as streams, woodland edges, fences and so on. Each compartment is given a reference number. If the trees within the compartment differ in species, age or condition, the compartment can be further divided into 'sub-compartments', each of which will comprise a 'stand' of trees. A stand is a group of trees of more or less uniform species composition, age, condition and growth rate. The sub-compartments are referenced as shown below, and the information is included on the woodland map or management plan. The system should be kept as simple as possible.

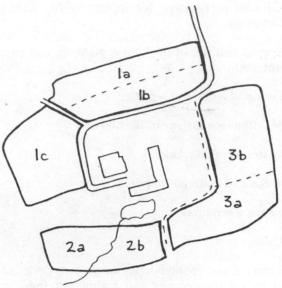

COMPARTMENT RECORD

Sub-cpt	area	species	planting yr	work proposed
1a	..	..	..	.....
1b	..	..	..	.....
1c	..	..	..	.....
2a	..	..	..	.....
2b	..	..	..	.....
3a	..	..	..	.....
3b	..	..	..	.....

Compartments are useful for identifying the different areas of the wood, and for drawing up work plans over a number of years.

Stand Groups

The identification of stand groups within a semi-natural woodland is a method of woodland classification by George Peterken, and is fully described in his book 'Woodland Conservation and Management' (1981). There are several different systems for classifying ancient and semi-natural woodland. The Peterken system is described here because it is fairly simple to use, and is relevant for both woodland ecology and for management.

Apart from its value for ecological studies, identification of stand groups is of direct use when drawing up management plans for semi-natural woods, as it indicates which species should be planted to perpetuate that particular woodland type, and which species are inappropriate. Many semi-natural woods will contain several different stand groups, and by identifying them and using appropriate management methods the internal variation of the wood will not be destroyed by the indiscriminate planting of artificial mixtures of native species.

Note that this classification by stand groups should only be applied to woodlands of coppice origin, for the reasons given below. This includes derelict coppice, or high forest formed from singled coppice shoots (see p36), but excludes any woodland that has been planted.

Basis of the Peterken classification

The system aims to identify natural stand types, so it was drawn up by studying woodlands which are as similar as possible to the natural woodland cover. As explained on page 8, coppice woodlands are thought to be the nearest to the natural woodland, because many have never been planted, but are the direct descendants of the woodland coppiced by early man. Peterken studied 700 sample stands in semi-natural coppice throughout Britain. Each sample stand comprised an area 30 x 30m (32 x 32 yds), and the data collected included a list of all tree and shrub species present, together with the cover of each species and the structural type, ie standard, coppice, shrub and so on. All vascular plants were listed, the soil strata in a 300mm (12″) pit examined, and tests done on soil pH at 100mm (4″) depth, and on soil texture.

The data was analysed to show which species tended to grow together, and these various groupings were termed the 'stand groups'. The results, presented as a constellation diagram, are shown below.

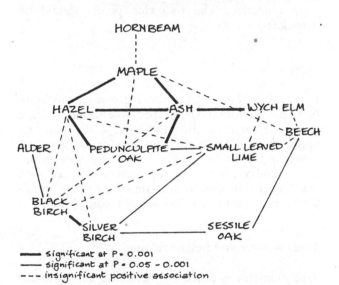

——— Significant at P = 0.001
——— Significant at P = 0.05 - 0.001
--- insignificant positive association

Peterken identified twelve different stand groups, which are defined by the presence of certain tree species that are faithful indicators of a certain range of soil and climatic conditions. The stand groups can be subdivided into stand types, which differ in their botanical and environmental features.

This is preferable to the alternative method of characterising a wood by its dominant or abundant tree species. Species abundance is likely to have been strongly affected by past management, whereas the presence of the 'indicator' trees, irrespective of their abundance, demonstrates that the site has the soil and climatic conditions necessary to support them. It is necessary to assume that the wood has not been so changed by management that indicator species have been entirely removed, or have been planted where they would not otherwise be present. Peterken considers that this is valid for long-established coppice woods.

The stand groups, and the species associations supporting them, are given below:

Group no	Group name	Defining species	Species association
7	ALDERWOODS	Alder	Alder–Birches
8	BEECHWOODS	Beech	Beech–Sessile Oak
9	HORNBEAM WOODS	Hornbeam	None
10	SUCKERING ELM WOODS	Suckering elms (1)	None
11	PINEWOODS	Pine (2)	None
1	ASH–WYCH ELM WOODS	Wych elms (3)	Ash–Wych Elm
4	ASH– LIMEWOODS	Ash and lime (4)	Ash–Pedunculate Oak–Lime
5	ACID OAK– LIMEWOODS	Lime (4)	Pedunculate Oak–Lime–Birch
2	ASH–MAPLE WOODS	Field maple	Ash–Maple–Hazel
3	HAZEL–ASH WOODS	Ash	Ash–Oaks–Hazel
6	BIRCH–OAK WOODS	Oak (5)	Birch–Sessile Oak
12	BIRCH WOODS	Birches	Black Birch–Silver Birch

Notes on species:
(1) Ulmus species except U. glabra
(2) Pinus sylvestris – ie native Scottish pinewoods only
(3) Ulmus glabra
(4) Tilia cordata – Small-leaved lime
(5) Quercus petraea and Q. robur. Most oaks are hybrids, and so these two species cannot often be reliably separated.

The first five groups above the line are defined by the presence of their five dominant tree species, which commonly do occur in more or less pure stands, and are rarely mixed together.

To quote Peterken (1981, p116), 'the remaining groups form an attenuating sequence whereby, for example, ash is present in Group 3, and may be present in any group above it in the table, but must be absent from the groups below (ie 6 and 12).' Thus, the mixed deciduous woods below the line are split successively on the presence of species with an increasingly wide range, ie from the relatively narrow wych elm and small-leaved lime to the relatively wide birch and hazel.

The sequence wych elm – lime – maple – ash – oak – birch, is thus a sequence of species with increasingly wide range of tolerances for soils, climatic and other conditions. Wych elm, at the top of the sequence, is the most restricted species and only occurs in Group 1. Birch, at the bottom, has the widest tolerances, and can occur in any Group. It only forms a birch wood if none of the other defining species are present.

Key to Stand Groups

To identify which group a stand of trees belongs to, use the key below:

a Select a typical part of the stand as a sample. In

most woods you will need to first walk around to familiarise yourself with the various features of the wood, and so to recognise areas which are obviously different in their species composition, and which thus constitute separate stands. Map these roughly as you go. Then select a typical part of each stand, and either run through the key, or note down all the tree species present to be keyed out later as convenient. Normally it is advisable to key out straightaway, so that any queries can be sorted out there and then.

With practice, you should be able to key out and identify the stands as you walk around a wood, thus giving a rapid classification.

Use the key by starting at the top, and selecting one of the alternatives under each number. These lead either to another number, or 'key out' at a Group, which is in italic.

1. Alder, beech, hornbeam, suckering elm or Scots pine (a) present (b) 2
    The above species absent 4
2. Only one of the above species present 3
    Two or more of these species present ....
    .... *Intermediate*
3. Alder present .... *Group 7*
    Beech present .... *Group 8*
    Hornbeam present .... *Group 9*
    Suckering elms present .... *Group 10*
    Scots pine present (a) .... *Group 11*
4. Wych elm present .... *Group 1*
    Wych elm absent 5
5. Lime present 6
    Lime absent 7
6. Ash present with the lime .... *Group 4*
    Ash not present with the lime .... *Group 5*
7. Field maple present .... *Group 2*
    Field maple absent 8
8. Ash present .... *Group 3*
    Ash absent 9
9. Oak present .... *Group 6*
    Oak absent, birch present .... *Group 12*

Notes:
    (a) Scots pine should be discounted where it is an obvious introduction, as it is in woodlands south of the Highlands.
    (b) 'Present' means long-established individuals, and not obviously planted. Planted individuals, seedlings and saplings should be ignored when using the key. Dead individuals should also be discounted, except for recently dead elms which are sprouting again from the base.

A problem in using the key may be, for example, how much field maple is needed at choice 7, to count as present? Obviously one maple in 4 hectares of ash-hazel-birch woodland is not sufficient for it to qualify as Group 2. In assessing your sample stand, you should imagine it divided into 30 x 30m squares (the original basis of the classification). If maple occurs in most squares, then the stand is in Group 2. If it occurs in a minority of squares, then the stand is in Group 3, 6 or 12. If it occurs in about half or

one third, then the stand should be recorded as Group 2 but transitional to Group 3, 6 or 12. If the maple occurs in a minority of squares, but these are clumped, then this comprises a separate stand type.

Using the classification

Draw in the boundaries of the stand groups on a map. These stand groups then form the basis of management compartments. Descriptions of the stand groups, together with their subdivisions (called stand types), are given in Appendix B. From these descriptions, appropriate management methods and species for replanting can be decided. Full descriptions, together with lists of the associated field layer plants are given in 'Woodland Conservation and Management' (Peterken, 1981).

Stand Condition

A survey of the stand condition is important if management for timber production is to be the main objective. The following points should be considered.

Species

If not already noted for stand group classification (see above), note the main species. This information is needed for estimating the natural life span and optimum rotation length, and also for assessing the value of the timber. Very high value species are cherry and walnut, with top quality oak, ash and beech also valuable. Mature timber of other broadleaves and mature conifers are of medium value.

Tree diameter and timber volume

Tree diameter is noted by measuring the diameter at breast height (dbh). For method see below. It is usually worth measuring all the trees over 300mm (1') dbh in a small wood, and a representative sample of the smaller ones. The measurement of timber volume is discussed below.

Age

For estimation of age, see details below (p27). Some woods will be fairly even-aged, others may have distinct components such as coppice with standards, or ages may be mixed throughout. Note the age of any distinct components, or a representative sample of a mixed age wood.

Stocking

The stocking of a stand can be estimated by looking at a sample area, say 20 x 20m. Count the number of usable trees (ie over 70mm or 3" dbh), and measure the dbh of each of these trees. Work out the average dbh for the sample area. Then multiply the number of usable trees to give number per hectare (one hectare = 10,000 sq m, therefore in this example multiply by 25) to give number of trees per hectare. Then use the table below to indicate whether the stand is overstocked, normal, understocked or very understocked. Note that these rates are for timber production, and other values such as wildlife are not taken into account.

| Average diameter of trees (cm) | Description of stand | | | |
	Overstocked (trees/ha)	Normal (trees/ha)	Understocked (trees/ha)	Very Understocked (trees/ha)
	more than		less than	less than
Below 10	4500	1200–4000	1000	500
10–20	2500	800–1700	600	300
20–30	1100	300–600	200	100
30–40	600	200–400	120	70
40–50	400	150–300	100	50
50–60	200	100–150	70	40
Over 65	150	50–100	40	25

This table is adapted from 'Management of Farm Woods' Leaflet 2 (MAFF, 1986).

Health and growth

Check the stand for obvious signs of disease or die back. This may show by defoliation at the crown, sparse foliage or the presence of fungi or fluid on the bark. A felled tree or stump which shows recent annual rings getting closer together indicates that growth is slowing down, and that health may be declining.

Stand quality

Straight, defect-free trunks are the most valuable for timber, and any natural regeneration from such trees is likely to be of reasonable quality. Twisted or forked trunks, or those with branches low on the stem are of less value for planking, but may have a particular value for specialist craftsmen. Further details are given in chapter 9. Natural regeneration from poor quality stands is not worth promoting for commercial production.

Other factors

The type of access is important when assessing the commercial potential of a piece of woodland, as poor access will greatly increase management and extraction costs. The distance and type of access from the woodland to a lorry loading point should be noted, together with internal access within the wood.

The area of the woodland affects its commercial viability. A small isolated woodland is of less value than the same area within a larger woodland, as management costs per unit area will decrease as the area increases. Small woods have a greater length of woodland edge per unit area than large woods. The conditions of light and space at the woodland edge encourage trees to spread and branch, which lowers the timber value.

trees at woodland edge have spreading shape

Timber Measurement

Timber measurement involves a variety of techniques for measuring diameters, lengths and volumes of standing and felled timber, and for estimating the age of a tree from its diameter. Various formulae can also be employed for working out the basal area of a tree, estimates of basal area of a stand of trees and so on. These are detailed in the publications referred to below.

Timber measurement is important for estimating the commercial value of a stand of trees, and thus for making decisions about the management of a woodland. There are various conventions and methods in timber measurement which should be followed, in particular so that a person buying standing timber has a clear estimate of the volume, based on an agreed standard method of measurement. The subject is fully explained in the Forestry Commission Booklet 39 'Forest Mensuration Handbook' (1975). Their Booklet 49 'Timber Measurement', from which some of the following information is taken, is a useful field guide.

The Forestry Commission and most of the bulk dealers in timber have been working in metric units since 1971, but most of the private forestry sector and many smaller merchants still use imperial measurements. Forms for grant aid, forestry legislation, British Standards and so on all use metric measurements. The details below are given in metric, but some conversion factors are included for use as necessary. An imperial system peculiar to forestry and still in widespread use is 'Hoppus Feet', which is a measure of volume that includes a large allowance for waste. It is named after a surveyor, Edward Hoppus, who drew up timber measuring tables in 1736. As a further confusing factor, note that metric details given here use the centimetre measure, following the convention used by the Forestry Commission. This is in spite of the fact that the British Standard metric system is based on the millimetre, as used elsewhere in this handbook. Always keep your tape measure, conversion tables and calculator handy!

Cubic metres to Hoppus feet   ×27.736
Hoppus feet to cubic metres   ×0.036
Cubic metres per hectare to Hoppus feet per acre
      ×11.23

·Hoppus feet per acre to cubic metres per hectare
×0.089
·Cords to solid cubic metres ×4.28
·Stacked cubic metres to Hoppus feet ×20.82

The details below give basic methods suitable for surveying a small area of woodland.

Measuring length and height

All lengths should be measured in metres, rounded down to the nearest tenth of a metre for lengths up to 10m, and to the nearest whole metre for lengths greater than 10m. The length of a piece of timber should be measured with a tape following the curvature of the log.

The total height of a standing tree is the vertical distance from the base to the uppermost point (tip). The total height of a felled tree is the straight line distance from the base to the tip.

The timber height (or timber length) of a tree is the distance from the base of the tree to the lowest point on the main stem where the diameter is 7cm overbark. In hardwoods, and occasionally in conifers, this point may alternatively be the 'spring of the crown', which is the lowest point at which no main stem is distinguishable.

Measuring the length of a fallen tree can be simply done with a tape. There are two instruments which can be used for measuring the height of a standing tree. A hypsometer measures directly an observed vertical distance, and a clinometer measures an observed angle. Both require the horizontal distance from the observer to the tree to be measured. These instruments should be obtainable from specialist forestry suppliers, or from suppliers of surveying equipment.

Two alternative methods, using simple equipment, are given by Alan Mitchell in 'A Field Guide to the Trees of Britain and Northern Europe' (1974, p26).

a Before going out in the field, cut a cane or suitable piece of timber to the exact distance measured from your eyeball to the farthest stretch of your grasping finger and thumb. In the field, stand at a distance

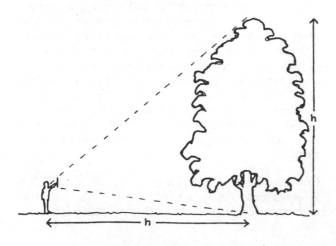

from the tree to be measured, holding the cane vertically at this same outstretched reach. Then walk back or forth until the tip and base of the tree are exactly in line with the upper and lower end of the cane. Then mark the ground directly below the cane. The height of the tree is equivalent to the distance from this mark to the centre base of the tree.

b The second method requires two people, and a 12″ ruler, notched or otherwise clearly marked at the one inch mark. One person holds the ruler vertically at arm's length, and moves until the tree is aligned vertically between the 0 and 12″. The second person holds a narrow strip of white card or similar against the tree, and is guided by the calls of the first person ('up a bit, down a bit' etc) until the white card aligns with the notch on the ruler. This point is marked on the tree. The height of this point above ground, in inches, is equivalent to the height of the tree in feet. For trees over 80′ tall, make a notch at the half-inch mark, and the resulting height in inches is half the height of the tree in feet. For metric, a 30cm ruler notched at 3cm gives a mark one tenth the height of the tree.

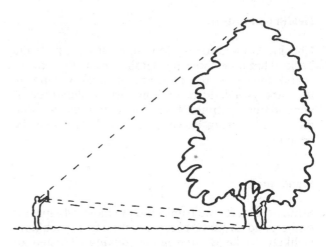

Whatever method is used, it should be noted that it is only in spire-topped trees, such as young conifers, that the apparent top shoot is the true tip of the tree. On wide-spreading trees, the shoots on the nearest branches will appear higher than the actual tip. Wherever possible, walk around the tree and study it from several angles before choosing the point which appears to be top centre.

Alan Mitchell also makes the following observations on estimating heights without experience. Trees of 7–15m height are nearly always under-estimated, and trees of 30m or more are greatly over-estimated. However, really tall trees of 50–60m may be under-estimated as the upper part is foreshortened to the observer beneath, and often they are amongst other tall trees which mask the scale. Tall, narrow trees look taller, and broad, domed trees look shorter than they actually are.

Tree diameter

Tree diameter should be measured in centimetres, rounded down to the nearest centimetre for individual trees. Mean diameters are recorded to the nearest whole centimetre.

Diameters are usually measured with a special girth tape, available from specialist forestry suppliers, which is placed around the circumference of the tree or log. Diameters can also be measured with calipers. Stumps and ends of logs are measured with a ruler or standard tape.

The diameter of standing trees is always measured at breast height point on the trunk, which is taken at 1.3m above ground level. On sloping ground, this is ground level on the upper side of the tree. On trees that lean on level ground, this is ground level on the underside of the tree. This measurement is called the diameter at breast height or 'dbh'. Trees with a dbh of less than 7cm are conventionally classed as 'unmeasurable'.

Age

If the wood is a plantation, or has been systematically managed, the owner may have records of planting dates. If not, the age can be roughly estimated from the diameter of the trunk, as given in the table below, from 'Practical work in farm woods' leaflet 2 (MAFF, 1986).

Approximate relationship of tree diameter to age:

dbh (cm)	10	20	30	40	50	60+
Species	Age in Years					
Beech	35	55	75	95	115	140
Oak	30	50	70	90	120	150
Ash, sycamore, cherry, walnut	20	30	40	60		
Alder, birch	15	25	35			
Pine	20	40	60	80		
Spruce	25	40	55	80		
Larch	15	30	45	70		

Note that these ages are averages only, and the site, soil and density of stand will affect the rate of growth. Open–grown trees will normally grow faster than those in dense woodland.

An accurate age can be obtained from counting the annual rings of a felled tree. It is worth getting into the habit of counting the number of rings of any felled tree you come across, to take both the opportunity of accurate recording, and of gaining practice in visual estimation of tree age.

Volume

All volumes should be recorded in cubic metres, to two or three significant figures as required. The conventional top diameter limit for volume is 7cm overbark, or the point at which no main stem is distinguishable, whichever comes first. Volume measurement may be required for estimating the volume of a standing tree, the volume of a stand, or the volume of felled timber.

There are several different methods of measuring volume, with varying degrees of accuracy. The method chosen should relate to:

a The reason for carrying out timber measurement. If the stand is being measured for sale, a more accurate method should be used than if the stand is being measured for drawing up a management plan.

b The value of the stand. Very high value stands should be sold only on the basis of measurement of the felled timber. High to average value stands should be measured by a method called tariffing, which requires the use of tables. Low value stands can estimated by a method using basal area. These methods are described in the 'Forest Mensuration Handbook' and in 'Timber Measurement'.

The methods mentioned above require not only the estimate of the volume of a selected tree, but an estimate of the number of trees within the stand to give the total volume. For small projects, such as the management of a small covert or farm wood, tree volume can be estimated from the table given below, by measuring the dbh of individual or selected trees.

Estimate of tree volume from diameter at breast height (dbh)

dbh (cm)	Estimated volume, over-bark (cubic metres)	
	Conifers	Broadleaves
5	0.01	0.01
10	0.04	0.04
15	0.1	0.1
20	0.25	0.25
25	0.45	0.4
30	0.7	0.6

The measurement of felled logs is normally done by the 'mid diameter method', which is described in the Forestry Commission publications previously mentioned.

Woodland Management Objectives

When planning the planting of a new woodland area, or the management of an existing wood, it is important that the objectives of the scheme are carefully thought through and clearly stated at the outset.

The various objectives of woodland management are as follows. Many woodlands can and should be managed for several complementary objectives.

NATURE CONSERVATION

This is considered in detail below (p45). For nature

reserves, SSSIs and ancient woodlands this will be the primary objective.

For other woodlands, the objective of nature conservation may be fulfilled by some of the following:

a Creating or maintaining an age range of trees and shrubs, with old trees and some deadwood.

b Creating or maintaining a structural diversity of trees, shrubs and ground flora.

c Creating or maintaining a range of habitats within or near the wood, including open glades, rides and woodland edges, streams, ponds, bogs, rocky outcrops etc.

d Protecting and encouraging the survival of any rare or unusual species of plant or animal within the wood.

The success of other objectives will often be directly related to sound management for nature conservation. For example, woods managed in this way are likely to be valuable features in the landscape, and to be attractive for recreation. When planting, the choice of species which suit the natural conditions of the site is also an important criteria for successful timber production.

LANDSCAPE

The importance of this objective will be related to the following:

a The amount of woodland in the locality. The landscape value will usually increase with increasing rarity in the area. On the other hand, some plantations or clumps of trees which are struggling to survive in exposed coastal or upland locations may be inappropriate.

Some areas rely for their character on the fact that they are very heavily wooded, and here the value is not related to the rarity of woodland, but to its completeness, and piecemeal loss will downgrade its value. Many of these areas are designated as National Parks, or Areas of Outstanding Natural Beauty, and woods may be protected by Tree Preservation Orders or other planning controls.

b The form of the landscape. Woods on hillsides and in undulating country are often visible for many miles, and may thus have visual importance over a wide area. The need to maintain such woods, and to do any regeneration with sensitivity, is thus important. Woods that are square or rectangular in plan, or that do not follow the natural boundaries within the landscape are likely to be obtrusive.

Most flat country in Britain is either urbanised or intensively farmed, and woodlands tend to be few and far between. Here the visual importance is less related to the area or outline shape of the woodland, than to its edge. Lines of trees, avenues, and

especially woodland edges along roads and housing areas are of great value. Clusters of trees around farms, churches and hamlets not only give shelter, but scale and interest in a flat landscape.

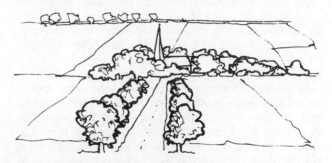

In urban areas, single trees, clumps, avenues, woodland remnants and parkland trees are all of importance in improving the urban environment.

c Where landscape objectives are amongst the most important, proposals for woodland management should consider immediate, short and long term effects of any work. For example, felling and replanting should, as far as possible, be phased over space and time so that the visual effects of any change are minimised. Silvicultural considerations must not be forgotten though, as sufficient felling will have to be done to give light and space for new planting to succeed.

Tree species may need to be chosen for the criteria of their appearance, as well as their ability to grow on the site. Mixtures, grouping of trees and woods should be designed for their visual effect as well as their silvicultural success. This is not always easy, especially where the need to choose the most economical fencing lines, ie straight lines, has to be reconciled with the desire to produce natural-looking woods and clumps.

RECREATION

Like many other objectives of woodland management, this cannot be considered in isolation, but surrounding influences and outside factors may be important. You should consider whether you wish to encourage or discourage recreation in the wood, and if the latter, whether it will be easy or even feasible to do so. Will recreation conflict with other objectives, particularly nature conservation or timber production?

a Look at existing rights of way around and within the wood. Are they over-used, perhaps heavily trampled, muddy, 'braided' (ie divided into many parallel tracks, usually to avoid muddy patches), and in need of management? If, on the other hand, rights of way are little used, would it be best, whilst fulfilling statutory requirements of signposting and stile provision (see Footpaths, BTCV, 1983), to maintain the status quo?

b Look for unofficial access in woodlands which do not have public rights of way. This may include evidence of parking at woodland edges or along roadsides, litter, paths, dens and tree-houses. Most woodland near densely populated areas will have this sort of use, and control may be very difficult, and even counter-productive when fencing gets persistently vandalised.

c Before encouraging the recreational use of a wood, either by upgrading existing public rights of way, or by opening up nature trails and walks, consider the likely effects on any surrounding areas. For example, a car–park for a woodland may also increase the accessibility of an adjacent pond or other habitat which is best left undisturbed. Often though, woodlands are well suited for recreation, as they can absorb a large number of people for a given area, whilst still giving the visitor a feeling of seclusion. Some of the wildlife interest can be retained, even if the woodland is heavily used.

d Recreational facilities need maintenance. It may not be worth putting in fences, gates, stiles, signposts and so on if there is no provision for any maintenance, or if there is likely to be persistent vandalism where a site is unwardened.

TIMBER PRODUCTION

As discussed by Evans (1984, p9), there is a great potential for increased production of hardwoods from British woodlands. The average yield of hardwood timber is just over 2 cubic metres/hectare/year, which is less than half the estimated mean yield class of British broadleaved woodland. The implication is that if all broadleaved woodland was managed for timber production, the national output could be doubled. Of course this would not be desirable, nor possible. Many woods have importance for other objectives which at present outweigh the need for timber production. Also many woods are too small, or the access is too difficult, to make production economically viable.

Nevertheless, timber production can be incorporated with many other management objectives, particularly where clear-felling is avoided. Planning for timber production can be difficult, as markets many decades hence cannot be predicted. Changes in grants and tax regulations may also alter the economic viability of a scheme. However, with the exception of a few high value timbers (details in Evans, 1984, p111), the best rule to adopt when planning any planting is to choose those species which will grow best on that particular site. The successful marketing of timber may depend on choosing the year when prices are right, or in seeking out particular markets or craftsmen for the product you have to offer (see p136).

Timber production for different woodland systems is considered further in chapters 3 and 4.

SHELTERED GRAZING (PASTURE WOODLAND)

As described in chapter 1, sheltered grazing is a traditional use for many woodlands, both in the lowlands and the uplands. It can be a useful technique on small farms and other land holdings where it gives flexibility in managing land and stock. It is currently being researched as a method of diversifying production on grazing land, by giving a return on timber as well as on meat and milk.

Any form of sheltered grazing needs careful management if it is to be successful. Trees may need some form of protection throughout their life in order to prevent browsing and bark damage. Heavy trampling or 'poaching' around the base of trees can also cause damage to the tree by impeding drainage. Heavy grazing will almost certainly damage the ground flora within the wood, and prevent natural regeneration. Rotational fencing is a method of allowing areas to be excluded from grazing whilst they recover, but is expensive to set up. It may also be difficult to combine sheltered grazing with recreation because of the need for fencing, the possibility of dogs worrying stock, and the likelihood of stock damaging the ground to the extent that walking is unpleasant. On the other hand, some pasture woodlands, such as areas of the New Forest, are kept 'open' by grazing, and so very attractive for recreation, as well as being of great importance for nature conservation.

Pollarding is a traditional method of cropping a tree so that grazing and wood production can exist together (see p107).

SHOOTING

Although shooting may at first seem at odds with nature conservation interests, it is due to their shooting value that many woods have avoided clearance in the last few decades. Management work for shooting is often compatible with traditional woodland management and conservation, and the income from shooting can help offset the cost of non-profitable operations.

a Pheasants require a sheltered woodland floor with areas of low vegetation for breeding cover. Such shelter benefits other forms of wildlife as well as encouraging natural woodland regeneration. Areas of low vegetation can be provided by coppiced areas and new planting blocks, which are of value for conservation as well as a part of commercial management for timber.

b Woods for game need wide rides for shooting operations, as well as for easy access. Such rides often support a very interesting flora, and are of value for management work and timber extraction.

c Control of deer can assist successful woodland planting and regeneration, and rough shooting of rabbits and grey squirrels, which can do serious damage to young and pole stage trees respectively, also benefits woodland management.

d Where magpies and jays are numerous they can damage pheasant shoots and the native bird life by taking eggs and young birds. Their control by gamekeepers can thus benefit the more vulnerable native bird species.

For further details on game and woodland management, see page 41.

Work Plans

Any work team requires clear instructions, and a written agreement with the client. This will prevent misunderstandings about the objectives of the project, or about what work is to be done. It is the means of communicating how the landowner's wishes are to be put into practice. A work plan must be concise, easily understood, and appropriate to the needs of the work team and the landowner.

The following are required:

a A map at 1:1250 or 1:2500. This must include a scale, north point, key, site name and grid reference. It should show the site divided into appropriate management compartments. Annotate the map with brief details of the work, including length and type of fencing; species and number of trees to be felled; number, size and species to be planted; tree protection; instructions on safety requirements; brief details of any other work.

b Estimates of materials required, costs, and a statement of who is responsible for obtaining the materials.

c Information on relevant grants. Draft grant applications should be included.

d Directions on what timber is to be felled, and estimates of volume.

e A statement on the intended use of the timber, and instructions on cross-cutting, stacking, conversion and extraction, as appropriate.

f A statement of when the work team is available.

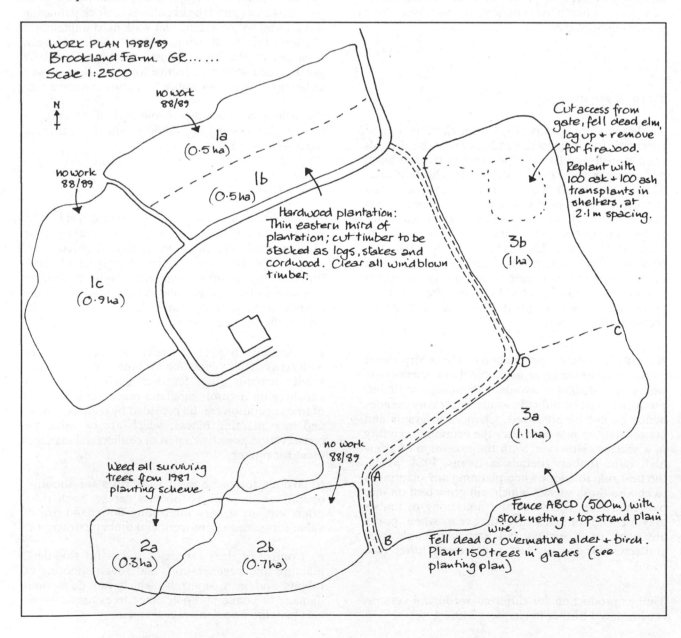

The management objectives must
– have been fully discussed with the landowner, and his site manager/agent
– be consistent with the order of priority of the objectives
– match the available resources, and efficiently use the available labour.

PLANTING PLANS

The purpose of planting plans are:

a to record on paper all the details concerning the planting scheme. These details are needed for your own information, for the owner or client, and for anyone responsible for management in the future.

b to communicate your instructions for the design and implementation of the scheme to your work team supervisor and work team.

Information required

The information presented on the plan should include:

a Location of planting areas

b The mixtures of species to be used in each area

c The type of nursery stock to be used in each area, for example whips, standards and so on

d The number of trees and the planting spacing for each area

e The method of planting, for example pit, notch and so on

f The use of planting aids such as rabbit guards, mulches, stakes

g Any requirement for soil treatments, pre-planting weed control, drainage

h Any further information on the grouping of species within each mixture, for example 'plant in groups of 3–5 individuals of each species', and whether in grid or randomly distributed

i Scale and north point

Presentation

The presentation should be simple and concise, preferably on one side of A4, with supplementary species lists as necessary. The information must be detailed enough for work to proceed without the designer being present, but not cluttered with unnecessary information which makes the plan difficult to understand. Note the following:

a For field use, it is advisable to keep the plans in resealable plastic envelopes (available from stationers), or attach a copy of the plan to a stout piece of card, possibly with any further information on the reverse, and then encase the whole thing in a clear polythene bag, sellotaped to fit neatly. Flimsy pieces of paper will not last long in the field. Always use a waterproof pen!

b Provide several copies, as the team may be working in different areas at the same time.

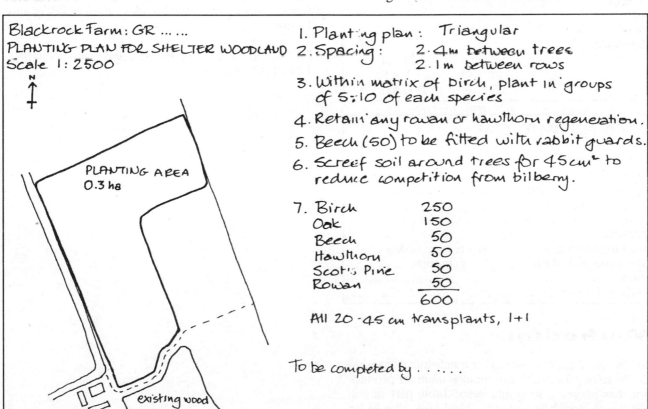

Blackrock Farm: GR ......
PLANTING PLAN FOR SHELTER WOODLAND
Scale 1:2500

N ↑

PLANTING AREA
0.3 ha

existing wood

1. Planting plan: Triangular
2. Spacing: 2.4m between trees
             2.1m between rows
3. Within matrix of birch, plant in groups of 5-10 of each species
4. Retain any rowan or hawthorn regeneration.
5. Beech (50) to be fitted with rabbit guards.
6. Screef soil around trees for 45 cm² to reduce competition from bilberry.

7. Birch   250
   Oak   150
   Beech   50
   Hawthorn   50
   Scot's Pine   50
   Rowan   50
                  600

All 20-45 cm transplants, 1+1

To be completed by ......

ESTIMATES

Planting

Having gathered the information for the work plan (above), an estimate can be made of the cost of planting. This is best done on a standard form, an example of which is given below. You will probably need to design your own standard form, to suit the working practices and conditions in your particular area.

```
PLANTING ESTIMATE FORM

General
Site ............................. Grid Ref ................
Area to be planted (ha)  ...
Site preparation .............
..................................................................
..................................................................
Planting pattern ............ Spacing ...................
No/ha .......................... No trees required ......

Details of trees
Species        No   Type/size              Cost
1
2
3
4
5 etc
                              subtotal

Accessories
Type                      No            Cost
Tree shelters
Mulching mats
Rabbit guards
Tree stakes
Tree ties
Peat
Mulch
Herbicide
                              subtotal
                                   VAT
                                 TOTAL
```

```
FENCING ESTIMATE FORM

Type of fencing .............................................
Total length ..................................................
Length of stock netting ...................................
Length of plain wire ......................................
Length of barbed wire ....................................
Number of:
straining/turning posts ...... struts ...... stakes .......
Gates (no and width) ............ gateposts .............
Stiles ..........................................................
Rails and other extras .....................................
```

Marketing

As discussed earlier, not only is it helpful for 'conservation to pay for itself', but management for production has played a long and respectable part in the history of British woodlands. Marketing should be considered at an early stage, both when managing an existing wood, and when designing and planting a new area of woodland. Consider the following points:

a The size of the parcel being sold significantly affects its attraction to buyers. Larger parcels attract a higher unit price, reduce haulage costs and increase the scope for mechanisation. It may be possible to amalgamate small parcels into saleable units. Co-operation, joint tendering and careful presentation of the parcel may make an otherwise unsaleable lot attractive to a large buyer.

b Access is extremely important in determining the value of a woodland crop, and may be the deciding factor in the cropping of existing woodlands. Sites for new woodlands should be chosen with this in mind, particularly for coppices, which produce a bulky, low value crop at relatively frequent intervals.

c Be prepared to put some work into researching local markets for timber, developing contacts and finding out who uses timber locally. Craftsmen, boat-builders and so on may be interested in small lots of particular types of shapes of timber that suit their requirements. The local office of the Rural Development Commission (formerly CoSIRA) will be able to provide a directory of craft users.

d Any 'processing' you can do may make the product marketable, and if so, should certainly add value. This could include fencing stakes, bird and bat boxes, or simply the bundling of garden poles.

e Find uses for timber within the estate, or for Conservation Trusts and similar organisations, on nearby reserves and holdings. Uses may include fencing, step and bridge building, farm building and heating.

Further information on marketing is given in chapter 10 and Appendix E.

3 Management for Timber Production

This chapter looks in greater detail at systems of woodland management where timber production is combined with management for conservation, shooting and other interests. These include coppices, plantations, farm woods and scrub. Information is given on establishment, spacing, rotations, enrichment, thinning and other practices. Details of how to do the practical work are given in chapters 6–10.

Coppice Management

EFFECTS OF COPPICING AND ITS DECLINE

Broadleaved woodlands which have been coppiced over a long span of time are rich in wildlife, especially flowering plants, birds and invertebrates. Coppicing retains an overall continuity of woodland cover so that species which have difficulty in colonising new habitats, including many rare and local plants and invertebrates, are able to survive. Coppicing maintains a small-scale structural diversity, with a constantly changing pattern of cut-over areas, scrub-like thickets and open canopy. In the first few years after felling, herbaceous plants germinate and flower, and then survive as seeds during the period when the canopy is closed, until the next felling allows the cycle to continue. In coppice derived from natural woodland, groupings of native tree and shrub species are able to persist indefinitely, with the loss of only a few species which do not tolerate coppicing.

Where coppice management is discontinued, more uniform conditions gradually develop, with fewer clearings and a less varied structure. This results in the decline or disappearance of many of the habitats which are maintained under continuous coppice management, along with the species which depend on these. Ride management is usually discontinued, to the detriment of the relict old-grassland flora which often survives along rides within ancient woods where management is maintained. In derelict coppice, leaf litter and dead wood accumulate, enriching the soil. If coppicing is reinstated a more luxuriant ground flora, such as heavy growth of brambles, may take over at the expense of the more interesting woodland plants of relatively nutrient-poor soils. On the plus side, old-wood and dead-wood habitats, which are rare in coppices which are 'tidied up' under traditional management, tend to increase, to the benefit of lichens, mosses, fungi, invertebrates and hole-nesting birds.

Where coppice woodlands are converted to high forest, the floristic and structural diversity decreases, and the amount of woodland 'edge' available for birds and insects declines. The ground flora changes most if the coppice species are felled and the site is replanted with beech or evergreen conifers, less so when oak, ash or larch are used. When conversion is done by singling (see p36), the effects are less drastic.

However, in spite of the benefits to nature conservation described above, coppicing is by no means the panacea for all situations, and should only be started or re-established after careful consideration. Historically, coppicing has not always been good for nature conservation, as many semi-natural woods were damaged by the planting of hazel and oak, to the exclusion of lime, ash and other species. As mentioned above, the absence of old-wood and dead-wood habitats in working coppice is a limitation to nature conservation value.

Although practiced in most areas of the country to some degree, coppicing is more appropriate to the woodlands of the south and east, where the soils and climate can support the necessary rate of growth. Woods on exposed or infertile sites will not have the ability to withstand repeated cutting, and are likely to be of greater conservation and landscape value if managed in other ways.

It is easy to get carried away with enthusiasm for coppicing, but there is little point in resuming a coppice programme for a woodland unless there is reasonable certainty that it can be sustained. The conservation value comes with the range of habitats which develop under a continuous cycle of coppicing. Neglected coppice, that has gone beyond its normal rotation, may be better converted by singling to high forest, rather than cut, only to be neglected again.

TYPES OF COPPICE

Evans (1984, p69) recognises the following different types of coppice:

1 Simple coppice. This is worked on one cycle, so forming an even–aged stand. Nearly all sweet chestnut is worked in this way.

2 Coppice with standards. This forms a two-storey woodland, with coppice beneath and a scattering of trees being grown as standards, usually oak. The coppice component is also known as 'underwood'.

3 Stored coppice. This has been left to grow on beyond its normal rotation, usually through neglect. There are many woods of this nature, now resembling high forest, due to the decline in coppice working early this century.

4 Short rotation coppice. This is worked on a rotation of less than 10 years, to provide material for wicker work, spars, hurdles etc.

PRODUCTIVE COPPICING

The table on page 157 lists coppice species and their uses. Many traditional uses are now obsolete, but not all are beyond recovery. Sweet chestnut is still in demand for fencing. Hazel is still used for hurdles and thatching spars, and osier willow (though not a woodland species) for basket making. One former use which is now being revived is the production of charcoal (see p140), with barbecue charcoal being a particularly suitable form for local marketing. Various species are likely to find continuing outlets for fuel, fencing, turnery and garden use. Pulpwood is a relatively new outlet, especially for large poles from stored coppice. Another new market is in woodchips for fuel, mulch and surfacing material. A final commercial possibility is mixed management to produce a marginally viable underwood product, such as pulp, along with high-quality standard trees for veneer and large timber.

Firewood coppices

With the increasing use of wood-burning stoves, firewood is becoming a more important product. Evans (1984, p86) estimates that an annual increment of 2–3 tonnes of air-dry wood/ha can be expected from a 10 year rotation. For householders interested in establishing their own fuel supply, it is calculated that 8 tonnes of air–dry wood are needed per year to heat an average three-bedroomed house. To produce this amount, a 3–4 hectare (7–10 acre) area of coppice will be needed, with about one–third being cut each year. Higher productivities, up to 6 tonnes/ha/year are possible with fast growing species such as native willows and poplars, and exotic alders, eucalypts and Southern beeches. Suggested native species are as follows:

Wet ground	White willow
	Crack willow
Moist but well drained	Common alder
	Black poplar
	Hairy birch
	Silver birch
Heavy ground	Ash
	Hornbeam
	Field maple

ESTABLISHING A COPPICE

In principle, this is similar to establishing any other type of woodland (see ch 6). The spacing of the new plants is related to the length of rotation. For example, hazel worked on a 7–10 year rotation is planted at 1500–2000 stools per hectare (600–800 per acre), whereas sweet chestnut on a 15 year rotation is more thinly planted, at 800–1000 stools per hectare (320–400 per acre). Oak and ash on 23–25 year rotations usually have 200–500 stools per hectare (80–200 per acre).

As with any wood, species should be chosen first to suit the available site and soil (see p71), and then according to demand. For care in the early years after planting, see chapter 7. Weeding is particularly important, to encourage vigorous growth of the young trees.

Coppicing can begin either as soon as the trees are established, ie at 5–8 years, or when the crop reaches marketable size. An early cut will encourage a better yield in the first crop, but will delay it by a few years. The first coppicing of young trees should be done in March or April, so that the new shoots emerge in June, after any risk of frost.

CONSERVATION COPPICING

Conservation coppicing aims to maximise the wildlife value of coppice woodlands, with the production of marketable wood as a secondary consideration. The following details are based on Peterken (1972), Mummery and Tabor (1978) and Ranson (1979) and on the experience of volunteer groups in this field.

Resumption of coppicing

Woodlands which are to be coppiced for conservation purposes are often more or less derelict. However, coppicing can be resumed, even after 50 years of neglect. Renovation can be costly, at least in terms of labour. Until a full rotation is re-established the material produced is often low grade and suitable only for firewood or pulp, though sale of this will help offset labour and other costs.

When planning how big an area to coppice each year, consider the available labour supply, as well as the woodland size, type and other factors. Often it is best to restore 0.2–0.4 hectare (½–1 acre) each year, until the rotation is in order, before attempting more extensive coupes. Initial cutting is much more laborious than re-cutting on rotation and it is easy to take on too much and do a poor job. Consider also other options, such as converting some areas to high forest by singling.

Old neglected coppices are often poorly stocked as a result of stool death, and gapping-up (p35) may be needed.

Rotation

The planned rotation must take into account the rate of regrowth, the size of underwood needed for any marketable products, and the total area to be coppiced. Many traditional uses required 7 to 15 year–old material, but some of the modern commercial uses take material up to 30 years old. Normally, the best flowering of herbaceous plants is in the second and third spring after coppicing. Ten-year old coppice is about at its best for nesting birds, while after about 20 years it begins to decline for this purpose.

Coppice plots are customarily described according to the winter in which they are cut, eg '1987 coppice' indicates cutting in the winter of 1986–87.

Size of coupe

The size of coppice plots may be anything from a minimum of 0.1 hectare (quarter acre), 0.2 hectare (half acre) in larger woods, to a maximum of 1.2 hectares (3 acres). Although traditional coupes were often 4 hectares (10 acres) or more in size, such large plots tend to suffer from exposure unless subdivided by windbreaks. Large plots also require a greater commitment of labour when the time comes to re-cutting. However, small plots are more vulnerable to damage by deer (see below), and to shading by surrounding trees.

Extraction

Even when the wood has a commercial use, extraction may be difficult, especially on steep hillsides, wet sites and where ride systems have fallen into decay. If extraction is considered, it is essential to re-open rides in advance of coppicing to provide a route to a paved road.

Start coppicing the more inaccessible coupes first, so that any wood which you plan to extract can be taken out through older woodland, though this must be done with care to minimise damage. Coppice the areas near to rides or roads in later years. This way you won't have to drag the wood out through dense young undergrowth.

Wood boundaries

It is best not to coppice wood boundaries at the same time as the adjacent interior coupes, to avoid loss of shelter. But boundary coppicing at some stage is important to maintain the woodbank flora and to reduce shading of neighbours' land. Where the woodland is surrounded by a hedge, it is well worth reviving this feature by cutting and laying, especially if livestock need to be excluded. See 'Hedging' (Brooks, 1975) for details.

Coppice with standards

Most old coppice has standard trees, which may be cut or left according to management aims. Where standards are quite small, it is generally best to leave about 25 per hectare (10 per acre) for the time being. Where they are large, 12 per hectare (5 per acre) is best. If there are more than about 50 per hectare (20 per acre), some should be cut out to improve the underwood and ground flora. One of the main objectives in coppice management is to maintain low cover (1–5m, 3–15'), but many underwood shrubs such as hazel as well as field–layer plants, cannot flourish under the dense shade of timber trees. In commercial coppice with standards, where the field–layer is not valued, as many as 100 standards per hectare (40 per acre) may be stocked.

If you thin out the standards, try to leave trees of a variety of sizes and age. Include at least one old tree,

perhaps on the fringes of the coppice plot. Be careful not to overthin, if natural regeneration is poor. Where there are too few standards, you may want to plant or to protect existing seedlings or promote standards from selected coppice poles. There are problems with the latter procedure, called 'singling'. If young, the promoted stem may tend to bend over in the wind, and if older, may unbalance the stool and pull it over. Regrowth from the rest of the stem will be retarded and twisted.

Oak is the most common standard tree, and is usually grown for 5–6 coppice cycles (100–130 years). Ash is grown for 3–5 cycles (60–100 years). Hazel excepted, standards can be the same species as the coppice, or can be different. Beech is unsuitable as a standard because of the heavy shade it casts. Because of the spacing of the standard trees, they tend to develop open crowns, and pruning may be necessary to produce top quality lengths of timber.

Stocking

Never try and 'thin out' the coppice by cutting stools here and there through the wood. This tends to promote the growth of brambles at the expense of other woodland plants and is not a solution to problems of shading. Some cut stools die, whilst others expand to fill the space available. The wood remains as shady as before, with fewer but larger trees.

Where coppice stools are sparse, or where stools have died or been damaged during extraction operations, their density can be increased directly by layering (p119), or by propagating new plants by stooling or layering, and then transplanting these to fill gaps. In ancient semi-natural woods, avoid using purchased plants or plants from another woodland, as these will be of a different genotype to the existing coppice. When transplanting, try to minimise the distance from the mother plant, to retain the original pattern of genotypes with the woodland.

Stooling involves coppicing the stool in the normal way (p118), but leaving several stems untouched. Then pile earth over the stool, and new shoots will grow with roots formed in the loose soil, making them easy to detach.

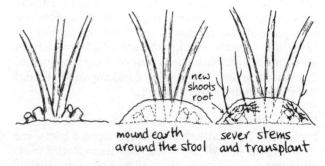

mound earth around the stool   sever stems and transplant

Gapping up should be done at the same time as the coupe is felled, as layering and stooling fit in with the felling operation, and the young plants will have a few years of higher light levels to become established. Mark the site of any layering, stooling or transplanting so that the plants can be easily found again. There are various ways of managing the young plants, which will need to be kept free of herbaceous growth in the first few years, and protected against deer and rabbits. One method is to use tree shelters (p90) for protection and to enhance the growth rate. These will disintegrate after about five years, leaving single stemmed trees which can then be coppiced to form a multi-stemmed stool the next time the coupe is felled. Alternatively, one year old layered plants or transplants can be cut back to near ground level during the winter, and they will then sprout several shoots the following spring. These cannot be protected by a tree shelter, so other forms of protection may be needed (see below).

Harvesting

Harvesting can be done by professional woodmen or by volunteers. Commercial firms may charge for the work, unless the material is readily saleable, in which case they may do it for free or pay for the crop.

Volunteer work parties provide a good source of labour where commercial harvesting is not feasible, and where more than a small amount of overgrown coppice is to be cut in a season. It is essential that volunteers have basic felling and coppicing skills, and are instructed as to the height to cut stools, species to be retained and so on. It takes a group of volunteers, with hand tools and a chain saw, up to 300 man-days to clear and sort material from one hectare (120 man-days for an acre) of derelict coppice. Work may be two or three times faster on 15–20 year old coppice. Professional woodmen with chain saws can do the equivalent work in as little as a third of the time.

Protection

Coppice regrowth needs at least three years free from heavy browsing. Coppice plots often need protection from the browsing of deer and livestock, and in the case of cattle or horses, protection from trampling which damages the ground flora. In the past, some woods were permanently hedged or fenced, while others were treated as 'rolling enclosures'. In the latter system, coupes were fenced for the first part of the rotation, and then opened up to browsing animals and for the use of commoners to glean firewood. This works best on long rotations of 20 years or more. For details of fencing see p56, and the BTCV handbook 'Fencing'.

Deer in any numbers are incompatible with coppice regrowth, especially ash. Where coppice plots are small, even one or two deer can denude the plot, and some form of protection will be necessary (p102). Occasionally rabbits may be a problem (p101). Deer damage may be tolerable in large coupes, where browsing pressure will be lower, and deer are less keen to browse in the centre of the coupe, at a distance from shelter. In some cases regrowth may be slowed, but not stopped. Brambles can give useful protection to the young shoots, though if bramble cover is very thick it can suppress the coppice growth.

Rate of growth

Regrowth varies according to the site, the condition of the stools and the species. Where unchecked by browsing, regrowth may be as much as 3m (10') in the first season for willows, 1.5–1.8m (5–6') for ash, hazel, sycamore and sweet chestnut, 1m (3') for aspen and field maple, and 600mm (2') for hornbeam. Growth then slows in the following years. The canopy may close in the second or third year for the more vigorous species.

In the first year after coppicing, a large number of shoots emerge, typically 50–150 per stool. Self-thinning takes place, so that by mid-rotation about 5–15 live stems remain. Artificial thinning is not often done, although this can be used to maximise growth per stem, where demand is for larger size poles.

Coppice can be worked indefinitely, but site exhaustion and stool mortality will cause yield to decline eventually. However, there is no evidence that the vigour of shoots from any one stool declines as the number of previous coppicings increases.

CONVERSION TO HIGH FOREST

This can be used to increase structural diversity within a large area of woodland, to manage neglected coppice where resumption of coppicing is not feasible or appropriate, or where the commercial return from larger timber is necessary to maintain the woodland.

Conversion can be done by singling of existing coppice stems, by promoting the growth of suitable self-sown species such as oak, ash or sycamore, or by replanting. The latter method will require a certain amount of clearance, which must be carried out with care where conservation value is important. Commercial replanting normally requires complete clearance of the existing woodland, which is highly destructive.

Singling or 'storing' is done by cutting all but the best stem from each stool, leaving a density equivalent to not less than half the stocking rate of a conventionally managed plantation of the same age (see p24). Any gaps over 30m diameter should be replanted, and where commercial considerations prevail, a fast-growing species should be chosen, to mature at the same time as the older surrounding trees. In later years, thinning is done as for plantation management. Hazel cannot be singled, as it is an understorey shrub.

The quality of stored coppice timber may be of inferior quality due to decay entering at the base of the trunk from the stool, and the curved butt or base. The process of storing is not irreversible, and coppicing can be revived even after 50 years interval.

Plantations and High Forest

FORESTRY PRACTICES AND THEIR EFFECTS

Silvicultural systems

In Britain, most productive forestry uses a monoculture system, rather like that of intensive arable farming. Planting consists of large stands of a single species (with or without a nurse tree) chosen for quick growth, early returns from thinning and selection for a final clear-felled harvest, after which the 'crop' is replanted. Typically, the system uses nursery stock selected for best growing qualities, irrespective of the native stock existing on the site.

A few forests are managed on the selection system, in which felling and replacement, often by natural regeneration, are distributed widely throughout the wood. This system is much more common on the Continent. Such a woodland has a more 'natural' and varied structure and appearance, and generally more wildlife value, than a monoculture forest, but it lacks the open-ground and thicket stages of replanted stands of monoculture trees.

In recent years, a number of woodlands, particularly broadleaved woods in areas of high landscape and wildlife value, have come to be managed by the 'low-input' approach. In low-input forestry, the need for intensive measures such as drainage, weeding and straight-line single species planting are minimised through the retention of suitable existing trees, the use of natural regeneration when possible, and the wide-spaced planting of relatively large 'whips' rather than smaller transplants (see below p74). Felling practices are, in effect, a compromise between clear-felling and selective felling, with some reduction in productivity in order to maintain the site's wildlife and amenity value.

Afforestation

When open uplands are afforested, conditions are often created which are suitable for many ground and fieldlayer woodland plants, insects, birds and small mammals, at the expense of the open-country species which formerly inhabited the site. As the canopy closes, these conditions deteriorate due to shading and the buildup of leaf litter. This is especially the case in conifer plantations (other than larch), and in oak and beech plantations. Thinning temporarily improves a stand's habitat value, but it is only as some stands mature and are felled and replanted that a more diverse overall structure results. A few animals, including red and roe deer, pine marten, wildcat, badger, fox, some predatory birds and a few seed-eating birds and insects are particularly benefitted by upland afforestation, especially where plantations are over 4 hectares (10 acres) in size.

Re-planting

Where existing broadleaved woods are replaced by conifers, there is a loss of semi-natural habitat and a decline in the number and interest of plant and animal species. This occurs to a somewhat lesser extent where mixed broadleaved woodlands are converted to single-species broadleaved plantations. More intensive maintenance of rides and other open areas may produce some increase in 'edge' habitats, with benefit to species which require these conditions.

Clear-felling

When a stand of trees is clear-felled, more rain, sun and wind are able to reach the ground, until such time as the canopy closes over again. This often results in the replacement, perhaps temporarily, of the rather specialised shade-bearing woodland herbs by species which demand more light and nutrients, and which are often of less conservation interest. The resultant flora may be very luxuriant unless heavily grazed or browsed. Bracken, which competes with tree and herb seedlings for nutrients and water, often flourishes when the canopy is opened up.

Where the soil is churned up by forestry work, soil compaction may occur and drainage is likely to be impaired. The water table may rise for a time after felling, due to compaction and the reduction in transpiration which accompanies the loss of trees. This can affect plant succession and limit the success of trees on poorly-drained sites, as well as damaging rides and woodland roads used for hauling timber. On slopes, and shallow or loose and sandy soils, erosion is likely unless care is taken to restore the ground surface. In such situations, wind-throw of remaining trees and those at the edges of felled areas may occur.

MANAGEMENT FOR WOOD PRODUCTION

This section is based on Evans (1984), and relates mainly to broadleaved woodland. Although management for wood production is the primary aim, this does not preclude other management objectives of landscape, conservation and amenity.

Oak is the principal species of about 30% of all high forest in Britain, with beech, ash, birch and sycamore making up a further 47%. Most of this woodland is in the southern half of England. The rotation length is the main factor in management, as the size at harvesting is closely tied in with the end-use and successful marketing of the timber. For prime timber and veneers, long rotations are needed.

The management of high forest for wood production must aim at stand and tree quality, as much as maximising yield. For broadleaves, sites must be reasonably sheltered to produce quality timber, and careful management is needed to minimise defects in the timber. There is no market reason for planting particular species of hardwood, and it is much more important to choose a species which is suitable for the site.

Planting and spacing

In the past, broadleaves were always planted very close, at 1–1.4m (3-4½′) spacings, to ensure good development of stems in the early years, and to leave plenty of choice for thinning and final cropping. However, the number of plants needed, and the costs of early weeding and cleaning meant that establishment costs were high. Now it is more common to plant at 1.8–2m (6-6½′) spacings. The reduction in choice of final crop makes it important to choose stock genetically selected for timber production, which lessens the conservation value of the woodland. Where there is a good market for thinnings, such as for firewood, close spacing may be viable.

As well as normal care in the first few years after planting, particular attention should be paid to clearing any climbing plants, to ensure good stem development of the young trees. Pruning may be necessary to improve quality.

Mixtures

In woods primarily planted for production of broadleaves, it has been and remains common practice to plant a mixture of broadleaves and conifers. There are two reasons for this. Firstly, the conifers act as a nurse crop, providing side shelter for the broadleaves, which, provided the conifers are not allowed to dominate, grow better in a mixture than in a pure stand. This is particularly the case in frost pockets, on exposed sites and in the uplands. Secondly, the thinning and sale of the nurse crop gives an early return. Conifers are the usual nurse crop, but alder is sometimes used on infertile sites for its ability to fix nitrogen in the soil.

There are problems with planting mixtures. Firstly, they look very un-natural in the landscape, as they are usually planted in rows. Secondly, it is difficult to ensure the crop is not swamped by the nurse, and frequent and costly thinning and cleaning is often necessary. With knowledge of the site conditions, it is possible to choose compatible species (see below). The use of tree shelters (see p90) to favour the final crop species seems to be a promising technique.

Making a mixture visually acceptable is difficult. One method is to keep the species separate by planting in blocks, with broadleaves planted on areas with major visual impact, and conifers in hollows and other areas mainly hidden from view. However, this would seem to reduce the shelter effect of the conifers, although they still have value as an early

crop. Where Norway spruce is used as a nurse crop, and then sold for Christmas trees, planting in alternate lines is usually acceptable as the conifers are removed before they have much visual impact.

There is less problem of compatability in broadleaved only mixtures, as the difference in growth rates between main crop and nurse crop is less than with a conifer nurse crop. The visual effect of the planting pattern is also less significant.

Evans (1984, p29) recommends the following mixtures of broadleaves, provided the site and soil conditions are suitable:

ASH with common alder or sycamore
BEECH with cherry
OAK with common alder, ash, cherry or sweet chestnut.

'Self-thinning' mixes can also be used, which should require no thinning of the nurse species. The nurse species are either understorey shrubs such as hazel, or fast-growing, light-demanding species such as rowan, which become suppressed as the canopy closes.

Thinning

Thinning of broadleaves should normally commence when trees are 8–10m (26–33′) high, the smaller size being applicable where there is a market for the thinnings. Usually the number left after the first thinning should be equivalent to two to four times the eventual crop, to allow for further selection. In France, the system used is to leave spacing of 50–75% of the intended final spacing.

Thinning of broadleaves should always be selective according to tree health and form, and not simply by position or row. In contrast, conifers are thinned to maximise total production per hectare.

Where broadleaves and conifers are being grown in alternating bands of three to four rows, thinning should start with the line of conifers nearest the broadleaves, and the broadleaves selectively felled.

Thinnings are done at five to seven year intervals in young stands, eight to ten year intervals in middle age stands, and 15 year intervals in older stands.

'Free growth' is a technique used for growing oak which involves heavy thinning at an early stage, to encourage rapid growth of the crop trees. For further information on this and other aspects of thinning see page 103.

Felling and Regeneration

Final felling should be timed to take advantage of any market opportunities, rather than taking place on a predetermined year.

There are various systems of organising and phasing felling and regeneration. In deciding which system to follow, one should consider not only silvicultural factors, but also those of landscape and amenity.

Evans (1984, p58) describes the following systems:

a Clear felling and replanting. This is the usual system in Britain, and has the advantages of concentrating work in one site, and results in rapid and uniform restocking. Felling of large areas is now avoided for landscape and amenity reasons, and coupes are usually 1–3 hectares (2½-7 acres). However, this can create problems with deer, as these smaller areas are favoured for browsing (see p101).

b Group felling. Under this system, a group of trees covering about 0.5 hectare (1 acre) are felled. It is usually more expensive than larger scale operations, but minimises damage to landscape, amenity and sporting interests. To allow adequate space and light for replanting, the diameter of the area cleared should be at least 1.5 times the top height of the remaining trees. Establishment and growth of young trees is usually good, because of the shelter created.

c Shelterwood system. This involves gradually removing the crop from an even-aged wood, to encourage restocking by natural regeneration. It is little used in Britain, but is common on the continent.

d Selection system. A wood managed under this system has the full range of trees from seedlings to maturity, and at intervals of 10–20 years a compartment is worked over, to remove the crop and to thin, clean and weed as necessary. This system maintains the 'natural' woodland appearance, but is little used in Britain.

e Two-storey high forest. A second crop is introduced into a wood part way through its rotation. This is used in Britain, where beech is planted in stands of birch, pine, ash or oak, to aid the establishment of the beech. The overstorey is removed a few years later.

Natural Regeneration

All British native broadleaves have the ability to regenerate naturally by seed, but produce seed only intermittently in 'mast' years. If thinning has been carried out properly, trees at rotation age should provide suitable seed sources. Felling should be done in the winter after a mast year, with trees extracted before April.

Either of these two felling systems can be used:

a Felling 50–70% of the mature trees, leaving the remainder as a shelterwood to shade out weed growth. These are felled within the next 10 years. Timing is very critical, as if felled too soon, weeds will become a problem, but if left too long, the young trees will suffer from lack of light. Careful thinning and some hand weeding may be necessary.

b Clear felling. This can be risky, as the expected regeneration may fail, and the site may also become very wet due to the loss of transpiration via the trees, and from compaction by heavy machinery. Weed growth is also more vigorous, but there is no damage to the new crop during final extraction.

For successful regeneration, the forest floor needs to be fairly clear of weed growth, and not too wet. In a good seeding year, glyphosate (see p97) can be used in August to clear weed growth. Fencing against rabbits and deer may be needed, and in some areas, control of mice may also be necessary (see p101). The use of tree shelters (see p90), placed over seedlings in the first year, should greatly improve growth and survival, and may do away with the need for fencing.

Natural regeneration also occurs vegetatively, including root suckers from species such as cherry and elm, or by stump regrowth.

CONSERVATION MEASURES

Choice of species and associated wildlife

Choose native species which occur locally in the area. If possible, use natural regeneration so local ecotypes of species are maintained. If this is not feasible, consider collecting seed locally and propagating the plants in a nursery prior to planting out.

Although native species are preferable for conservation value, recent research has indicated that some exotic species, such as sycamore, are not as poor in the wildlife they support as had been previously thought. Southern beech supports a richer wildlife than native beech.

In terms of numbers and species of birds, mixed broadleaved and conifer woodland supports the highest number, followed by broadleaved only, and lastly pure conifer plantations.

Woodland layout

Leave any wet, rocky or otherwise marginal areas to grow up naturally. These areas seldom repay ground preparation and planting, and by leaving them you provide for some continuance of grassland habitats, and for colonisation by native scrub species.

Provide or maintain associated habitat features such as rides and glades. Junctions of rides can be enlarged to create an open area within the wood. Once existing rides are in good order, you can increase the amount of woodland 'edge' by creating irregular margins around plantings and along roads.

Maintenance

Minimise operations such as clearance, drainage and weeding, and do only what is necessary to establish the new crop of trees. Avoid excessive 'tidying-up', which is costly as well as environmentally destructive.

Ivy, honeysuckle and other climbers are important food plants for butterflies, and should be left if possible.

Thinning, felling and extracting

Vary the age and class structure of the woodland by felling and thinning the canopy as often as is consistent with wood production objectives. This will help retain a wide variety of trees and shrubs, and maintain or encourage the development of a field layer.

Keep the felling coupes as small as possible, to increase the structural diversity and edge effects. In commercial woods, coupes should be of one to three hectares, but could be much smaller in amenity woods.

Phase clear-felling over a period of years, to reduce the apparent scale and visual impact of the work. This is especially important when felling woods on slopes and on other widely visible sites. In places, felling can be arranged to reveal a succession of views previously closed, thus adding interest to the landscape. On slopes, irregularly triangular clearings are best, with the acuteness of the apex increasing with steepness.

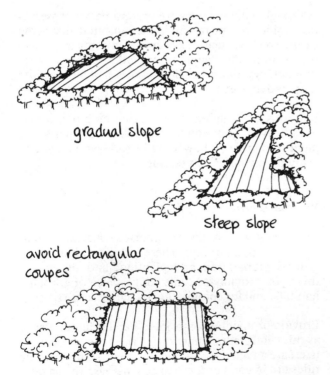

gradual slope

steep slope

avoid rectangular coupes

In phased or group felling of woods on gradual slopes, it is often best to start at the low end (especially if this runs along a road), and work progressively uphill so that new plantings have started to mask the felling of succeedings years' blocks. If possible, leave an irregular screen of roadside trees until the cut areas behind have regenerated.

Retain a few trees or small groups beyond their normal rotation, to provide lichen habitats and sites for hole-nesting birds, as well as the visual interest of very old trees. Provided they are not being relied on for a seed source, the most mis-shapen and least valuable trees can be left.

Take particular care with extraction on limestone, sand dunes and other easily eroded soils. Where the ground vegetation is of special interest, it may be necessary to carry rather than drag thinnings to collection points in order to reduce damage. Avoid extracting timber when soils are wet and easily compacted.

Farm Woods and Coverts

Woods on farms make up a very important part of the total amount of woodland in Britain. It is estimated (Forestry Commission Census of Woodlands and Trees, 1979–82) that small farm woods, of less than 10 hectares (25 acres) total 295,000 hectares (728,975 acres) in Britain, or 39% of the total of broadleaved woodland. In addition there are many clumps and lines of trees not included in this estimate.

Characteristics of farm woods

Many farm woods have suffered neglect in the last few decades, and now have spindly growth in need of thinning, or single age stands of mature and over-mature trees, with lack of regeneration. Whilst farming has been so profitable, there has been little priority given to woodland management.

There are problems in managing these small woods for timber production. Their small size means that woodland operations are more expensive per unit area, and often access for management and timber extraction is very poor. The long length of boundary for the area of woodland means that a high proportion of trees are along the edge, and are often leaning, heavily branched or in other ways poorly formed for timber value. This also makes fencing more expensive than for larger blocks of woodland.

However, the conservation and sporting value of farm woods is usually very high, and can often be enhanced by some management for wood production, thus making management worthwhile. Farm woods are often oases for wildlife in expanses of intensively farmed land, and many are of ancient origin.

Integration

By integrating farm and woodland operations, benefit can be given to both.

a Shelter for livestock is important in upland areas, and by careful management of planting and regeneration, need not be damaging to the long-term health of woodlands.

b Improving farm roads for woodland management is also beneficial for farming operations.

c Woodland management provides useful winter work for farm labour.

d Woods can provide estate needs for fencing material, firewood, woodchip fuel and animal bedding, as well as larger timbers for building.

Sporting value

Many farmers value their woods for rough shooting, pheasant shooting, and as fox coverts. Broadleaved woods are especially valuable, as their varied structure and species provide good sources of food, cover and shelter. The long and irregular boundaries of small farm woods maximises the important woodland edge habitat.

Pheasants require a fairly open woodland structure, so that sunlight and warmth reach the woodland floor. Shelter from the wind is also important, so some ground cover or a boundary hedge is needed. Wide, sunny rides are valuable for feeding sites.

Ideal tree species are sweet chestnut, oak, whitebeam and ash, with an understorey of hawthorn and rowan for their berries. For further information see the Game Conservancy Booklet 15 'Woodlands for Pheasants'.

In lowland woods, the priority is usually to let more sunlight into the wood, and open up rides and glades. In upland woods where conifers predominate, broadleaves need to be introduced and the structure of the wood diversified. 'Game strips' can be created, by planting irregular strips of broadleaves or pines and larches through spruce plantations. All these measures will improve the conservation value of the wood, and can be integrated with management for wood production. Comprehensive details on the subject of woodland design and management for game is given in 'Woodland Management' (Gray), available from the Game Conservancy.

Short-rotation coppices of 5–10 years, with good access along rides and paths creates suitable conditions for fox-hunting. Some hunts own and manage coverts in this way, specifically for their sport.

HEDGEROWS AND FARM TREES

Hedgerows and other isolated farm trees are especially important in areas where woodlands are scarce. In addition to their landscape value, they offer shelter and some wildlife habitat where these are often at a premium.

Hedgerow trees are an important source of hardwood, as together with timber from small woods of less than 2 hectares (5 acres), they contribute about 20% of the total output of hardwood in Britain. However, it is probable that this output is not being

replaced by new plantings. Traditionally, they also provided a useful source of pollarded poles, and can be coppiced for firewood, if fenced off from livestock.

In the last few decades, many hedgerow and other farm trees have been lost at an alarming rate, exacerbated by the ravages of Dutch elm disease. On many farms, hedgerow trees are disliked because they cost money to maintain, shade adjacent land and get in the way of machinery, particularly where fields are small. By careful siting however, farm trees can be replaced by planting field corners and boundaries where shade will not be detrimental.

Maintaining and replacing hedgerow trees

Keep in mind the following general points:

a Trees that are regularly cut, either as hedge shrubs or pollards, should continue to be managed in this way to preserve the vigour of the trees. Typical species for this treatment include ash, maple, willow, oak and elm. Pollarded trees are extremely long-lived and valuable for wildlife, and should be maintained even after their middles rot and the crowns start to die back.

b The simplest way to ensure that there are young trees to replace those which have died or become unsafe is to promote 'tillers' (saplings) which are already growing in the hedge. Where trimming is being done by machine, walk the hedge beforehand and tie bright bits of cloth or plastic around the stems which are to be left uncut. A further protective measure is to position a stout stake with an easily-seen painted top on either side of the sapling.

c Where the hedge is beyond recovery, or does not contain suitable tree species, new trees can be planted in or beside the hedge.

Planting in an existing hedge is laborious. Also, competition for light, water and nutrients from the existing hedge makes it hard for trees planted in this position to survive. Use tree shelters to enhance growth, and keep the hedge well trimmed around the trees to aid their growth.

Planting beside the hedge is easier, but you need to fence off the trees from livestock or provide them with individual guards, which is expensive. Trees planted beside the hedge take up more room than those planted in the hedge, and make mechanical trimming more difficult.

d The most promising locations for new hedgerow trees are along roadsides, especially internal or newly built roads which lack adequate screening and shelter, and where there is a 'waste' verge on one side of the hedge suitable for trees (see also point e, p50).

e Plant hedgerow trees at irregular spacings, and at least 10–12m (30–40′) apart to allow each tree to develop fully.

SHELTERBELTS

Shelter is a valuable function provided by all rough hedges and narrow woodlands, some of which – such of the 'shaws and rews' of the Sussex Weald – are characteristic and ancient features of the farming landscape. Management of these features should aim to protect their historic, landscape and wildlife value by reducing interference as far as possible. Maintenance may include essential trimming where they border arable land, and protection from grazing to allow natural regeneration, aided by replanting where necessary.

Shelterbelts as planned and planted features are mainly found in upland or very exposed areas where they provide protection for forestry plantings as well as windbreaks for buildings and shelter for crops and livestock. In such environments, careful design, siting and maintenance are needed to ensure the survival and usefulness of the shelterbelt. For details on design and siting see Caborn (1965), Ministry of Agriculture, Fisheries and Food (1977) and chapter 5 of Blyth, Evans, Mutch and Sidwell (1987).

Design

For optimum efficiency, shelterbelts should have about 40% permeability, so that the wind speed is slowed, without eddies forming. Shelter should be created for about 20 times the height of the belt on the downwind side, and about 3 times the height on the upwind side. The wind will sweep around the ends of a belt, leaving a triangular-shaped sheltered zone, as shown. To allow for variations in wind direction, the length of a belt designed for crop shelter should be about 25 times its expected height (Blyth, Evans, Mutch and Sidwell, 1987).

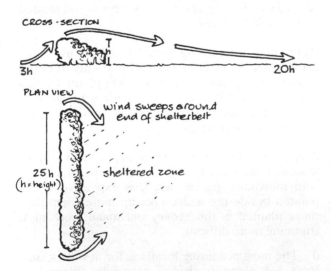

The most important part of a shelterbelt is the base, as if this becomes sparse, wind speeds are increased through the wood and the area beyond, and it becomes difficult to retrieve the situation as new plants cannot be established in such draughty conditions, unless artificial shelter is used. The base can be kept thick by correct choice of species and

suitable management. Shelterbelt trees should not be brashed.

Wider belts are no more efficient than narrower belts of the same permeability, so where crop protection is the main objective, and cropping space is valuable, a shelter of three, five or seven rows, up to about 20m width, is sufficient. However, narrow belts are difficult to regenerate without clear-felling and replanting, and are less attractive as landscape and wildlife features than wider strips.

Avoid gaps, openings and re-entrants on the windward side of shelterbelts. If an opening is required, make it oblique to the wind, and plant the edges with wind-firm species.

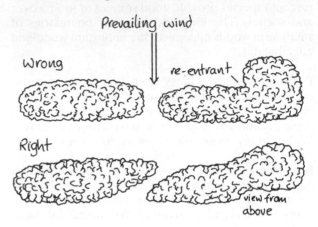

Planting

For most purposes, an A shaped profile is suitable, with the middle third planted with tall trees, and the outer thirds planted with smaller trees and shrubs. Where the aim is maximum shelter for minimum width, plant tall, wind firm species up to the windward edge, with smaller trees and shrubs along the leeward edge.

A shaped profile

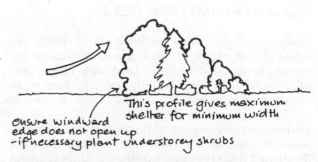

This profile gives maximum shelter for minimum width
ensure windward edge does not open up - if necessary plant understorey shrubs

Suitable species include the following:
TALL   Lime, oak, sycamore, Scots' pine

MEDIUM   Whitebeam, cherry, rowan
SMALL   Hawthorn, holly, hazel

In harsh, upland situations birch, alder and willow may be suitable on more fertile sites, with Scots' pine, and the non-native Shore pine and Noble fir best on infertile ground.

There are several ways of approaching establishment and maintenance:

a Nurse species can be planted, which will grow quickly and give shelter for the slower-growing longer-lived species. Suitable conifers include Scots pine, and introduced species such as Sitka spruce, European larch and hybrid larch. Of the broadleaves, willow and poplar can be used as a nurse. The nurse can either be planted in a strip along the windward edge with an outer strip of understorey shrubs, or mixed throughout the planting, but both methods present problems. When a windward strip is felled or deteriorates, the increased exposure may damage the remaining trees. Nurse crops that are mixed throughout need careful thinning and removal to make sure the slower-growers are not swamped.

b The belt can be established in two stages, planting half the width initially, and the other half as the planting begins to mature and become sparse at the base.

c Plant the full belt initially and thin it heavily at about 15 years, and more lightly thereafter at about 5 year intervals, at the same time under-planting with shade-bearing shrubs, small trees or successor species such as beech.

In extreme conditions, especially near the coast where salt air can burn foliage for several miles inland, it may be necessary to plant behind a fairly permeable screen (eg wattle hurdles, brashings, chestnut paling or slatted timber fences). Take a close look at site conditions and seek local advice on species which do well in the locality, since plants which are generally tolerant of salt winds may not be so in every situation.

Old, sparse, ineffective shelterbelts can be revitalised in several ways. Where a belt casts a heavy shade, plant a new margin one to three rows deep along its windward edge. Then thin and underplant the old belt. Alternatively, replant existing gaps in the belt and then gradually extend the replanted areas by further fellings. A third method is to cut a series of V-shaped wedges through the width of the belt, starting at a point on the leeward edge. These should be replanted and progressively widened out by further fellings until the whole belt is eventually replanted.

SHELTERWOODS

In upland and exposed areas, woodland may be planted to provide shelter for stock. Shelter is valuable for stock in bad weather, as this reduces the food intake they need to keep warm. It can also be helpful to the farmer, as the stock are easier to locate in bad weather, when they will gather within the shelter.

a Woods can be designed so that they offer shelter, whilst still being fenced against stock. On open land, where stock can move freely all around the perimeter, blocks of woodland will give some shelter whichever way the wind is blowing. Some woods are planted in the plan of an 'L' or 'X', to increase the amount of edge and shelter. Unlike shelterbelts, the permeability of the woodland is not significant, and any species that suit the site can be used. It may be possible to combine the shelter function with management for wildlife, landscape or timber value.

b Other shelterwoods are partly or completely unfenced, allowing access for stock. This gives better shelter, but management of the woodland is more difficult than for fenced woods. The ground can become badly trampled or 'poached', which not only destroys the ground flora but damages root systems of trees. Browsing and bark damage will occur, and natural regeneration will be halted. A better method is to divide the woodland into three or four fenced compartments, using one per season in rotation. Any natural regeneration may need extra protection, such as tree shelters, until large enough to withstand browsing.

Scrub or 'Poor Quality Woodland'

It is often the characteristics that confer the grade of 'poor quality' for timber production that are those of importance for nature conservation. For example, unmarketable species such as rowan, sallow, thorns and elder form valuable habitats for invertebrates and for nesting and feeding birds. Damaged or over-mature trees are valuable habitats for fungi, invertebrates, birds and small mammals, and the open glades of an 'understocked' woodland are important for flowering plants and insects.

However, many of these characteristics are not permanent, as trees age and die, and open glades succeed to scrub. Other factors such as grazing or increased recreational use may degrade the conservation value and make some intervention necessary. Often limited measures to produce some timber can combine with management for conservation.

Woodland is defined as poor quality if it has a poor stocking of marketable species (other than for firewood), and where more than half the trees are of poor form or defective. Poor stocking is evident if the distance between potentially usable trees is more than average tree height. Poor form includes trees which do not have a reasonably straight, defect-free butt of at least 3m length.

Species normally defined as 'unmarketable' include dogwood, elder, field maple, hazel, holly, rowan, sallow, thorns and whitebeam. This is because either

43

limitations of size or timber quality make them not readily marketable. However, most species can be coppiced for firewood or other uses, and the timber of mature trees of holly, field maple or other species may be of interest to craftsmen, sculptors, floral arrangers and so on. Such limited markets need to be found before any timber is felled, especially where timber value needs to be balanced against conservation interest.

MANAGEMENT FOR WOOD PRODUCTION

Many areas of scrub have very high conservation, landscape or sporting interest, and any benefit to be gained by management for wood production should be balanced against possible losses to these interests.

Especially in the lowlands, many scrub woodlands are on fertile sites, and have good potential for wood production. Evans (1984, p93) gives five main options which can be followed, the choice of which should be determined by the age and condition of the wood, and the finance and labour available for management.

Coppicing

This is a good choice where labour, finance and other inputs are limited, and where management is likely to be intermittent. It is feasible for many woods where small size or poor access makes other uses unsuitable. All broadleaved species can be coppiced, although beech does not respond well, and shrub species such as elder, sallow and thorn do not produce any useful timber. Coppicing is not worth starting if the wood consists mainly of shrub species, but only where tree species predominate.

Enrichment

This involves planting trees which will produce a marketable crop. Trees can either be planted in existing gaps, which should have a diameter at least one and a half times the height of surrounding trees, or in swathes cut through the scrub. The width of the swathes should be at least equal to the height of the adjacent trees, with 4m (13') the minimum practical width. This latter technique is more expensive in labour and planting costs, and can create an unattractive 'stripy' appearance.

Rapid establishment of the new trees is essential to compete with surrounding growth. Weeding, use of tree shelters, and cutting back of competing trees is necessary to produce a good crop.

The recommended technique is to use transplants, spaced 3–4m (10–13') apart. Tree shelters (p90) promote rapid growth, protect against browsing, and make the trees easy to relocate for maintenance. Regular maintenance is essential to ensure that trees do not suffer from competition.

Improvement

This is only worth doing if the stand contains trees which are worth improving. Individual stems which are suitable in species, form and quality should be marked, and then favoured by cleaning and thinning.

The aim should be to produce at least 100 trees/ha (40 trees/acre) of marketable potential. For pole-stage woods, which are those with trees over 10m (33') top height, the best course may be to fell all but the selected trees. This saves further thinning, and produces a quantity of timber immediately which should pay for the operation.

Woodland below pole-stage should be checked every four years and competing growth from trees, shrubs and climbers cleared from around the selected crop trees.

Thicket or pre-thicket woods require no intervention, apart from the clearance of invasive weeds such as rhododendron or bracken.

Non-intervention

Some scrub woodland will be in the process of naturally developing to high forest, and if at the 'thicket' stage (below 10m, 33' height), can be left to grow for 10 to 15 years before thinning is needed. Conservation or other interests may also dictate non-intervention, or the wood may simply be not worth attempting to manage for an economic return.

Replacement

This involves clearing the existing wood by machinery or herbicides, and then replanting. This is undesirable for conservation reasons, and there are also disadvantages for commercial operations. Clearance by machinery can badly compact the soil and increase surface wetness, which makes establishment of a new crop more difficult. There will be profuse weed growth, and the incidence of Honey fungus (p102) is likely to be high.

Replacement is only worthwhile if the new crop is to be of a high value. Replacement by conifers, which has been a common practice during the last few decades, is no longer the policy of the Forestry Commission (p18).

4 Management for Conservation and Amenity

This chapter looks firstly at the priorities in woodland conservation, and then at methods of managing woodlands and trees for conservation and amenity.

Priorities in Woodland Conservation

This section is based mainly on Peterken (1977 and 1977a) which should be consulted for details.

The general priority in woodland conservation is the conservation of ancient semi-natural woodlands.

As discussed in chapter 1 (p7), ancient woodlands are those which have existed continuously on a site since at least the year 1600. Such woods are characterised by the presence of certain 'indicator' species. These are plants or animals which have great difficulty colonising sites once they have been cleared. Their presence does not mean that clearance has never taken place, but that any clearance must have been so long ago that its effects are negligible.

The following plant species are those whose presence indicate ancient semi-natural woodland. Note that other factors should also be taken into account when assessing sites. Some of these species are now available either as seeds or plants, and may thus be introduced to sites.

Quercus petraea (Sessile oak)
Tilia cordata (Small-leaved lime)
Sorbus torminalis (Wild service tree)
Euonymus europaeus (Spindle)
Equisetum sylvaticum (Wood horsetail)
Ophioglossum vulgatum (Adder's tongue)
Polystichum aculeatum (Hard shield fern)
Helleborus viridis (Green hellebore)
Anemone nemorosa (Wood anemone)
Ranunculus auricomus (Goldilocks)
Aquilegia vulgaris (Columbine)
Corydalis claviculata (White climbing fumitory)
Cardamine flexuosa (Wood bitter-cress)
Viola reichenbachiana (Pale wood violet)
Hypericum hirsutum (Hairy St Johns wort)
Moehringia trinervia (Three-nerved sandwort)
Oxalis acetosella (Wood-sorrel)
Vicia sylvatica (Wood vetch)
Lathyrus montanus (Bitter vetch)
Geum rivale (Water avens)
Sedum telephium (Orpine)
Chrysosplenium oppositifolium (Golden saxifrage)
Chrysosplenium alternifolium (Alternate-leaved golden saxifrage)
Sanicula europaea (Sanicle)
Mercurialis perennis (Dog's mercury)
Euphorbia amygdaloides (Wood spurge)
Primula vulgaris (Primrose)
Lysimachia nemorum (Yellow pimpernel)
Myosotis sylvatica (Wood forget-me-not)

Veronica montana (Wood speedwell)
Melampyrum pratense (Common cow-wheat)
Lathraea squamaria (Toothwort)
Lamiastrum galeobdolon (Yellow archangel)
Scutellaria galericulata (Common skull-cap)
Campanula latifolia (Large campanula)
Campanula trachelium (Nettle-leaved bellflower)
Galium odoratum (Woodruff)
Adoxa moschatellina (Moschatel)
Dipsacus pilosus (Small teasel)
Convollaria majalis (Lily of the valley)
Ruscus aculeatus (Butcher's broom)
Endymion non-scriptus (Bluebell)
Allium ursinum (Ramsons)
Paris quadrifolia (Herb paris)
Luzula pilosa (Hairy woodrush)
Luzula sylvatica (Greater woodrush)
Narcissus pseudonarcissus (Wild daffodil)
Epipactis purpurata (Violet helleborine)
Epipactis helleborine (Broad helleborine)
Neottia nidus–avis (Bird's nest orchid)
Platanthera chlorantha (Greater butterfly orchid)
Orchis mascula (Early purple orchid)

'Semi-natural' woodlands include those which, on ancient sites, are made up mainly of native species growing where their presence is apparently natural, and not obviously planted. On recent sites, ie those that have grown up since about 1600, semi-natural woods are those which have originated by natural regeneration.

Ancient semi-natural woodlands are important for several reasons. They contain many features deriving directly from natural conditions. They cannot be recreated once they are destroyed. They provide homes for many 'extinction-prone' species, which include those with little ability to disperse or colonise new sites, relatively small populations, or those subject to large fluctuations in numbers. The viability of these species is made more precarious by the fact that, in Britain, woodlands exist as 'islands' within a virtual sea of cleared land. A rare plant or animal which occurs on one 'island' is often unable to colonise suitable habitats on another 'island', even if this is located nearby.

Ancient semi-natural woodlands may be grouped under four main headings according to their management history:

a   Relics of medieval pasture-woodland

b   Ancient high forest, mainly the 'native' pine-woods of highland Scotland, which may be treated as a geographically separate form of pasture woodland

c   Ancient coppice woods in which the coppice layer has not obviously been planted

d   Ancient woods on inaccessible sites such as ravines and cliffs

In addition, one type of recent woodland has a high nature conservation priority: woodland which has been formed by at least 150 years of natural succession and structural development.

As well as individual priority sites, there are several woodland areas where special sites may be difficult to distinguish but where the entire area has a high value. These include the Chilterns, the western Weald, the New Forest and surrounding districts, the Lower Wye Valley and Speyside.

Peterken (1977a, p231) estimates that of the total area of British woodland, no more than about one fifth falls into the above categories. This amounts to about 1.5% of the land surface of the country. Very few of these woods are economically viable in their present condition. In the past few decades many have been replaced by plantations or cleared completely, although with recent policy changes, the rate of loss should decrease. Protection of remaining sites is vital. Many priority sites are listed in Ratcliffe (1977), and in the NCC Register of Ancient Woodlands. Pasture-woodlands are covered in Rose and Harding (1978).

These high-priority woodlands are not the only ones which deserve conservation management. Many woods have a local importance which can be maintained or enhanced by volunteer effort. Even the least hospitable plantation has some conservation potential and can be improved by the adoption of appropriate management measures.

GENERAL PRINCIPLES

Peterken (1977) outlines general management principles for nature conservation, which on the whole can be applied to amenity and landscape management as well. The first five principles apply to general landscape policy:

a Distinguish between individual woods of high conservation value, woodland areas of high conservation value and other woodlands.

b Give special treatment to special sites and special areas.

c Minimise clearance of woodland to other land use. If clearance is required, it should avoid sites and areas of high conservation value.

d Accept afforestation, other than on sites of high conservation value, but not so much that non-woodland habitats are reduced to small islands within a sea of new woodland.

e When considering clearance and afforestation, develop large blocks of connected woodland while maintaining a scatter of small woods between large blocks.

The next three principles apply to the management of sites or areas of high conservation value:

f Manage a proportion of woods on minimum-intervention lines (see below) in order to restore natural conditions insofar as this is possible.

g Where traditional management is not feasible, introduce alternative systems of management which retain or enhance the conservation value of the site or area.

h Where traditional management is not feasible, introduce alternative systems of management which retain or enhance the conservation value of the site or area.

The remaining seven principles can be applied to woods and woodland areas generally:

i Minimise rate of change within woods, for example in the amount and distribution of tree species, in order to give wildlife time to adjust.

j Encourage maturity by maintaining long rotations between fellings. If this is not possible, retain a scatter of old trees after restocking.

k Encourage native tree species and use non-native species only where necessary.

l Encourage diversity of woodland structure, habitats and species of trees and shrubs, insofar as this is compatible with other principles.

m Encourage restocking by natural regeneration or coppice regrowth.

n Take special measures, where necessary, to maintain populations of rare and local species.

o Retain records of management.

MINIMUM INTERVENTION IN WOODLAND

On some woodland sites, it may be decided that a policy of minimum intervention or non-intervention is the best course to take in order to maintain the interest of the site. Sites which may benefit from minimum intervention are mostly those that have a structure similar to high forest. Long neglected coppice with standards may have this sort of structure. Some sites may be suitable for non-intervention; others will need control of exotics such as sycamore and rhododendron, or control of grazing and browsing.

Another approach is to allocate certain stands within a wood for minimum intervention, which can contribute to the value of the wood in the following ways:

a Dead wood is a valuable component of woodland ecology, which is mainly lost in managed woods. The amount can be increased by leaving perhaps four or five senescent trees per hectare in managed stands, but this is far less than would occur naturally, and the trees are usually left isolated in rather open conditions. The value of these isolated trees would be enhanced by the much greater amount and variety of deadwood occurring in nearby minimum intervention stands, from which the insects and other organisms of dead wood could spread.

b Any mature stands within woods which are otherwise under 50 years of age or so are particularly valuable, and minimum intervention should be practiced when possible. Maintenance of mature stands can also be achieved by managing stands on long rotations of more than 200 years. However, mature stands should only be felled where there are replacement stands coming up to maturity, ie where the age gap between stands is less than about 50 years.

c Little is known of the long-term effects of soil disturbance and compaction during forestry operations, therefore the maintenance of some completely undisturbed soil is important. Minimum intervention stands provide a 'control', against which ecological changes in managed stands can be measured.

Native Upland Woodlands

These include the native pinewoods of Scotland, and broadleaved woods in the uplands of England, Scotland and Wales. Some of these woods are remnants of the ancient natural and semi-natural forest, with others derived from ornamental planting, especially of beech and pine, during the 18th and 19th centuries. The patches of ancient wood have survived due to being on inaccessible sites such as steep slopes, glens and bogs, where they have remained unexploited.

These woods are of enormous value as ecological remnants, as features in landscape, and for the wildlife they support. They are of little commercial value, and their conservation is the management priority. The major problem with these woods is lack of natural regeneration (see p39).

MANAGEMENT OF NATIVE PINEWOODS

The native pinewoods of Scotland, particularly those in the Cairngorms, are among the largest areas of semi-natural forest remaining in Britain. In their totality they include a great variety of structure, from open parkland to densely wooded stands; with subsidiary habitats ranging from bogs and mires to cliffs, screes, rivers and lochs. They are valuable for their bird life and as sources of shelter and food for grazing animals, especially red deer in winter. In addition, they are important for timber production and as a scenic and recreational resource.

In many forests, overgrazing by deer and intensive forestry threaten to destroy the scenic character and wildlife importance of the pinewoods. The key to their long-term conservation is to sort out the remaining sites into categories which can be clearly distinguished by management goals. Forster and Morris (1977, pp118–119) propose the three following categories.

Strict Natural Zone

Management measures to include:

a Reduction of grazing pressure to allow natural regeneration, control of fire hazards and the removal of non-native species.

b 'Non-intervention' should also be practised so that wildlife is disturbed as little as possible, there should be no ploughing, screefing or drainage, no timber extraction, no tree planting, and no removal of windblown timber.

Managed Natural Zone

Management measures to include:

a Timber harvesting by selective thinning and small groups to produce a forest structure of mixed age, and capable of optimum timber production from a self-sustaining resource.

b Promotion of natural regeneration, but without ground treatment.

c No ploughing, drainage or tree planting. Removal of windblown timber if it is commercially desirable, or if there is a danger of spread of disease or pests.

Planting Zone

Management measures to include:

a Commercial forestry measures to obtain maximum productivity, provided no damage is done to adjacent 'Strict Natural' and 'Managed Natural' zones.

b No widespread use of fertilisers, herbicides or pesticides which might affect adjacent zones.

c Planting only Scots pine of local provenance.

The implementation of such a zonation system requires close cooperation between landowners and conservation bodies such as the Nature Conservancy Council. The main input from voluntary working bodies in these woodlands is in fencing and other measures to aid natural regeneration (see p39).

UPLAND BROADLEAVED WOODS

Evans (1984, p104) identifies the following four types of semi-natural upland broadleaved woodland. The dominant species is usually determined by the type of soil.

a Oak woods. These occur on acid soils in high rainfall areas. In south west England they are found as high as 400m (1320'), but in the highlands of Scotland they rarely occur above 200m (660'). Though dominated by sessile oak, other species of trees and shrubs occur, and at higher altitudes the woods merge into areas of rowan and birch.

b Ash woods. These are much less extensive than oak woods, and occur only on base-rich and calcareous soils in the Mendips, Derbyshire Dales and northern Pennines.

c Birch woods. Although often a successional stage between oak and pine woods, there are extensive semi-natural stands of birch in Wales and Scotland. Natural regeneration may be profuse at woodland edges or where the soil has been disturbed.

d Alder woods. These are widespread through Britain, but confined to wet soils beside streams or areas of impeded drainage.

Other upland woods are mainly planted, and include beech, Scots pine and sycamore.

Decline

Many surveys have shown that the area of upland woods are declining, and all attribute the primary cause to be uncontrolled grazing and browsing by wildlife and livestock, which prevents natural regeneration. In Snowdonia, 80% of the broad-leaved woodland area had negligible regeneration, in spite of the fact that over 90% are dominated by mature or overmature trees (Evans, 1984,p105).

Other causes for lack of regeneration are the irregularity of seed years, and uncontrolled burning of adjacent moorland which can spread into the woodland edge. Birch is particularly at risk, as it regenerates at the woodland edge. There may also be inherent problems with regeneration of oak and birch, which may be inhibited in dense stands by lack of light, the thick organic ground layer preventing sufficient rooting into the soil so causing drought of young seedlings, and defoliation by insect larvae.

A major problem is that many upland woods are valued by their owners for the shelter they afford to livestock, thus measures to encourage regeneration must, to be adopted, take this into account.

Possible measures include:

a Fencing of the wood, where this does not conflict with need for livestock shelter. Successive fencing of parts of the wood on a long rotation may be an alternative, so allowing areas to regenerate and recover before letting stock back in again. Regeneration is most susceptible at the seedling stage.

b Protection of individual seedlings by tree guards or shelters. This is best done in stages over a few years, to encourage a varied age structure. Like the use of successional fencing, this is more likely to be successful than attempting to secure regeneration in a single operation, which might fail due to drought, disease or some other calamity.

c A firebreak around the wood will prevent accidental burning. Evans (1984, p108) recommends spreading a heavy application of lime on a strip 10m (33') wide around the wood. This encourages the growth of sweet grasses, which will be preferentially grazed by livestock, so maintaining a close-cropped and fire-resistant sward. This method has the advantage of having little visual impact in the landscape.

d If regeneration follows a good seed year, gaps can be opened up in the canopy, equal to one and a half times the height of the stand. Where weed growth is dense, control will be necessary.

e If regeneration does not occur, planting will be necessary. If possible, use plants grown from seed collected locally.

Establishing upland broadleaved woods

Exposure and generally poor soils in upland sites means that establishing new plantings of broadleaves is difficult. Rowan, alder and birch are the most successful species. Planting mixtures of broadleaves and conifers will aid establishment (see p38). The most favourable sites should be chosen, in a sheltered aspect if possible, and with good drainage. Protection from browsing is essential.

Pasture-Woodlands, Parks and Avenues

The large numbers of very old or decaying trees typical of parks and pasture-woodlands have a special value for wildlife. They provide an abundance of dead-wood habitats which are often lacking in managed woodlands of predominantly young and healthy trees. This, plus the continuity of tree cover and the relatively stable conditions of light and humidity, makes ancient pasture-woodlands in some ways more typical of primeval forests than other surviving woodland types (Rose and Harding, 1978, p32).

Often parks and pasture-woodlands have great historic significance as well as being beautiful landscapes. Their trees should never be felled unnecessarily. Removal of dead wood should be kept to a minimum consistent with the need for public safety. They should be protected both from overgrazing, and from scrub encroachment and eventual overshading by younger trees due to the complete cessation of grazing and mowing. To whatever extent possible, agreement should be reached with surrounding landowners to limit air pollution and spray drift from agricultural chemicals which can seriously damage the lichen populations of old trees. Hollow trees are often the target of vandals, who set fire to them. In areas of heavy public access, fencing may be necessary.

PARKLAND PLANTINGS

Before the old trees die completely, replacements should be planted nearby to preserve something of the parkland landscape for future generations. In many cases it may already be too late to secure an unbroken succession of old trees, but 'conservation pollarding' (p107) of selected trees may help extend their lives until replacement plantings have matured. It is important that a study is made to try and find out as much as possible about the original design, particularly of the 18th and 19th century landscaped parks, in order to retain the character of the area.

In semi-natural pasture-woodland, natural regeneration or the planting of native trees of local provenance is preferable, but exotics have a place in landscape parks. Planted trees should be individually fenced against livestock. Planting is best phased over a ten to twenty year period, both to spread the costs and to avoid the risk of disastrous losses due to drought or other occasional calamities.

Parkland plantings for large-scale effect are best planned by a landscape architect. Especially important are the heights and crown patterns of the trees used. Foliage, flowers and changing character throughout the seasons should also be considered. Miles (1967, pp140–5) and Hilliers Manual of Trees and Shrubs list ornamental trees suitable for a variety of situations.

Park trees are usually planted singly or in widely spaced belts, groups, clumps or groves, depending in most cases on whether or not the land is in agricultural use. Single trees tend to develop much greater girth and branching than members of the same species in woodland. The following points are basic:

a Single trees should be shapely and symmetrical and not too numerous.

b Groups of three to five trees with their crowns in a compact mass produce a more solid effect than a single tree. Generally each group should be composed of just one species.

c Clumps can be used to provide a background, obscure or break up the skyline, and give depth and variety to the scene. A mixture of species and an irregular outline are usually best for informality.

d Groves can be used to break up an area into smaller sections, for example to separate formal parts of a park from the 'natural' landscape beyond. They can be planted along ridges, on high or broken ground, or as short rides or avenues on level ground. Normally, irregular areas of varying widths and broken margins look best, and the species of trees should be planted according to their function, such as shelter, screening or shooting.

AVENUES

Work may include planting of new avenues, as well as restoration of ones which have fallen into decay.

Avenues are usually of a single species. Some are broad and long enough to form a framework for a feature such as a house or monument. These can be 'patched' by interplanting young trees or by planting new rows within or without the original lines when the existing trees start to age and die off. Other avenues create a pleasing pattern of tracery and dappled shade when seen from beneath, and to achieve absolute symmetry it is necessary to replant this type of avenue afresh. In almost every case it is best to resist felling existing avenue trees until they die completely. Replacement planting should use descendants of the original stock if possible.

The width of an avenue depends on its length, the species planted and the number of rows. Normally an avenue 100m (100 yards) long is about 10m (10 yds) wide. An avenue 1km ($\frac{1}{2}$ mile) long may be 50m (50 yds) wide or more. Trees in rows may be planted relatively close, at 5–10m (5–10 yd) intervals, to eventually almost merge into a large scale hedge. Alternatively they can be planted further apart, at 20–40m (20–40 yd) intervals, to retain their individuality. Very large-scale avenues should be planted in widely spaced clumps so that replacement is easier, the effect is less artificial, and the avenue is not ruined if one trees dies.

Thinning may be necessary as trees in an avenue mature. At West Lodge Park, near Barnet, a double avenue of common lime was planted at three yard intervals in 1910. In 1976 every third tree in each row was removed, without regard to the size or shape of any individual tree. Ten years later the thinning was hardly noticeable, as smaller trees had caught up and spread to fill the gaps.

Urban Trees and Derelict Land

Management of trees in cities and waste places is a complex subject which can only be dealt with briefly here. Vegetation management and planting programmes should be developed within an overall landscape design policy. See Fairbrother (1974) and Clouston (1977).

URBAN TREES

Formal plantings

In formal plantings, such as in small squares or courtyards, arrange species to produce a balanced blend of foliage and flowers. Avoid planting too many species, which produces an unattractive hotchpotch. Consider the size of plants at maturity and the effects of seasonal changes in their appearance. Avoid straight lines and square blocks and aim for layouts which suit the landscape.

Plant shrubs and whips rather than standards when possible. Large trees give an 'instant' effect, but are expensive and less likely to thrive.

Informal plantings

In informal plantings such as public open spaces and school grounds, shrubs and whips can be planted at fairly close spacing provided that later thinning takes place so that the plants can grow to maturity. Barriers, clumps and thickets produce a more natural woodland effect, and are less prone to vandalism, than scattered or irregular planting.

Where space allows, plan woodland blocks or corner plantings with graded 'edges' for structural diversity. Use pioneer species or nurse trees to give diversity early on, and to provide suitable conditions for the 'climax' species.

Species

Use native species when possible, but recognise that some exotics also have great amenity and wildlife value, and may be more suited to areas of poor soil or limited space. You can use fastigiate (columnar) forms of trees such as oak, lime or beech, or slow-growing varieties where native species might grow too large or require lopping. Consider problems of public safety, and the effect of trees on soils and building foundations (see below). Native species which tolerate poor soils and air pollution are listed in the table on page 148. For further information on native and exotic species, see Hillier (1977) or Bean (1970).

Trees in confined spaces

Where space is limited, near buildings, in gardens and next to roads, the effect of plantings and the eventual size of the trees must be carefully considered in advance. The following points are based mainly on Edlin (1972, pp32-46).

a Map out trees near buildings or roads before planting, using a simple plan at a scale of 1:50 for small gardens and 1:100 for larger areas. Where trees are to be sited near buildings or overhead obstructions such as telephone wires, make an elevated sketch at 1:50 showing the outline of the trees at the time of planting and when mature. This provides a check against planting too close. As a rule of thumb, most open-grown conifers achieve a total crown spread of about 33% of their height at maturity. Broadleaved trees are more variable, but a spread of 40% of height is realistic.

b On your maps, indicate constraints on planting such as crowns and stems of neighbouring trees which are to be retained, buildings, fences, hedges and walls, posts and poles which carry wires, signs or lights, drains and sewers, water and gas mains, electric and telephone cables and building foun-

dations. Further constraints include sight lines at road junctions, supply of light to windows, patterns of light cast by street lamps, clear margins at road-sides and the attitudes of adjacent landowners who may be affected.

c Site trees no closer than 5m ($16\frac{1}{2}'$) to drains and sewage pipes. Keep the larger species of willows further away, as they are very prone to send roots into drains for water and block them as a result.

d Never plant poplars within 18m (60') of any building. Their roots are very aggressive and can damage foundations. They also cause shrinkage of clay soils, especially in areas subject to summer drought, such as London and East Anglia.

e Legally, no tree may be planted within 4.57m (15') of the centre of any made–up carriageway. For safety's sake, it is usually best to plant roadside trees at least 9m (30') apart in any direction. Keep trees at least 6m (20') from road junctions to leave sight lines clear.

TREES ON DERELICT LAND

Always survey the site before deciding what sort of management is necessary. Industrial wasteland and derelict urban sites often support surprisingly interesting plant communities which may be destroyed by too-hasty 'improvement' plantings. Given time, they may develop into perfectly good secondary woodland without any help or expense. Sometimes all that you need to do is to tidy up around the edges and to show that the site is cared for. Provide paths, benches or fencing according to the nature of the site and the type of access which is planned for it.

Soils

Sites vary greatly in their soils and suitability for various species. Spoil tips and slag heaps may contain heavy metals, such as copper or zinc, which limit reclamation to top-soiling and grassing over. They may be unstable and require landscaping with heavy machinery before planting can be considered.

Normal drainage channels may be blocked, soil is likely to have poor structure, if any, and surfaces are often compacted and eroded while lower levels may be porous and tend to dry out. At the opposite extreme, quarry workings such as chalk, sand and gravel pits, can have a porous dry soil which is liable to seasonal flooding or waterlogging. Clay soils or those which have been worked in wet weather are liable to be compacted, and need drainage before planting can take place. Coarse-structured soils can be treated by the addition of organic material and very acid soils can be limed. Gemmell (1977) gives details.

City sites often consist of rubble, which may vary from a fine dust of ground-up bricks to boulders and lumps of concrete. Once dug over and rototilled to reduce compaction, these sites can often support a surprising range of plants since they are often rich in calcium, and sometimes phosphate, from the mortar in the brick. Where trees and shrubs are planted, it is usually necessary to add topsoil to the planting pit, but broadcast topsoiling is expensive and may be unnecessary.

Refuse tips often contain much decaying organic material and make good sites for plants, but it may be necessary to first remove or bury the larger lumps of non-degradable debris. Tips are sometimes set alight or catch fire spontaneously and obviously must be put out before planting begins, since otherwise they may continue to burn below the soil surface.

Species

Species which are useful on a variety of sites include grey alder (a non-native), birch and Scots pine on light soils, larch and oak on intermediate soils, and poplars, willows and the native common alder on wet soils. Beech, and the non-native species of sycamore, Austrian pine and western red cedar are suitable for calcareous soils.

Associated Woodland Habitats

RIDES, GLADES AND WOOD MARGINS

Rides, glades and wood margins provide conditions which are open and sunny, yet sheltered and humid, and suitable for many plants and animals which cannot thrive in dense woodland. They also provide 'edge' habitat which is often particularly rich in species. The rides, glades and margins of ancient woodlands have often evolved over many centuries of management, and provided an appropriate level of use and maintenance is applied, they generally retain much more interest than similar but newly created features. For this reason it is much more important to maintain, and if necessary rehabilitate existing features, rather than to create new ones.

Rides, roads and paths

Access routes in woodlands can often be distinguished under the three categories of rides, roads and paths (Mummery and Tabor, 1978, p7). Rides are generally straight arteries through a wood, traditionally 6m (20') wide, ditched and often drained, compacted and able to carry vehicles at almost any season. They have a predominantly grassland flora. Roads are about 2.5m (8') wide, often winding, not ditched or permanently compacted, and used for periodically extracting material from the wood when the going is firm. They have a woodland flora. Paths are pedestrian ways winding between trees, to give access to points of interest or to enable working parties to take short cuts through the wood.

Not all woods have these features, and often the

rides are ancient while at least some of the paths and roads may be recent. At Chalkney Wood, Essex, access has been made at random through the coppice stools, leaving a maze of old cart ruts.

Keep in mind the following points when considering the maintenance of existing rides and roads (Mummery and Tabor, 1978, p9):

a Rides need as much light as possible to maintain their grassland flora. This is best achieved by rotational coppicing along the ride, preferably to at least 100m distance from the ride, rather than in narrow 'linear coppice' of for example 8m strips. The disadvantage of 'linear coppicing' compared with wider coupes are that less sunlight reaches the ride, extraction of material cut in subsequent years may have to be brought through the young regrowth, and such narrow strips provide less freedom from disturbance for birds and insects.

b The flora of woodland roads is best maintained by alternating periods of light and shade. This can only be provided by siting coppice plots beside the roads and allowing coppice to regenerate naturally. Failure to coppice leads to the loss of vigour rather than loss of species of the woodland flora. Worse than not coppicing is to prevent regeneration of the coppice, or to convert the road into a ride, since this tends to encourage the growth of rank invasive plants such as brambles, willowherb and thistles.

c Roads and rides should be used regularly to maintain their condition, provided vehicle use is avoided when roads are wet and soft.

d Where management of ride and road margins is by mowing rather than coppicing, it is best to vary the frequency of mowing to create a graded edge.

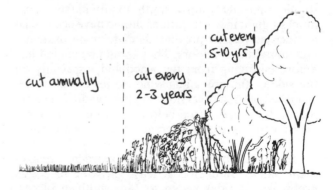

Diversity is increased if alternate edges are mown in different years. A typical mowing regime, from Monks Wood NNR, is shown below (Steele and Welch, 1973, p314).

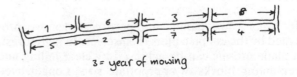

Mowing should be done between October and March, if possible, to allow tall herbaceous plants to flower and set seed, and to allow invertebrates to complete their life cycles. Some rides and roads may have to be cut along the centre strip two or three times a year, to allow vehicle and pedestrian access, but elsewhere summer cutting should be avoided.

New rides, roads and paths are required in newly afforested areas, and occasionally in existing woodlands. Details of the design of rides to standards suitable for vehicle access and timber extraction is given in Blatchford (1978). When designing these features for wildlife and amenity consider these points:

a Paths normally develop haphazardly, as trees grow up and people or animals find the easiest routes through the woods. Follow these natural bends and curves when laying out or opening up a path.

b Bridleways should be at least 2.5m wide (8′), and trimmed up to a height of at least 3m (10′) to provide clearance for riders. Footpaths can be narrower, and allowed to grow over above head height where you wish to discourage use by horse-riders. For further details on footpath and bridleway management see 'Footpaths' (Agate, 1983).

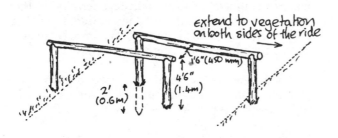

c Ride orientation should be determined by access requirements, but where possible at least one ride should run roughly north-south, to provide the maximum sunlight in winter. Rides should have occasional distinct curves, to prevent them forming draughty and uninviting corridors. They should be angled just before emerging from the woodland, especially on the side of the prevailing wind, to lessen the wind-tunnel effect. For diversity, vary their width in places, scallop their edges (see below), and maintain some overhanging branches to create areas of open shade.

d In conifer plantations, rides between management blocks should be at least 9m wide to act as firebreaks. If rides widen to 18m width in places, they will combine some of the features of rides and glades.

Glades

In coppice woodlands, temporary glades are provided by the coppice plots themselves. In high forest, a glade mosaic can be achieved by clear felling and replanting blocks of appropriate size. Longer-lived glades are also valuable because they provide a more stable habitat. The following points apply to creating and maintaining glades:

a Glades which are linked to ride systems are generally more useful to wildlife than those which are isolated. This is especially true for plants and animals which may be unable to find new clearings in the midst of woods. Glades which are to be maintained should be accessible by motor-mowers.

b Small natural glades often form where trees are hit by lightning or are blown down. The remains of the dead tree should be left to rot, and herbs and shrubs allowed to grow up around it to improve its wildlife value. Good locations for purpose-cut glades are around ponds or swampy areas, where trees grow poorly, and at the corners of intersecting rides.

c Glades should be at least 0.2 hectare (half acre) in size, if fringed with big trees, to ensure that sunlight reaches the ground even in winter. Glades can be as small as 0.1 hectare (quarter acre), if fringed with a margin of shrubs and small trees. Remember when cutting new glades that the crowns of the existing trees will expand and reduce their effective area.

Small glades receive more light in winter if they are elongated on a north–south axis. Ideally, large woods of 40 hectares (100 acres) should contain some larger glades and fields up to 2 hectares (5 acres) in size.

Light-canopy trees such as birch and aspen can be left to provide dappled shade in parts of larger glades, to increase their variety.

d Where it is not possible to have a big enough glade within the wood, one edge, preferably on the south or west side, or a ride margin, can be deeply scalloped to create a partially protected open area. Scalloped margins increase the amount of edge and provide more varied conditions of light and shelter.

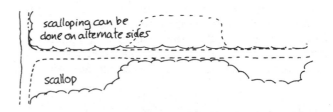

e Glade margins should be cut to form a graded edge in the same way as rides. Traditionally, large glades were managed by being enclosed and left to grow up to late hay, and after cutting livestock were let in to graze on the stubble. This helped to create floristic diversity by keeping down the accumulation of litter and preventing coarse grasses dominating.

Where grazing is not feasible it may be best to remove the litter by hand, or burn the cut litter over part of the glade each year. Management may have to be tailored to meet the needs of any rare or interesting species, such as the Black Hairstreak at Monks Wood, or flowers which require freedom from mowing to set seed. Mowing should generally be done between October and March, as for rides.

Wood margins

Wood margins can, in general, be maintained in the same way as ride or glade edges to provide a variety of sheltered conditions. In ancient woods the margins are usually defined by banks and ditches, which are often of great historic interest. Wood-bank trees should usually be left untouched. Sometimes these are species unusual for the site, such as beech planted in damp oakwoods, or they show signs of pollarding or laying as hedges. Not infrequently, they are the oldest trees in the wood. It may be worth renewing pollarding or hedging, bringing only a proportion of the wood-bank into rotational cutting at any one time, and leaving some trees to continue to age without interference.

PONDS AND STREAMS

Open-water habitats are often very valuable in their own right, and their presence in a woodland greatly increases the site's diversity, as well as improving its amenity value. Aquatic and amphibious plants and animals in woodland ponds and streams are often more free from disturbance than in ponds located in the midst of agricultural or urban land. Where enough suitable habitat is available, selected ponds can often be used for field studies or for fishing without damaging their interest.

Pond and stream management is covered in detail in 'Waterways and Wetlands' (Brooks, 1976). The following points are basic:

a Woodlands with poor drainage or a high water table are often rich in wildlife. Drainage should never be undertaken unnecessarily or without a clear idea of the ecological effects.

b Where woodlands lack watery habitats, it is often possible to diversify them by damming small streams or digging out, and if necessary, lining ponds. Ponds can also be useful for fire-fighting.

c Woodland ponds and streams tend to silt up quickly and become overshadowed by trees. Heavily shaded watercourses are almost barren of wildlife, although moderately shaded streams are ideal for bryophytes. Overshaded ponds and streams should be opened up along parts of their south sides to let in sunlight. The sunniest bank is the north bank, which should be managed for herbaceous and low shrub vegetation. Parts of the margin should be left shaded, especially by overhanging roses, brambles or hawthorns which provide food for aquatic animals. Some ponds, especially those in ancient woodlands, should be left undisturbed to allow natural succession to take place, and to avoid destroying the record of woodland history which is contained in their sediments.

d Pond banks should be gently shelving, at least in places, to allow a full zonation of marginal plants to develop, and to create landing places for ducklings and amphibians. If possible, ponds should be at least 1.8m (6′) deep at the centre in order to maintain open water.

e Felling, extraction and work such as ride improvement should be done with great care on slopes and near ponds and streams, which may otherwise be badly damaged by siltation and disruption of drainage. A wide fringe of shrubs and trees is useful to intercept excess runoff and prevent soil erosion and silting.

OLD TREES AND DEADWOOD HABITATS

Old and dying trees, and standing and fallen deadwood provide habitats for almost a thousand animal species, of which most are insects, but include other invertebrates, bats and hole-nesting birds. Lichens, fungi and mosses are also abundant. These habitats are particularly important for many rare and restricted species.

Traditional woodland management emphasised 'cleanliness', to prevent the spread of pests and diseases harboured in dead wood. Use could also be made of materials such as brashing and lop-and-top which no longer have much value to people. Woodland management for conservation purposes often aims to increase the amount of old trees and deadwood habitats. Hygienic measures are still important in productive conifer plantations, but dead conifers can safely be left to rot where no productive plantations occur nearby. Their presence is especially valuable in remnant Highland pinewoods, in secondary woods on the sites of old plantations and in relicts of coniferous plantings within existing broadleaved woods.

In broadleaved woodlands, insects and fungi of deadwood (other than honey fungus) rarely affect healthy trees so forest hygiene is less important. But keep in mind the following restricting factors:

a In actively coppiced woodlands, it is normally more practicable to burn cuttings than to leave them to rot (p124). Where the cuttings are to be used for pea sticks and so on, some of the stacked material can be left over one winter, to provide shelter and spring nest sites, and then removed later for sale.

b Where public safety is paramount, it may be necessary to lop dead limbs and to fell standing trees. But even here, some dead wood can be left on living trees, and dead trees can be left where fallen.

c Elms are a good deadwood habitat, but the risk of Dutch elm disease means that on sites where some elms are free of the disease, dead or dying elms should be felled, and the bark removed from the stems and larger branchwood and burned.

Stubbs (1972) suggests a number of additional management principles for the conservation of old trees and deadwood habitats:

a Maintain a continuous supply of dead wood in a

diversity of sizes and of each of the following four types: living or partly living standing trees: boles of trees with the tops broken off: logs of various sizes: residual stumps.

b Leave at least a few trees, scattered through the wood, to reach the maximum size and age practical, since certain lichens only grow on trees older than 200 years, and large dead trees provide better habitats and more stability than small ones. Lichens require dappled shade, so be sure the old trees aren't completely overshadowed.

c Leave dead or dying wood on standing trees for as long as possible. With felled trees, leave as much of the bole as possible, including the thickest parts. Leave portions of all sizes of side limbs scattered about, with some limbs leaning against the tree with their shattered ends uppermost. Do not break up stumps or disperse piles of dead and rotting wood. An intact fallen tree is better than one which is fragmented. Pile brushwood nearby.

d Dead wood should be protected from intense sun, otherwise it dries out and becomes useless to all but a few invertebrates. Maintain at least a partial canopy over dead boles, and allow the field layer to grow up to increase humidity. A diversity of settings is valuable, for example some dead wood in glade edges, under moderate canopy and in dense shade. Dead wood near nectar-rich flowering plants such as hawthorn, elder and umbellifers, and near damp areas and streams, supports a more interesting animal life than dead wood far from these resources.

e You can increase the amount of dead-wood habitat by felling or ring-barking standing trees. Do this in winter or spring, since bark beetles and other creatures which colonise new dead wood cannot usually make use of summer or autumn felled trees. If decay is by fungi along, it proceeds much more slowly than when invertebrates are present from the beginning.

For further information see 'Wildlife Conservation and Dead Wood' (Stubbs, 1972).

BRAMBLES AND CLIMBERS

Brambles are sometimes routinely cleared from woodlands, although they can be useful for management as well as for wildlife. They can help shield tree seedlings from deer and rodent attack, and in woods open to the public can be useful for managing access. Brambles bear flowers which are important to butterflies and other insects, and should be left except where they threaten to overwhelm young trees, or where they cover large areas and shade out interesting low-growing herbaceous plants. As newly-planted trees grow up, they eventually shade out most of the brambles except along sunny rides and in glades.

Honeysuckle and clematis (old man's beard or traveller's joy) twine around stems and can strangle or smother young trees. They should be controlled in young plantations, but once the trees are established and have closed the canopy, honeysuckle generally causes little problem. Clematis may need continuing control, especially in hedgerows and in base-rich soils where the vigour of other trees and shrubs may be reduced.

Ivy neither strangles nor smothers young trees, although it may compete with them for water and nutrients, and smother the crowns of old and already moribund trees. There is seldom any reason for cutting it out. Climbers provide food, cover and nest sites for invertebrates, birds and mammals. Honeysuckle is especially good for butterflies and is used by nesting dormice, while the autumn flowers and late berries of ivy provide an important wildlife food source at a season when other food is scarce. Climbers should normally be allowed to develop in established woodlands and along ride margins.

Woodland Regeneration

Not all woodlands are self-maintaining, but may need help to keep some of their characteristic trees and shrubs from dying out. These are typically woods in areas of climatic extremes, those under heavy grazing pressure, and those where coppicing has been long neglected.

In upland areas, many semi-natural woods are vestigial. Even the cessation of grazing, which usually still occurs sporadically, may not be enough to prevent them gradually succumbing to unfavourable climatic conditions. In other woods, the long-term balance between tree species may be changing due to marginal changes in soil nutrient levels (especially phosphorus), litter accumulation, the water table or to fluctuations in the populations of rodents, deer and other animals which feed on seedlings and young trees. Oak, particularly, is often said to have a regeneration 'problem', although this is usually on sites where its apparent dominance may be due to 19th century planting practices and where, under more nearly natural conditions, it may maintain itself as just one of several major constituents in a mixed woodland. Scots pine, in some of its native Highland locations, is another 'problem' tree which is often said to require help if it is to survive.

On sites where nature conservation, rather than forestry, is the main aim, it is important to keep the problem in perspective. Long periods of apparent non-regeneration may mean little on some sites, such as good oak areas in parts of the New Forest, where individual trees may live 400 years or more. The maintenance of woodland cover may be due to very occasional periods suitable for oak regeneration. For details on oak regeneration see Morris and Perring (1974).

The time scale may be almost as long in native pinewoods if, as one hypothesis suggests, regeneration may depend on infrequent catastrophic storms which uproot many of the existing trees and expose fresh mineral soil to seedling colonisation (see Goodier and Bunce, 1977, p80).

In such areas, too-hasty attempts to aid regeneration may cause more harm than good. Even if woods are gradually dying out due to natural factors such as climatic change, it must be asked whether this should, in every case, be resisted.

Where regeneration is deliberately aided, methods should be tried on a small scale first. Every site differs, and failures may be costly and result in environmental damage. In addition to fencing against rabbits, deer and farm stock, the following measures may be used:

a Opening the canopy by thinning, limited clear felling or rotational coppicing, in order to let in light for seedlings. This is especially helpful for some species, such as oak and pine, which are light demanding. Under natural conditions, these species regenerate best on the margins of woods rather than within the woods themselves. Other species, such as beech, ash, wych elm and wild cherry, grow up more easily under moderate woodland cover.

b Cultivating the ground prior to and during seed fall, and delaying the felling of parent trees (if felling is necessary) to a year later, when it can be seen if regeneration is occurring. At this stage the ground should show a 'bristle' of small seedlings which are little damaged by extraction of the seed trees.

Most seedlings germinate and grow best in soil which has been harrowed or otherwise deeply scarified, so that the surface vegetation and leaf litter has been broken up. Large-seeded species such as oak can germinate and root through a grassy cover, but small-seeded trees such as birch germinate successfully only on bare soil or decaying humus. Scots pine can seed into short heather but seedlings are smothered in tall heather or deep moss. Ploughing in the vicinity of parent trees can aid Scots pine regeneration on upland sites.

An alternative to cultivation is the controlled burning of heather and other vegetation to aid Scots pine regeneration. This also releases nutrients which may be important in stimulation of cone production (Carlisle, 1977, p74).

c Where natural seeding is insufficient, larger seeds such as oak mast, beech and hazel nuts can be collected and planted, preferably with protection from rodents (see p101). Sowing of seeds in pre-erected tree shelters (p90) is a new technique which appears promising. In the Highlands, the Nature Conservancy Council have had success with direct sowing of alder seed in areas of purple moor-grass (*Molinia caerulea*) and bog myrtle where pines do not grow. In drier areas of the same plots, birch has been seeded successfully using locally collected seed plus added leaf mould.

d It may be necessary to plant nursery stock of species which do not seed adequately or whose seedlings have a poor survival rate. If possible, nursery plants should be raised from seeds of selected trees on site. This is especially important on ecologically valuable sites, where it is important that the local genetic types should be maintained (p73).

For felling systems to encourage natural regeneration in commercial broadleaved woods see page 39.

5 Trees and the Law

This chapter covers legal considerations which are most likely to affect the conservation and amenity management of trees and woodlands. It does not deal with trees and shrubs as boundary features. Problems of ownership, trespass, damage to neighbouring property and nuisance are summarised in 'Hedging' (BTCV, 1975). James (1972) and Pollard (1975) discuss these topics as well as others such as insurance and taxation.

Information in this chapter is mainly from the Department of the Environment Circular 36/78 (Welsh Office Circular 64/78), 'Trees and Forestry' (available from the Forestry Commission), which should be consulted for details.

Felling

FELLING LICENCES

The regulations are set out in the booklet 'Control of Tree Felling' (Forestry Commission, 1986), from which this information is taken. These regulations do not apply to Northern Ireland or the inner London Boroughs.

A licence from the Forestry Commission is normally required to fell growing trees (though not for lopping and topping), but in any calendar quarter up to 5 cubic metres may be felled by an occupier, provided not more than 2 cubic metres are sold.

Licences are not required to fell trees if any of the following conditions apply:

a The felling is in accordance with an approved plan of operations under one of the Forestry Commission's grant schemes.

b The trees are in a garden, orchard, churchyard or public open space.

c The trees are all below 8cm (3") in diameter, measured 1.3m (4'3") from the ground; or in the case of thinnings, below 10cm (4") in diameter; or in the case of coppice or underwood, below 15cm (6") in diameter.

d The trees are interfering with permitted development or statutory works by public bodies.

e The trees are dead, dangerous, causing a nuisance or are badly affected by Dutch elm disease.

f The felling is in compliance with an Act of Parliament.

Application

The application for a felling licence should be made by the landowner, tenant, or by an agent acting on behalf of owner or tenant. Applications should be submitted at least 3 months before felling is due to commence, to the relevant regional office of the Forestry Commission (addresses on page 163), on forms obtainable from them. Felling must not commence until a licence has been issued.

Usually the Forestry Commission will arrange for the trees to be inspected. Consultations may be made with the local authority and any other statutory authority concerned, in order to ensure that relevant environmental or land-use aspects of the proposal are taken into account.

Where forestry or amenity considerations are important, a licence may only be issued on condition that re-planting is carried out. A licence for the felling of broadleaves will normally be conditional on their being replaced with broadleaves. Any such conditions will be discussed with the applicant before the licence is issued. Planting grants will normally be available where a re-planting condition has been imposed. Information on grants is given on page 154.

Provision is made for appeal against refusal of a licence, and for appeal against replanting conditions.

The licence is valid for a set period of years, and if it expires before felling is completed, a replacement licence must be applied for and issued before felling can continue. Any felling without a licence is an offence and carries a liability to a fine not exceeding £1000 or twice the value of the trees, whichever is higher.

In certain circumstances, whether or not a felling licence is needed, permission may be required for any proposed felling. This may include Sites of Special Scientific Interest, Conservation Areas, or where a Tree Preservation Order applies.

TREE PRESERVATION ORDERS

Tree Preservation Orders (TPOs) are the principal means of planning control over the felling or maltreatment of amenity trees. Further information on TPOs in England and Wales is given in the leaflet 'Tree Preservation – A Guide to Procedure' available from the Department of the Environment.

Tree Preservation Orders may be made by a local planning authority (county or district council, or London borough) to cover individual trees of exceptional amenity value, groups of trees, woodlands or all trees within a specified area, whether urban or rural. TPOs do not normally include blanket protection over large areas. Orders are designed to protect amenity trees which might be at risk, but not to hinder careful silvicultural management, so they are not usually made over areas where for many years a high standard of woodland husbandry has been maintained, and where no change of practice or ownership is likely.

A Tree Preservation Order may:

a Prohibit the damage or destruction, felling, lopping, topping or uprooting of trees except with the consent of the local planning authority.

b Ensure the replanting according to specified conditions of any part of a woodland area which is felled as part of permitted forestry operations.

c Require the replacement as soon as reasonably possible of any tree (other than one which is part of a woodland) which is removed or destroyed in contravention of the order, or which dies.

A landowner whose trees are made subject to a TPO must be informed by the Council making the order, and the trees identified on a map. A seller of land is bound to inform a buyer about any TPOs that apply to the property. Anyone can check whether TPOs are in force on any trees, by contacting the relevant District Council.

Should an owner wish to fell trees covered by a TPO, there are two possible courses of action:

a If the proposed felling comes within one of the exceptions from felling licences listed above, an application for consent to fell should be made direct to the planning authority.

b If the proposed felling requires a licence, an application must be made in the first place to the Forestry Commission, who will forward it, together with their comments, to the planning authority so that it may be dealt with as an application for consent to fell under the TPO.

CONSERVATION AREAS

With certain exceptions, anyone proposing to cut down, top, lop or uproot a tree in a Conservation Area is required to give six weeks' notice of their intention to the District Council concerned. If the work is not completed within two years of giving notice, a further notice is needed. A felling licence is required for the felling of trees in a Conservation Area, unless any of the exceptions (a–e above) apply. The trees may also be subject to a Tree Preservation Order, in which case the details given above apply.

RIGHTS OF WAY AND PUBLIC SERVICES

Local authorities can cut back or fell trees and bushes which obscure public rights of way, including footpaths, which obstruct light from street lamps or the sightlines of car drivers. Railway authorities, land drainage authorities, electricity authorities and British Telecom can require removal of trees or parts of trees which may obstruct railways, river banks (where machines are used for dredging), power lines

or telegraph lines. Railway and electricity authorities must pay the costs involved and compensate the owner. Electricity authorities pay a continuing annual compensation for loss of the use of ground. British Telecom does its own lopping, and pays no rent for land occupied by its poles or for wayleaves. Similar powers are available to public bodies that operate water mains, gas mains, oil pipelines and airports, to prevent risk of accident or damage to the installation or to provide access to service routes.

The Wildlife and Countryside Act

SITES OF SPECIAL SCIENTIFIC INTEREST

Under the Wildlife and Countryside Act 1981, the Nature Conservancy Council may designate Sites of Special Scientific Interest (SSSIs), for their geological or ecological value. The intention is that the occupier of the land should not operate in any way which would destroy or damage the special features noted in the designation.

The NCC has to notify the landowner of the boundary of an SSSI, and of any operations or management practices which would affect the site. The landowner must notify the NCC of intention to carry out any of the operations given in the SSSI notification, in time for discussions to take place.

As far as woodland work is concerned, this not only affects woodland SSSIs, but also proposed planting on non-wooded SSSIs. Examples might include downland or wetland, whose value would be reduced if planted with trees. These habitats are not just affected by the shading and other changes brought about by tree cover, but also by operations such as drainage, fertilising or herbicide application which may be part of the tree planting programme.

The following section from 'Control of Tree Felling' (Forestry Commission, 1986) outlines the procedure regarding felling operations on an SSSI. Where felling operations are involved, notification must be given to the NCC, whether or not an application is to be made to the Forestry Commission for a felling licence. In circumstances where a licence from the Commission is required, the notification to the NCC should be given at the same time as an application is made to the Commission for a licence. Subsequent discussion with the NCC on the application will be conducted as part of the normal consultation procedures carried out by the Commission on felling licence applications. Similar arrangements will apply when felling is proposed under one of the Forestry Commission's grant schemes.

SPECIES PROTECTION

The Wildlife and Countryside Act 1981 also controls the disturbance, killing and removal of various plants and animals. Protected birds are listed in Schedule 1, animals in Schedule 5 and plants in Schedule 8.

Copies of the Act and Schedules are available at public libraries.

Pests and Diseases

The Plant Health Act, 1967, provides measures to prevent the introduction or spread of plant pests and diseases. Orders may be made by the Forestry Commission on forest trees and timber, and by the Ministry of Agriculture, Fisheries and Food. In addition to orders prohibiting the landing or transport of certain articles or requiring the destruction of plants or seeds liable to aid the spread of diseases or pests, numerous orders have been made which require the felling and burning of affected trees. For example, the Watermark Disease (Local Authorities) Order 1974, gives powers to certain local authorities to order the destruction of diseased willows, with the aim of protecting commercial plantations of cricket bat willow. The order was amended in 1986, and now covers the counties of Bedfordshire, Essex, Hertfordshire, Norfolk and Suffolk.

Under the Forestry Act, 1967, the Forestry Commission may authorise the destruction of rabbits, hares, squirrels and other vermin which are damaging or likely to damage trees. If the landowner does not take sufficient steps to prevent such damage, the Commission may authorise any competent person to enter the land for this purpose and charge the occupier for the work.

Miscellaneous

UNSAFE TREES

The owner of a tree will not be held responsible in law for damage caused by it falling or losing branches if the failure of the tree could not reasonably have been forseen or prevented. However, if the tree had obvious signs of disease or weakness, the owner might be sued for any damage caused. It is therefore very important that trees under which the public have access are regularly inspected to check on their condition. For further details see Forestry Commission Arboricultural Leaflet 1 'The External Signs of Decay in Trees'.

WATER RIGHTS AND ANGLING

There are particular responsibilities on the owner of woodland regarding neighbours' water rights. The cultivation of land for tree planting, or the use of herbicides or fertilisers must not damage water rights, fisheries or angling on neighbouring property.

6 Safety, Equipment and Organisation

The following information on safety and equipment is basic to many aspects of woodland and tree management work.

For further information on these topics, see the Forestry Industry Safety Guides produced by the Forestry Safety Council.

Safety Precautions

GENERAL

See also pages 96 and 109 for additional precautions when using herbicides and when felling.

a Have a suitable first aid kit at the work site (see below).

b All volunteers should have been immunized against tetanus.

c Do not work in soaking rain. Once gloves, tools and the ground become sodden and slippery, the chance of hurting yourself greatly increases.

d Wear suitable tough clothing (see below). Thorns and brambles are a hazard, especially when weeding or clearing scrub. Most vulnerable are hands and wrists, followed by knees and face. If you sometimes wear glasses it is best to wear them when working as a precaution against jabs in the eye.

Attend to splinters promptly. Don't ignore even the smallest, as they can cause serious infection. Go to a doctor immediately if you have any serious pain or swelling.

e Never try to lift more than you are capable of, and if you can't get help, move logs by rolling or skidding. When lifting heavy weights, bend your knees, not your back, and lift using your leg muscles.

f Never walk backwards when you are carrying anything, as you may trip. Take particular care when working on a slope.

g Always clear up as you work, and don't leave cut material or debris littering the area.

h If you bring bags with cameras, food and other items, put them safely out of the work area. They may either get crushed, or cause someone to trip.

TOOL USE

Further details are given where appropriate in later chapters. The following points are basic.

a Never use an unfamiliar tool until you have been shown the proper technique. Only trained operators are allowed to handle chain saws.

b Take care with billhooks, slashers, axes and saws. All edged tools are safest when sharp. Check that the tool head is secure and that the handle is free from splinters and cracks. Keep a safe distance from other workers when using edged tools.

c Axes and other cutting tools are brittle when very cold. Warm them before starting work in hard frosty weather. Sharpening will protect the edge. Avoid cutting icy wood, as it will damage the edge.

d Always make sure there is a clear path to swing the tool. Even a small twig may deflect it and cause injury. Never cut towards yourself with an edged tool, as it is likely to slip or bounce off the wood. When using a short-handled tool, keep your free hand well away from cutting direction. Be alert for hazards such as wasps' nests, adders, stones and so on.

e Carry edged tools at their point of balance, just below the heads. Carry them at your side with the edges pointing down and slightly away from you. If you trip, swing the tool away from you and let go. Bow saws should be carried with the blade protected by a plastic sleeve. Never carry more tools than is safe, which usually means just one in each hand.

f Do not leave tools lying about on the woodland floor, as you are likely to either lose them, or discover them the painful way, by treading on them. Never leave edged tools with their cutting surfaces upward.

Prop tools against a nearby tree or stump, or keep them together in a hessian sack. Store your tools centrally so you and any other users know where to find them.

g   Chainsaws must only be used by trained operators, who must wear full safety gear. For further details see 'BTCV Chainsaw Policy' (1986).

WORKING ALOFT

Only trained and properly equipped people should work aloft, and then only when absolutely necessary. The following points are basic:

a   Never work aloft in a high wind, or when branches are wet or covered by frost or snow.

b   When climbing in a tree, move slowly and with care. Don't jump on branches to see if they are sound. Remember that the branches of some species such as horse chestnut, Douglas fir, larch and poplar tend to be weak or brittle. Test hand holds before using them.

c   Volunteers without special training should only work from ladders. Before using any ladder, check that it is in sound condition. Place the top of the ladder squarely against the trunk or main branches of the tree, with the base resting firmly on solid ground. Test the ladder's stability before climbing it. Often it is safest to rope the top of the ladder to the tree. Have a helper stand on the lowest rung of the ladder to steady it.

FIRES

See page 124 for fire lighting and tending. See page 67 for fire-fighting equipment. Blatchford (1978, pp52–9) gives details.

If you are faced with a wildfire, remember the following basic rules:

a   If you see a fire starting, tackle it.

b   If after a few minutes the fire is clearly out of control, leave it and get help immediately. Call the fire brigade.

c   If you are with other people, one of you should run to report the fire while the others stay to fight it.

d   If in doubt, get out! Never put yourself in danger by working beyond your endurance or by neglecting your line of retreat.

e   Work from the flank of the fire to keep the flames from spreading. Beating, earthing and the controlled use of water to cool the hottest spots are generally most effective. Where the blaze is in trees above waist height, go to the far side of a firebreak or barrier and concentrate all efforts on preventing the fire sparking onto your side of the barrier.

Clothing

The aim is always safety and comfort first. Special protective clothing is required when using herbicides (see page 96). For general work you will need:

a   Overalls or close-fitting work clothes. Loose clothing is dangerous when working with edged tools and among branches and brambles. Don't wear a floppy coat or scarf. Be especially careful when working aloft, as even a belt can snag and cause injury.

b   Boots. Heavy leather work boots with spiked or deep moulded soles and protective steel toe-caps are best. In wet and muddy conditions, wellingtons with steel toe-caps are suitable. Plimsolls, light shoes and standard wellington boots do not give adequate protection.

c   Gloves. Essential when dealing with thorns and brambles, and for handling wire rope. A glove is best not worn on the hand holding an edged tool, as this makes the handle harder to grip. Gloves with gauntlets are preferable as they protect the wrists.

d   Helmet. When felling trees, working aloft or near machinery wear a safety helmet complying with BS 5240. Increased protection is needed for chainsaw users, as detailed in 'BTCV Chainsaw policy' (1986).

Tools and Accessories

Items are listed by category, according to their most important type of use. Many items are used for more than one purpose, but are listed only once.

FOR ALL PROJECTS

First aid kit. Keep this with you at all times. Splinters are the most common problem, but wounds may be serious when they do occur. BTCV can supply standard first aid kits which comply with the 1981 Health and Safety Regulations (First Aid). For six to ten people, the contents are:

1 guidance card
20 individual sterile adhesive dressings
2 sterile eye pads with attachments
2 triangular bandages
2 sterile coverings for serious wounds
6 safety pins
6 medium size sterile unmedicated dressings
2 large size sterile unmedicated dressings
2 extra large size sterile unmedicated dressings

From experience on projects, the following 'welfare kit' is also found to be useful: 100mm crepe bandage, tweezers (round-nosed), scissors (round-nosed), insect repellant, antihistamine cream for insect bites, sunscreen cream, mild antiseptic cream, aspirin, eye lotion and eye bath.

A list of local hospitals with casualty departments should also be to hand.

PLANTING AND EARLY CARE

For general use

a   Heavy-duty treaded garden (digging) spade

b   Heavy-duty garden (digging) fork

c   Grubbing mattock

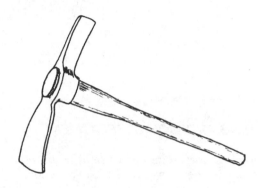

Nursery work: additional tools

a   Garden roller, for preparing seedbeds

b   Garden rake

c   Sharp knife or secateurs, for light pruning

d   Wheelbarrow

e   Hoe

Drainage tools

See 'Waterways and Wetlands' (Brooks, 1976) for details.

a   Round-mouthed (taper-mouthed) shovel or Devon shovel

b   Rabbiting spade or long-handled drainage spade

c   Rutter and hack, for cutting drains in peat

Fencing tools

See 'Fencing' (Agate, 1986) for details.

a   Mell, maul or 'Drivall' for driving posts (and tree stakes)

b   Crowbar, for making pilot holes for fence posts

c   Wrecking bar (swan neck)

d   Claw hammer

e   Fencing pliers

f   Wire strainers

g   Heavy-duty wire cutter (bolt cropper)

h   Tinsnips, for cutting netting

i   Shuv-holer for removing soil from straining post holes

Specialist planting equipment

a   Schlich or Mansfield planting spade. Both types have a ridge or bulge across the face of the spade which makes a hole for planting when thrust into the ground.

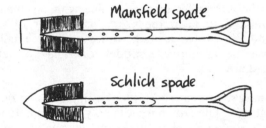

Some people dislike these special-purpose spades and prefer a small garden spade, such as 'lady's' spade for all-day notch planting work.

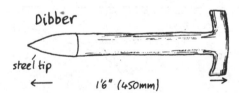

b   Dibber (dibbler, planting arrow).

c   Surveying poles or marker canes, for use in line planting.

d   Bags with shoulder straps, or buckets, lined with peat moss, earth or sawdust, for carrying small transplants so that they don't dry out. Bags are best for lightness and convenience, and can be made up out of hessian, denim or canvas. If fertilizer is to be applied at the time of planting, it is best if the bags are divided into two sections, one for plants and one for fertilizer. At a pinch, you can use the bottom half of an old fertilizer sack, well washed out, with a strap of baler twine tied to the two corners.

Clearing tools

a   Weeding hook or Dutch weeding scythe, for herbaceous and light woody material.

Reap hook (sickle, bagging, fagging or paring hook)

and the somewhat stronger bean hook and its variants (eg 'Gamekeeper Jungle Knife').

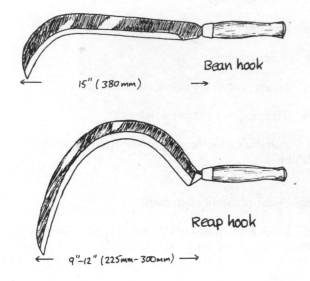

Bean hook

15" (380mm)

Reap hook

9"–12" (225mm–300mm)

Reap hook handles may be in line with the blade, or cranked to keep the user's hand clear of the ground. If you use a hook with a cranked handle, choose the appropriate model for right– or left-handed use.

Ordinary scythes are useful for cutting grass on rides and glades. The Dutch weeding scythe is sometimes preferred over weeding hooks for clearing brambles because it can be used in a more upright position.

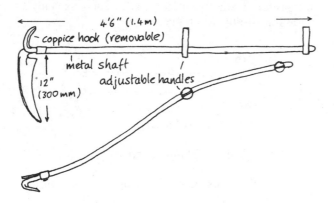

4'6" (1.4m)
coppice hook (removable)
metal shaft
adjustable handles
12" (300mm)

b Brushing hook or slasher.

The heavy pattern slashers and hooks generally have rather less curve than their equivalent light versions, and are more suitable for tougher, older weed growth. Some are fitted with rings and bolts where the blades fit the handles, to give extra strength. None of them are sturdy enough for use on material over about 25mm (1") diameter.

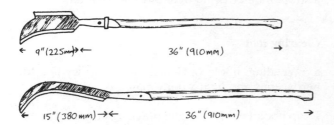

9" (225mm)   36" (910mm)

15" (380mm)   36" (910mm)

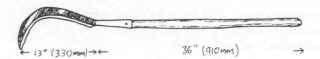

13" (330mm)   36" (910mm)

c Crooked stick, for use with weeding hook.

PRUNING AND WOUND TREATMENT

a Pruning saws. The most useful all-purpose pruning tool is the bow saw (discussed under felling tools, below). Its main drawback is that it is hard to use on a close-branched tree. For versatility and accuracy when working aloft, the best additional tool is a one-handed pruning saw, which cuts on the pull stroke.

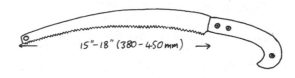

15"–18" (380–450mm)

Pruning saws often come with replaceable blades. For a slightly longer reach, the handle can be replaced with a 600mm (2') fawn's-foot handle cut down from an old axe haft. For high pruning, standing at or near ground level, use a two-handed pruning saw. This has a similar blade to the one-handed saw, but comes with a light alloy handle in detachable or telescoping sections, 1–3.6m (3'–12') in length.

b Toggle lopper or long-handled tree pruner. Loppers and pruners, if sharp and in good condition, give very clean cuts and are ideal for use by unskilled workers. However, they are rather slow for woodland work, and light-weight models can easily be strained or twisted out of alignment if used on material beyond their capacity.

The toggle lopper, which is useful for brashing and woodland path clearance, as well as for general pruning, can cut up to 32mm (1.25") branches with ease. The toggle action gives much greater power than ordinary shears.

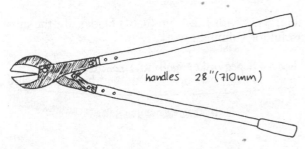

The long-handled or long-arm tree pruner is useful for cutting higher branches.

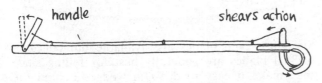

c Rope, for slinging and hauling up tools, and for use in felling.

d Firmer chisel, 25mm (1″) width or larger.

e Ladder, preferably non-rusting light metal alloy.

FELLING, EXTRACTION AND CONVERSION

With the amalgamation of the edged tool industry and changing forestry practices, many traditional felling and conversion tools are no longer being manufactured. Some of these, such as certain types of billhooks and the side axe and froe, are still important in coppice management and in making coppice products. Volunteer groups can help keep these tools available by pooling bulk orders to larger manufacturers, and by seeking out blacksmiths willing to experiment with traditional designs. It is also worth keeping a lookout for second-hand tools in patterns which are now out of production.

For general use

a Billhook, for very light scrub clearance, coppicing, hedging and general light trimming work,

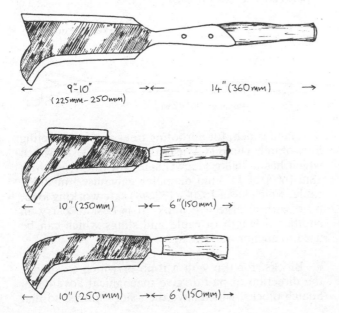

such as preparation of bean poles. There are many patterns, varying in size, blade curvature and balance.

For general woodland work, a fairly light single-edged tool with a moderate hook is probably best. Some volunteers have trouble managing the heavy Yorkshire billhook one-handed, or must grip the handle so high up that it becomes awkward to use. Never swing a double-edged billhook straight up towards your face!

b Bow saw, for felling and cross-cutting material between 50mm (2″) and 300mm (1′) in diameter.

The small triangular-shaped saw is best for coppicing, hedging and pruning where close-growing stems or branches prevent the use of larger D-shaped saws. The latter are more suited to use on stems in the 100–600mm (4–24″) range; the size of material which they can handle being limited by the width and depth of the bow. The 910mm (36″) saw is best used as a two-man tool.

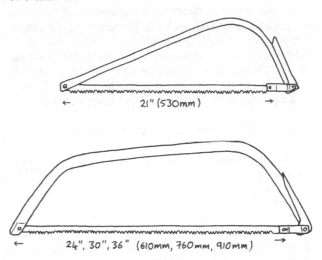

Blades are usually hard-point (non-resharpenable and non-resettable) although sharpenable blades are available. In practice, 'throwaway' blades are cheapest and most efficient unless one of your passions happens to be saw-doctoring.

c Axes. Preferably a felling axe for laying-in large trees, and a lighter snedding axe for snedding, trimming and coppicing.

There are two main patterns, as shown. English axes (known in America as brush or pole axes) have long edges for the size of their heads and little shoulder. This gives a broad, deep cut, suitable for felling big hardwood trees very low to the ground. In keeping with their main purpose, English axes tend to be heavy, with heads of 2.3–3.2kg (5–7lb). This gives maximum 'bite' with every swing. A straight handle ending in a 'swell knob' is traditional on English axes, but these days most woodmen prefer to fit both types with curved fawn's-foot handles.

Wedge axes have relatively broad shoulders and shorter edges, and tend to have heavier polls than their English counterparts. The poll gives extra

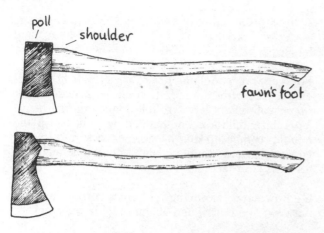

poll

shoulder

fawn's foot

weight to the head to increase momentum. Wedge axes tend to jam less easily in softwoods than English axes, and they split out larger chips of wood when cutting out sinks. They are also somewhat easier to use in confined situations. They are usually lighter, at 2–2.3kg (4½-5lb) for felling work, and 1.6kg (3½lb) or lighter for snedding.

Axe hafts come in different lengths according to the weight of the head and the physique of the user. Felling axes usually have 910mm (36") hafts, while light snedding or trimming axes have 660–760mm (26–30") hafts. If the handle is too long, then replace it. Don't cut it down to size, as the tool is slippery and dangerous to use without the fawn's-foot end.

d Sharpening stones (whetstones) and file.

e Power chain saw. To be used only by trained operators.

f Chopping block (p126).

g Saw horses, for cross-cutting. The design shown (from Mummery, Tabor and Homewood, 1976, p12) is strong and easy to make.

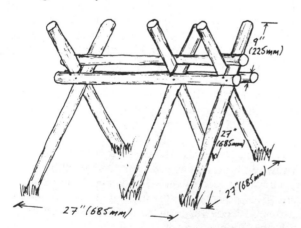

9" (225mm)

27" (685mm)

27" (685mm)

27" (685mm)

h Wheelbarrow, for moving tools and short logs. The best type is heavy-duty steel, with a single wheel and long handles for leverage and balance. Pneumatic tyres are essential for work in soft ground.

For large or difficult trees; additional equipment

a Two-man cross-cut saw, if a chain saw is unavail-

able. Saws with 1.2–1.5m (4–5') blades are the most useful for volunteer work.

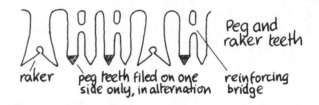

Two-man peg-raker tooth saw, concave back
handles detached

Two-man, peg toothed saw, straight back

Straight-backed blades are available but concave-backed blades are generally best for felling since they make it easy to drive in wedges behind the blade to keep the cut open. Handles are secured to the blades by means of bolts and wing nuts, so that they can be removed when necessary to extract the blade from the cut.

Teeth patterns vary, but most are peg-and-raker types. The peg or cutting teeth are sharpened on alternate sides, to cut a channel or kerf in the wood. The raker teeth clear sawdust from the kerf.

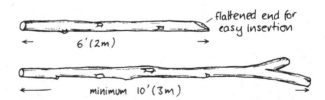

Peg and raker teeth

raker

peg teeth filed on one side only, in alternation

reinforcing bridge

b Wedges; magnesium, plastic or wood. When felling, it is useful to have either a high-lift wedge, or three or four wedges, varying from 75mm to 150mm (3" to 6") in length. You need a maul or a wooden mallet for tapping in the wedges. For splitting logs, steel wedges are needed, and a sledge-hammer for knocking them in. Wear goggles when doing this.

c Progs (stout forked poles), for directing trees, and levers for shifting logs.

flattened end for easy insertion

6' (2m)

minimum 10' (3m)

d Hand winch, for uprooting trees and for directing lines of fall. The BTCV uses the 'Tirfor TU 16' winch which has a 760kg (15cwt) safe working load, with 18m (60') of 11.3mm diameter galvanised maxiflex cable, which has a 1620kg (32cwt) safe working load, fixed with a large eye hook. It is best to carry an additional length of cable and slings which can be used to anchor the winch.

e Blocks, for use with a rope or winch to change the direction of pull or give mechanical advantage. Snatch blocks, which have their sides hinged so that a rope can be admitted without having to be threaded through, are especially useful.

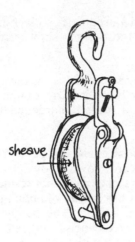

sheave

Choose blocks to fit your ropes or cables, which must be strong enough to take the planned load. Ropes and cables should fill the grooves of the sheaves so that they are fully supported without any hint of binding. The greater the number of sheaves in a set of blocks, the greater the mechanical advantage, but the more rope required. There is no mechanical advantage gained simply by using a single block to change the direction of pull, but if the block is used with one end of the rope anchored, there is a mechanical advantage of two.

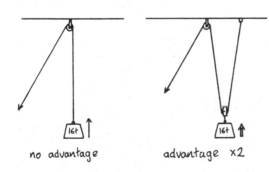

no advantage   advantage ×2

Firelighting

a Matches

b Dry newspaper, and firelighters or used sump oil. Do not use old car tyres, as they leave behind a tangle of wire which needs clearing up, and also release large amounts of trace elements such as cadmium into the soil, which effectively poisons it.

c Pitchfork or small prog, to keep the fire under control.

Specialist aids

a Breaking bar. This is designed to help control the direction and timing of fall, especially in one-man working. Several types are available.

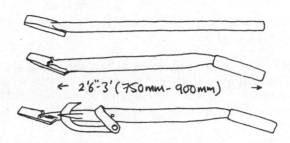

← 2'6"-3' (750mm - 900mm) →

b Sappie, for moving logs over short distances and for stacking poles and battens.

The sappie can be used as a lever, to move the pole over obstacles, or driven into the poles to pull it along the ground.

On steep ground, where logs only need occasional nudging, this tool is safer to use than a rope because it can be pulled quickly away from the log.

c Hand tongs or lifting hooks, for two-person carrying of poles and for handling and stacking logs which have been cut into short lengths.

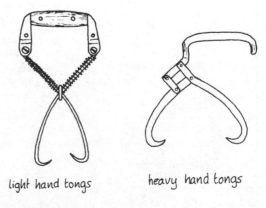

light hand tongs   heavy hand tongs

Small, light spring-loaded tongs have a 280mm (11″) opening and weigh 0.7kg (1.25lb). Heavy tongs, not spring-loaded, give a 290mm (11.5″) opening and weigh 1.7kg (3.75lb).

Take care when using tongs to jam the hooks well in and lift gently at first to make sure the tongs are secure. To release tongs from the log, push downward to open the jaws and twist sideways to clear.

d Pulphook or lumber hook, for lifting, loading and stacking short logs and billets.

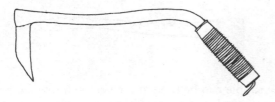

To use the pulphook, drive it into the side of the log to pull logs off a stack. Drive it into the end of the log when carrying, to give a good grip.

Conversion

For simple cradles, brakes etc to hold material, see page 129.

a Side axe (broad axe), for hewing and pointing.

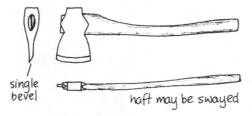

single bevel

haft may be swayed

Unlike felling axes, the side axe blade is bevelled on one side only. The other side is flat, to allow the axe to cut along the wood without biting too deeply into it. The haft is often bent or swayed away from the flat side, to protect the hands when in use. If you don't have a side axe for pointing, use a froe, billhook or hand axe (hatchet).

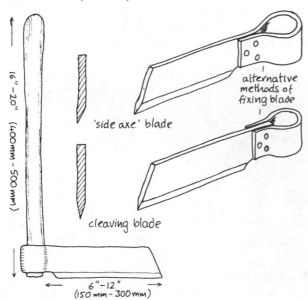

16″-20″ (400mm - 500mm)

'side axe' blade

alternative methods of fixing blade

cleaving blade

6″-12″ (150mm - 300mm)

b Froe (cleaving-axe), for hewing and cleaving. Single-bevel froes can be used instead of a side axe for hewing. For cleaving, a double-bevel type is best.

If you can't find a used froe, a blacksmith can make one to one of the designs shown (from Lambert, 1957, p24).

The size of the tool depends on the weight needed for the job. The blade is of 44 x 6mm (1.25 x 0.25″) tool steel with a forged, hardened and tempered cutting edge.

c Mallet, of a size and shape to suit the work. Three examples are shown below. One-piece mallets may be of ash, hazel or any other resilient hardwood. The third mallet has a head of apple, pear, beech or elm with an ash handle. The handle should taper slightly (larger at the head end) so that the head jams securely onto it with use.

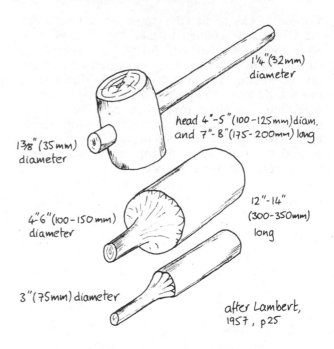

1¼″ (32mm) diameter

head 4″-5″ (100-125mm) diam. and 7″-8″ (175-200mm) long

1⅜″ (35mm) diameter

4″-6″ (100-150mm) diameter

12″-14″ (300-350mm) long

3″ (75mm) diameter

after Lambert, 1957, p25

d Draw knife, for rinding and shaving.

Draw knives may be straight or curved. Curved types can be home-made from sections of old weeding hooks.

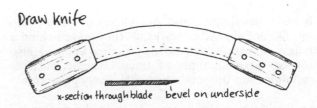

Draw knife

x-section through blade   bevel on underside

e Bark peelers. Swedish peelers with detachable blades are best for conifers and general work. English

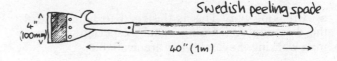

Swedish peeling spade

4″ (100mm)

40″ (1m)

66

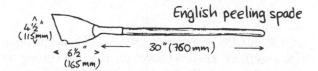
English peeling spade

peelers are mainly used for peeling tanbark from large oak logs.

If you don't have a peeler, use a worn-down, sharpened garden spade.

FIRE FIGHTING

Much fire fighting equipment duplicates items used for other purposes, such as billhooks for preparing beaters, axes for cutting fire breaks, spades and mattocks for cutting trenches and shovelling earth onto flames, and crowbars to clear obstructions. The following additional equipment is necessary:

a   Fire beaters

b   Rakes, to rake off surface litter to form a fire line

c   Buckets, preferably canvas

d   Torches or hurricane lamps, for use at night

e   Wire cutters, to clear old fencing

Tool and Equipment Maintenance

Proper maintenance of tools and equipment is essential for safe and efficient working. People who own their own tools usually take good care of them. Volunteer groups which keep a stock of communally used tools should encourage the same attitude of personal responsibility towards their use and upkeep. It is essential to have a tools officer or organiser to take charge of the tool store, ensure that tools go out on task in a good state and check them over afterwards. On task, the leader should be sure that volunteers know how to sharpen, clean and store tools as well as how to use them safely.

This section includes general points on storage, transport and care of tools, and techniques for sharpening edged tools in the field. Jobs for the workshop, such as filing and grinding of edged tools, and replacement of hafts and handles are explained in detail in the 'Tools Workshop Manual' (BTCV, 1988).

STORAGE AND GENERAL CARE

a   Keep all tools clean and dry. Carry a rag with you to wipe them off in wet weather – especially handles, which are slippery when wet. Keep edges free from mud, otherwise they dull very quickly. Clean tools immediately after use. If mud is left to harden, the tools will be more difficult to clean, sharpen and oil.

b   Oil all metal parts before storing to prevent rust. Use clean oil, not used sump oil which contains metal fragments that can hurt your hands.

Wipe wooden handles with linseed oil when new and occasionally thereafter, as this helps keep them supple. You can also oil with lanolin, which protects metal, wood and your hands all at once.

c   If handles are scored, rough or splintery, sand them smooth. File out nicks in metal handles.

d   Store tools under cover, preferably in racks or on wall brackets. Organise tools by type, with all tools of a type arranged the same way. Keep edged tools stored well out of the way, or provide individual guards for the blades.

e   Store bow saws with the tension released.

f   Transport tools under vehicle seats or in a trailer or roof boxes to prevent accidents. Don't overload vehicle roof racks, as this can affect vehicle stability. Wrap edged tools in sacking or provide individual guards, for safety and to prevent them damaging each other. Guards for axes and cross-cut saws can be made from old fire hose.

g   Hang ladders securely out of the way. Make sure wooden ladders and extension ladders with rope fittings remain absolutely dry. Repair or replace any loose or weak rungs immediately.

SHARPENING EDGED TOOLS IN THE FIELD

Edged tools should go into the field sharp. It is hopeless to try to carry out major sharpening while on task – filing and grinding are workshop jobs.

a   Sharpen tools at least twice a day when in use, or more often as necessary. Some tools, including sickles and scythes, need very frequent honing. A quick touch-up every ten minutes is not excessive. Others, such as axes and billhooks, can be used longer without sharpening but should be checked whenever you stop to rest.

b   Carry the correct sharpening stone (whetstone) for the job. Fine cylindrical (cigar-shaped) stones are needed for sickles and scythes. They may also be used for billhooks and slashers, along with flat (canoe-shaped) stones. Canoe-shaped or flat rectangular stones are best for axes. Flat round axe-stones, although commonly used, are dangerous and difficult to hold.

A useful sharpening kit is available which consists of a gauge, rectangular sharpening stone and carrying frog. The gauge has slots indicating the correct edge for reap hooks, slashers, billhooks and axes. The stone has two different faces, coarse and fine, for general sharpening and final honing. The canvas frog, which loops over a belt for carrying, is designed to protect the stone and gauge. The set is available from Stanton Hope Ltd.

c Stones are fragile – treat them with respect. Wrap them or carry them separately or in a frog. Broken stones are dangerous and should not be used.

d Always wear a glove on the hand holding the sharpening stone. Place the tool on a firm surface such as a stump, with the edge projecting, or sit down and steady the tool on your knees.

Spit on the stone to moisten it, as if used dry, it wears away quickly. Hold the stone at an angle conforming to the existing taper of the blade. If using a combination stone, use the coarse side first to eliminate any flaws and bring to an edge, and the fine side afterwards to give a good polish and even taper. Sharpen with small circular motions – this is safer than sweeping the stone along the edge and gives better results for inexperienced workers.

Take particular care to sharpen the hooked part of billhook and slasher blades, as this often neglected part does most of the cutting work. On single-bevel tools, sharpen the bevelled side only. To finish, remove the burr on the flat side with a few light strokes.

e Don't touch the blade to see if it is sharp, but check by sighting along the edge. You should see a uniform taper with no light reflected from the edge itself. Reflected light indicates a dull spot, so keep sharpening until this disappears.

f Certain trees, such as Sitka spruce, are particularly hard on axes. To prevent the edge turning or chipping, first hone it in the usual way. Then, working only on the extreme edge, alter the angle of the sharpening stone and make a few strokes with the fine side, cutting diagonally in towards the edge on both sides to give a slight chisel effect. This should be only just visible – you don't want to actually dull the tool, just strengthen it.

SAW MAINTENANCE

a Oil blades frequently. When sawing through resinous trees, keep blades clean and free-cutting by dousing them with an oiling mixture of 7 parts paraffin, 2 parts white spirit and 1 part lubricating oil.

b Sharpen saw blades (or change the blades of hardpoint bow saws) when the saw takes more effort to use than is normal, when it produces fine dust rather than 'crumbs' or small chips of wood, or when the teeth have lost their set or become damaged or broken.

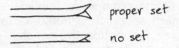

To change the saw blade, first release the tension. If the tension lever is hard to release by hand, put the saw on the ground with the frame upright and pull back on the lever, using a metal bar if necessary.

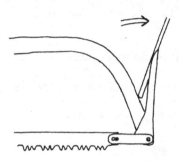

Next, hold the saw vertical with the frame towards you and the lever against the ground. Put your foot on the lever to hold it and push the saw frame away from you.

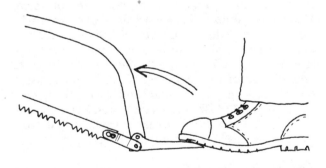

Remove the rivets and put them in a safe place. Position the new blade, replace the rivets and retension the blade by pressing the lever against the ground until it closes.

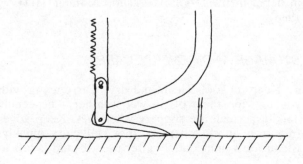

Blades which are to be sharpened in the workshop should be reversed in the saw (points into the bow) to make them easy to identify later. Blades which are beyond help should be taken out of the saw and broken in two, and the pieces removed from the work site for disposal.

c Touch up hardpoint bow saw blades, when dull, by running a whetstone once lightly along each side, with the stone held flat against the blade.

d If a bow saw blade tends to 'run' (cut in a curve), reverse it in the frame. If this is ineffective. adjust the set on the 'gaining' side by running the whetstone over it as for sharpening.

e Sharpenable bow saw blades must be touched up regularly. If they have raker teeth these must be adjusted at each sharpening and kept below the level of the cutting (peg) teeth. Setting is required less often. Cross–cut saws should not be touched-up, but used until they require a complete stripping, sharpening and setting. This may be every one to three weeks if in frequent use, or only very occasionally if in infrequent use.

Sharpening and setting is best left to a professional 'saw doctor'. Although volunteers can learn this skill, it requires special files, vices, setting pliers and other tools and is slow, painstaking work. Many ironmongers can recommend a saw doctor or do the work themselves.

Organising Group Work

Organisational points are included where appropriate in the following chapters. For all tasks note the following:

a Volunteers work best if someone responsible for site management is on hand to explain the purpose of the task and to work alongside them.

b Before starting work, the leader should explain the task (if this has not already been done by the site manager) and set the day's objectives. It helps greatly if the leader has visited the site in advance and has the job clear in his or her own mind. The introductory talk should cover the reasons for the work, care of tools and a demonstration of their use, and the standard of work expected (eg low-cut stumps, general tidiness, avoidance of unnecessary damage). The leader should be sure that volunteers know which species of plants are to be cleared or left. For this purpose, it helps to assemble a tree 'library' in one corner of the work site, consisting of marked specimens of living or freshly cut material (buds are especially important) so that volunteers can check out unfamiliar trees as they work. A tree key or a good field guide is also useful.

c Small groups should work methodically on one goal at a time, rather than fragmentarily on several things, none of which may get done by day's end.

Large groups may, of course, do several things if they are sure of finishing them. It boosts morale, especially on long tasks, to see that a measurable amount of work has been accomplished.

d Some woodland work can be done in teams, while other work is best done with workers well separated for safety and efficiency. Whatever the division of labour, don't leave anyone out. People of all strengths and abilities must find a place. Give new volunteers instructions and put them to work alongside experienced workers, if possible.

e Keep an eye on how volunteers use tools. Don't hesitate to offer advice to even the most experienced volunteer, as otherwise new workers may pick up bad habits. If the volunteer doesn't have enough skill for the job, tactfully suggest a change of tool or activity. Axes have a special appeal to the novice, and are particularly dangerous for the untrained. Count out and count in the tools at the start and finish of work and note any which need repair.

f Every situation differs. Use your imagination. Adapt these 'rules' to the occasion. Local conditions, the weather, and the ages and wishes of volunteers may make all the difference in the approach. Aim for efficiency and good quality work, but never at the expense of safety.

7 Tree Planting

Among the most important conservation and amenity reasons for planting trees and shrubs are:

a To replace hedgerow, farmland and amenity trees which have been lost through felling, disease or old age.

b To supplement natural regeneration where this is inadequate in felled or derelict woodland.

c To diversify wildlife habitats or provide shelter in open areas, or to stabilise easily eroded soils and spoil tips.

d To improve landscape amenity, or to screen and improve the appearance of buildings.

Planting – Site Assessment Checklist

The following notes provide a checklist of points which should be considered when planning a new planting scheme. These are taken from a leaflet 'Assessing a Site for Tree and Shrub Planting' by Jerry Langford (BTCV, South Glamorgan, 1985, photocopied). These points should be considered during the process of forming a management plan (p18).

Should trees or shrubs be planted at all?

a Who owns the site? Will the owner give permission for planting?

b What is the site used for? Will planting affect this use?

c Why plant trees on this site? Will they increase the wildlife interest? Will they provide or improve an attractive amenity? Will they provide useful timber?

d Will tree planting damage interesting habitats that are already present? New planting may shade out old grassland, streams or ponds. Thickets and old orchards are valuable habitats which should normally be retained, and any bogs or very damp ground should be left unplanted.

e Are young trees already growing of their own accord? If so, is extra planting really justified? Natural regeneration is preferable for wildlife interest, and is cheaper. It can be encouraged in a number of ways (p54).

f Will the trees you plant have a secure future? May the site be developed in the future resulting in loss of the trees? Seek assurance from the owner about the future of the site.

g There may be a good reason for the site being treeless, for example thin or polluted soil, exposure, waterlogged ground or heavy grazing. Perhaps only certain parts of the site are suitable for planting?

The choice of tree and shrub species

a Look at any existing trees or shrubs on the site. These may indicate a remnant of semi-natural cover, or in the case of obviously planted trees, will indicate which species are likely to be successful on the site.

b Consider the location. In a rural site you should choose species in keeping with any existing woodland. In an urban site consider whether you want to create an attractive ornamental planting, or a 'natural' area. Will the use of introduced species be acceptable?

c Consider the eventual height of the trees. Is there enough space for forest trees such as oak, ash or beech? Will the trees shade gardens or windows, interfere with overhead lines or overhang roads? Will they grow to block attractive views?

d Is the soil natural or has it been disturbed? Soil on building sites or derelict land may be badly churned up, mixed with rubble and rubbish, or completely removed. It may be polluted with chemicals or be very low in nutrients. If there are no trees or other vegetation already growing, you may have problems. Consult the local planning authority.

e Plant species which suit the soil type, whether sandy or clayey, acid or alkaline, well drained or subject to waterlogging.

f Is any part of the site very exposed to the wind, or are there hollows where frost will be severe?

g Is air pollution a problem, or is the site on the coast and exposed to salt winds? Either of these will limit the choice of species.

Planting

a What size of young trees should you plant? Which planting method should you use? Do the trees need stakes?

b Will the trees need protection against browsing by farm stock, or against rabbits or deer? Either fence the site or use individual tree guards, whichever is the cheaper.

c Is vandalism likely? If so use small trees and thorny shrubs, and plant brambles to protect the trees. Avoid using stakes or guards which draw attention to the planted trees.

Aftercare

a Watering, weeding, removal of ties and stakes, and replacement of dead trees may be needed. Who will do this?

b Most sites will need weeding for the first three or four years. Mulches or herbicides are the best methods for encouraging good growth of the young trees. What mulching materials can you obtain? If you decide to use herbicide, is there someone properly trained who will be able to do the work?

c Will the trees be easily visible amongst the weed growth, by the time the herbicide is applied?

d Any guards or tree shelters remaining after five years or so should be removed. Can you ensure this will be done?

e If trees die will you be able to replace them? This may be a condition of grant aid.

f Do you have proper records of the scheme, so that anyone taking over can continue with the maintenance?

Choice of Species

The table below is a summary of the site requirements and characteristics of 28 native species of trees. This table is an outline guide only, and should be used in conjunction with careful survey of the site and locality. Further information on these species, and on many native shrubs, is given in Appendix C. The choice and planting of native trees and shrubs is fully covered in Beckett (1979), a particularly useful book for conservation purposes as it gives details on characteristics, requirements, wildlife value, propagation and natural distribution in Britain. Evans (1984) gives silvicultural details on many broadleaved species.

The range of species can be greatly increased by including introduced species, which although of less value for nature conservation, may be more suitable than any of the native species for certain sites and situations. Some of these are discussed below. Of the many books which describe introduced tree species, Rushforth (1987) is one of the most comprehensive.

Urban areas and amenity planting

Most areas available for tree planting in towns and residential areas are fairly small, often with limited space both for top growth and root growth. Other limitations include disturbed, polluted, heavily compacted or even non-existent soil, polluted air, and the need to choose species which do not inconvenience or endanger the public by heavy leaf-fall, honeydew or brittle branches. However urban areas do offer at least one advantage in that average temperatures arc slightly higher than in surrounding rural areas, which

TABLE 7A   SITE REQUIREMENTS AND CHARACTERISTICS OF NATIVE TREE SPECIES

	Wet ground	Light dry soils	Heavy soils	Acid	Alkaline	Withstands shade	Average ultimate height 0.5–5m	6–15m	16m+	Growth rate Fast	Medium	Slow	Tolerant of pollution	Tolerant of coastal sites	Tolerant of exposed sites	Bird value	Insect value
Alder	*				*	*		*		*					*		*
Ash	*	*		*	*				*		*		*	*	*		
Aspen			*	*	*			*	*	*			*	*	*		*
Beech		*			*	*			*		*						*
Birch, Downy	*			*			1	*	*				*		*		*
Birch, Silver		*		*				*	*				*		*		*
Cherry, Wild		*			*			*			*		*			*	
Crab Apple	*	*	*	*				*				*	*			*	*
Elm, Wych			*	*	*				*		*		*	*	*	*	
Hawthorn		*		*	*		*					*	*	*	*	*	*
Hawthorn, Midland			*	*	*	*	*					*	*			*	*
Hazel				*	*	*	*			*							*
Holly		*	*	*	*	*					*		*	*	*	*	
Hornbeam			*	*	*			*			*				*		
Juniper		*		*	*		*					*			*		
Lime, Small-leaved			*	*	*				*		*						*
Lime, Large-leaved			*		*				*		*				*		*
Maple, Field			*	*	*	*		*			*			*			*
Oak, Pedunculate			*		*				*		*				*	*	*
Oak, Sessile	*	*	*	*		*			*		*				*	*	*
Pine, Scots		*		*					*		*				*		*
Poplar, Black	*	*	*		*				*	*							*
Rowan		*		*			*			*			*	*	*	*	*
Service Tree, Wild			*		*	*	*					*					*
Whitebeam, Common		*	*		*		*					*		*		*	
Willow, Crack	*				*		*			*			*	*	*	*	*
Willow, White	*				*		*			*			*	*	*	*	*
Yew		*		*	*	*	*					*	*		*	*	

71

can give a longer period of growth and increase the range of species that can be grown.

These limitations restrict the use of the large native trees (see table 7a), leaving only a few natives which are suitable. In such small clumps of trees, isolated from other semi-natural habitats, the use of natives is less important than elsewhere, as the opportunity for recreating a 'woodland' habitat, with its assemblage of dependent insects, birds, fungi and so on, is greatly limited. It is therefore reasonable to use cultivars of native species, plus naturalised and long-introduced species, particularly if these make tree-planting acceptable and appreciated on a site which might otherwise not be planted at all.

A 'cultivar' of a species is one which has either been bred for horticultural purposes, or has arisen naturally, either in the wild or in cultivation, and has then been selected, named and propagated. These forms are selected because of desirable qualities of height, shape, colour of foliage or blossom, autumn colouring and so on. By using a cultivar of a native species, you are perpetuating some of the ecological value, whilst growing it in a form which is more suitable for an urban area. Examples include weeping or 'fastigiate' (upright) forms of the large native trees such as ash and beech, holly and yew in various shapes and colours, and the many forms of hawthorn, wild cherry, myrobalan, rowan and whitebeam which have been selected mainly for their blossoms and berries. The best source of information on these trees is 'Hilliers Manual of Trees and Shrubs', but note that only the more commonly planted cultivars will be easily obtainable.

The most obvious effect of using non-native trees is their appearance, which, with a few possible exceptions such as sweet chestnut, is immediately associated with gardens or parks. In recent years there has been a strong movement away from the 'mown grass and ornamental trees' type of urban park, and towards more natural plantings of trees and shrubs with areas of long grass, damp ground and so on. In large areas such as parks, derelict building plots, and sites adjoining 'waste' land or railway embankments there is considerable value in using natives, both for their own appearance and in their potential for supporting wildlife, thus effectively recreating a piece of native habitat.

Polluted or disturbed soils

Many urban sites will have either very thin or non-existent soils, or be polluted from industrial activity. Special measures may need to be taken, such as fertilising or providing top soil. Suitable species are those that are available to 'fix' free nitrogen in the soil, such as the introduced grey and italian alders, or common alder in wet conditions. Birches and willows are also useful. These pioneer species can be used to establish cover, into which other native species may be planted at a later date when soil conditions and shelter have improved.

Coastal or exposed locations

Sites which are exposed to cold or salt winds are very restricted in the tree species they can support, and under natural conditions, would probably not be wooded. However, tree planting may be desirable to provide screening of car parks or buildings, or shelter for livestock, and the use of introduced species which will succeed on such sites is therefore justified.

Timber production

Most timber production in this country is of introduced species, because of their fast growth and tolerance of cold or exposed sites. Conservation plantings will normally avoid these species, but there may be instances where it is important to gain some fairly quick financial return from a woodland, in order to make it viable. There are also a few species which may be worth planting, because their timber is of a high value, although these do take many decades to mature. A mixture which includes some non-natives may therefore be used.

Site Selection and Layout

Selection

If possible, choose a site which butts up against an existing copse, hedgerow or woodland remnant, or incorporate any mature trees within the new area. This will greatly increase the wildlife value of the new planting, as the woodland remnant will contain plant and animal species, many of them hidden or inconspicuous invertebrates, fungi and lichens as well as seed, which can then spread into the new planting. If instead, the new planting is isolated by perhaps 100 metres of arable land, many of these species will never make it to the new planting area.

Avoid planting up areas of boggy ground or old grassland, which are better maintained as they are. However, ponds and boggy ground can be incorporated within tree planting areas, although they should be left open to the sunlight and not planted on their southern sides. Avoid trees which rapidly seed and colonise new areas, such as birch, or the open boggy ground will soon become thicket.

Field corners that are unproductive for arable farming provide possible sites for tree planting, and are usually of limited existing wildlife interest due to the use of herbicides. Note the following:

a Modern cultivators and harvesters require a turning radius of approximately 15m (50'), leaving a corner about the size shown below. If the field is not going to be grazed for at least 10 years, it is cheaper to protect the trees with individual tree shelters. Where grazing is possible, the trees should be protected by fencing, as sheep and cattle will rub against and damage the young trees, even if they do not browse them.

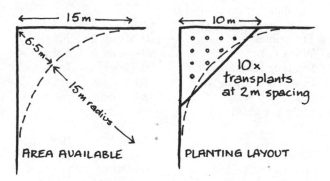

AREA AVAILABLE   PLANTING LAYOUT

b If possible, amalgamate the corner plantings to give one large plot, rather than several separate plots. A single plot will be about 80 square metres (1/50 acre), with two adjoining plots about 135 square metres (1/30 acre). At least 400 square metres (1/10 acre) is needed to create a reasonable area of habitat, and fencing costs become cheaper as the area increases (see below).

Layout

You will need to balance the various advantages and disadvantages of larger blocks of planting against those of more varied outlines.

Concentrating planting into one block with a regular outline is the cheapest solution where a fence has to be constructed all the way around. A circle gives the greatest area for the shortest perimeter, but is not usually the cheapest because a strained wire fence cannot easily be constructed in a curve, and more expensive forms of wooden fencing need to be used. Circular woods can be very effective as hilltop clumps, but otherwise look rather out of place in semi-natural landscapes, and do not fit in easily with other land uses. Squares and oblongs are the next most efficient shapes for fencing. For further details on tree protection see page 86.

Blocks of woodland have advantages for wildlife, as they are of sufficient size to provide the shaded and sheltered microclimate which many woodland plants and animals need, and large enough for viable populations. On the other hand, blocks of single age trees, particularly when past the thicket stage, may be poor in wildlife because of the lack of habitat variety. Often the most valuable part for wildlife is the woodland edge, where the varied structure of herbs, shrubs and small trees can flourish in the space and sunlight. Therefore a varied outline, which increases the length of the woodland edge, is beneficial to wildlife. However, too much emphasis on creating 'edge' can result in patchy and sinuous plantings, which never develop the sheltered conditions of woodland. Taken to extreme, small isolated clumps of trees support only a meagre wildlife.

Where space permits, the optimum to aim for is a basic block of woodland which is cheap to fence, and within that create sheltered glades, rides and

areas of thicket and scrub to provide a variety of habitat. This in effect provides 'edge' within as well as outside the wood, and is of course closer to the natural conditions in which the plants and animals of the woodland edge developed. Such layout is extravagant of space where timber production is an objective, and also has the disadvantage that any trees growing along an internal or external edge will have a spreading and branching form, which is less productive in timber.

Supply of Trees

SOURCES

Wherever possible, planting stock should be raised from the seed of trees growing on or near the site to be planted. This is not just because it's fun to start your own tree nursery. Raising trees of local provenance (p170) helps to ensure the survival of local genetic strains, which may be swamped by the widespread planting of trees of non-local or even non-British provenance. Information on how to gather, store and propagate seeds of native trees, plus other methods of propagation, are given in the BTCV booklet 'Tree Nurseries' (Liebscher, 1984). For those interested in large-scale work, Aldhous (1972) gives full details.

If purchasing trees from a nursery, check the provenance of each species, and be wary if the nursery are unable to supply the information. Some nurseries list the provenance of each species in their catalogue. Many nurseries now have a policy of increasing the use of seed from British seed sources.

Some nurseries will raise plants from seed of acceptable provenance if collected and supplied by the customer. Where there is a choice, use seeds from trees of provenance to the north of the planting site rather than to the south, as these are liable to grow better in your area.

It may be worth transplanting wild seedlings or suckers, where they would otherwise be cleared from a site or would die due to shading or trampling. Their growth qualities cannot be assessed in advance, so such plants should not be used as timber trees or specimen plantings.

If you buy plants from a nursery, you can purchase seedlings and line them out for a year or two before transplanting. This is cheaper than buying larger trees, especially if you purchase wholesale, provided you have a suitable lining-out site and can plan the programme in advance.

Alternatively, you can buy nursery transplants for planting out directly on site. You pay more per tree this way, but save the cost and time involved in developing a nursery. Most forestry and amenity planting is done this way. Prices vary according to the species and size of tree, with discounts for quantity purchases. Packing and transport charges may be extra.

For certain species, you can take cuttings or buy rooted or unrooted setts for lining out in the nursery, or for direct planting. Poplars and willows may be propagated this way, as well as some ornamental trees and shrubs. This is quicker and easier than propagation by seed, and ensures that the parent plant is reproduced without genetic change.

ORDERING NURSERY PLANTS

Local suppliers of trees may be listed in the Yellow Pages under 'Nurseries-Horticultural' or 'Garden Centres', but most of these will be suppliers of container-grown ornamental stock. For native trees in quantity, your best starting point is to contact the local tree officer at the County or District Council, who should be able to give you the names of local suppliers. Look in the 'countryside and farming' section of your local newspaper, and for larger growers, in the national forestry and horticultural magazines such as 'Forestry and British Timber', 'Horticulture Week', 'Nurserymen and Garden Centre' and 'The Grower'. Each August, 'Horticulture Week' publishes a booklet of 'Nursery Stock Suppliers', which gives current details of the majority of suppliers in the UK. Although mainly for amenity stock, this includes information on suppliers of forest seedlings. The National Farmers Union and the Horticultural Trades Association will advise on specialist suppliers. The Forestry Commission sell surplus planting stock through their various conservancy offices, and seeds through the Seed Branch at the Forest Research Station.

It is best to place orders as early as possible, by July or August for supply in the late autumn/winter. Lifting of open ground stock will take place from October/November, depending on the species concerned, and the season. If mild weather continues late into the autumn, lifting will have to be delayed as this cannot be done until cold weather has stopped plant growth and hardened shoots. When placing an order, request delivery by a certain date if necessary, but be prepared to be flexible, as either mild or very wet weather can affect lifting, just as very wet or cold weather can delay planting. For inspection and pre-planting care, see page 76.

Preparation for Planting

SIZE OF TREES TO PLANT

The table below gives the nomenclature for trees of various sizes, along with the usual planting distances for each size. This metric system is standard throughout the nursery trade.

'Feathered' trees are well furnished with branches from low on the stem. 'Standard' trees have a specified length of clear stem below a crown of branches.

Name	Overall height	Planting distance
Seedling (one year old in Japanese paper pot)	variable	2–3m
Transplant	20–40cm	2m
Whip	60–90cm	3–4m
Whip or feathered whip	90–120cm	4m
Feathered whip	150–180cm	4–5m
Feathered whip	180–210cm	6m
Light standard	250–275cm (150–180 stem)	10m plus
Standard	275–300cm	10m plus
Selected standard	300–360cm (180–215 stem)	10m plus
Extra heavy nursery stock	5m plus	20m plus

When deciding the size of tree to plant, keep the following points in mind:

a Trees for forestry use are usually planted as '1 + 1' (one year seedlings transplanted for one year) or '2 + 1' (two year seedlings transplanted for one year). Such transplanted seedlings are much hardier than plants of equal size which have not been moved prior to final planting out.

One year seedlings in Japanese paper pots are becoming more popular, as their use maximises the benefits of using tree shelters (p90). Planting with the rootball intact results in high survival rates and strong early growth, and the planting season can be extended. They are more expensive and bulky to transport than plants supplied bare root.

Small trees survive transplanting better than larger ones of the same species, as large plants may check after planting and be slow in establishing. The optimum size for most broadleaved species is 25–50cm. More important than the height is the root collar diameter, as thin, spindly plants are more likely to die than shorter but sturdy plants. For plants in the 25–50cm range, the root collar diameter should be at least 5mm.

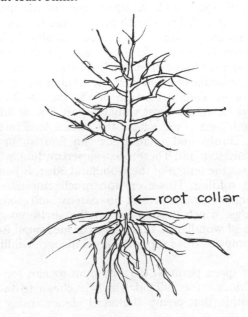

← root collar

An exception is alder, which should be 45–70cm ('1 + 1'). Alder seedlings grow rapidly but '1 + 0' plants are not recommended because survival is often poor (Evans, 1984, p31).

Container grown transplants appear to be more successful than field grown transplants in difficult soils, as well as allowing for early or late season planting.

b Plants for shelterbelts and hedges are often planted somewhat older and larger than those for forestry use, '1 + 2' or '2 + 2' plants, 30–60cm tall.

c Experimental work is currently being done by the Forestry Commission to compare the survival and growth of transplants, whips and standards, with and without chemical weed control (see Arboriculture Research Note 67:87:ARB). Results after three years showed the transplants (40–70cm) growing at the fastest rate, but that they had not yet caught up with the standards (1.8-2.3m). However, the most important factor was the chemical weed control, which for all sizes resulted in much better growth than the unweeded trees. This highlights the importance of weeding (see p95), but also disproves the assertion that standards have the advantage of needing less weeding than transplants in the first few years after planting. In the experiment, the unweeded standards were the least successful plants, with many dying back.

PLANTING SEASON AND WEATHER PRECAUTIONS

Plant fully hardy trees any time over the season (October to March or April) other than in hard frosty or cold windy weather. Hard frost is most likely in January and February. Plant half–hardy species (suitable only for western coastal districts) in spring.

Hardy deciduous trees are best planted before Christmas. They will survive spring planting but are more likely to suffer from drought than if planted in the autumn or early winter. Birch and beech, especially, are bad risks if planted after the end of February.

Evergreens are best planted either early or late in the season, when their roots are somewhat active. Spring planting should take place when the soil has begun to warm but before the first flush of new growth.

In dry areas early autumn planting is best for most species, other things being equal, to give the trees a chance to become established before spring droughts. In wet areas, early spring planting is generally best, to minimise the risk of uprooting in winter gales.

Avoid planting in sunny, windy, drying weather. Choose cloudy and drizzly weather is possible. Be sure to firm up trees (p94) if hard frosts or storms occur in the weeks after planting.

Although container grown plants can be planted at any time of year, the above guidelines will give best results. If planting is done in late spring or summer, plants should be watered during dry spells for the first growing season.

SITE PREPARATION

Clearance, cultivation and drainage

Large-scale clearance, cultivation or drainage of planting sites is costly, requires equipment and skills beyond the scope of volunteers, and may be environmentally very destructive. It is best to avoid the need for such measures by choosing suitable trees for existing site conditions, and by not planting under heavy shade or in boggy patches where trees will do poorly. On grassland sites, it is very important to destroy the sward at each planting position by screefing (p81) or herbicide application, as grass competes strongly for moisture and nutrients.

See Blatchford (1978, pp22–7) for further information.

Fencing

It is usually necessary to fence around newly planted or coppiced trees, to prevent damage by rabbits, livestock or deer, and to reduce trespass. Design and materials are given in the BTCV handbook 'Fencing' (Agate, 1986), and Pepper and Tee (1972). For details of individual tree protection see page 86.

Keep the following points in mind:

a Note the points above (p73) on the most economical shapes to fence, and on comparative costs of fences and individual guards (p87).

b Post-and-wire fencing is usually the cheapest and most effective type, especially against rabbits and deer. Ordinary strained wire is often adequate but high tensile spring-steel fencing may be preferable, as fewer posts are required to erect a taut and stock-proof fence. This is especially useful in either stony or very soft ground where it is difficult to erect posts. See 'Fencing' (Agate, 1986) for further details. Where rabbits and deer are not a problem, consider renovating and maintaining any existing hedges or dry stone walls rather than replacing them with fences. (See 'Hedging', Brooks, 1975 and 'Dry Stone Walling', Brooks, 1977, for details). Post-and-rail or chestnut paling fences may be more appropriate in parkland or amenity areas, or on ground where straining posts cannot be secured firmly.

c Include gates and stiles where necessary for access. If you have to put netting across an existing badger run, put in a badger gate (see Rowe, 1976, for details).

d When fencing against rabbits, make sure the bottom 150mm (6″) of netting is turned outward, to prevent rabbits from burrowing underneath. Hold the netting down with thick turfs, stones or wire pegs. Rabbits must be eliminated from the fenced area before you plant.

e Do not use barbed wire in deer fences, nor as the top wire when fencing against horses, as these animals are easily injured by the barbs.

See page 87 for information regarding the height of fence required against different animals.

LIFTING, TRANSPORTING AND PRE-PLANTING CARE

Every year, thousands of trees are planted which are already dead, due to careless handling between the time they are lifted from the nursery and final planting-out.

In order to try and prevent these losses, the Committee for Plant Supply and Establishment, which represents various professional organisations, has issued the 'Code of Practice for Plant Handling' (revised 1985). This three part code comprises the following – Part 1: Specifications for packaging and transporting nursery stock; Part 2: Recommendations for plant handling from lifting until delivery to site; Part 3: Recommendations for plant handling from delivery to site to successful establishment.

Any plants received from a commercial nursery should be packaged, handled and transported in accordance with the code. If this is not included by the nursery as part of their normal terms of business, the purchaser can stipulate that the supplier adheres to the code in any contract to supply plants. The code is also a useful practical guide for all aspects of plant handling, whether you are growing your own plants, or buying in. Copies of the code, in a booklet called 'Plant Handling' are available from the Horticultural Trades Association.

It is essential to:

a Prevent drying of the roots. Hele the trees in or, for short periods of storage, put them in plastic bags. Keep them shaded and out of the wind (see page 78).

b Keep as much short fibrous root on the trees as possible.

c Avoid damaging the roots, breaking the stem tops or stripping bark from stem or roots.

d Prevent heating, by maintaining air circulation around the stems and foliage of trees in storage or transit. Heat is generated by bacteria and micro-organisms on the plants, especially on the leaves of evergreens. Plants are seriously weakened and may be killed if they become warm to the touch at any stage between lifting and planting.

Lifting small trees

Lift and shift seedlings, transplants and whips as bare-rooted plants, ie with no ball of soil around the roots.

Lift the trees using a garden fork, rather than a spade which may damage the roots. Work from the outside edge of the seedbed, or along the transplant line.

1 Insert the fork vertically to the full depth of the blade and push the handle down until it is about 45 degrees from the vertical.

2 Repeat this process as necessary to loosen the soil. Then grasp the plants by their tops, lift them gently and shake loose the excess soil from the roots. If there is going to be more than a few minutes delay before the plants are sorted, then put them directly

into plastic sacks or lay them in a barrow or trailer with the roots covered with plastic. Plants are particularly vulnerable at this stage.

3   Take the plants immediately to a cool shed, or behind a screen out of sun and wind, for sorting. As you sort, cut off any roots over 150–175mm (6–7″) long, which can be a nuisance when planting. Trees planted with bent-over roots often develop crowded, weak or unbalanced root systems. Prune off any multiple leaders to leave a single strong leader on each tree.

Ruthlessly cull and burn all diseased, spindly or damaged plants and those with inadequate root systems, as these are not worth planting.

4   Count and bundle the plants into suitable units while sorting. Tie the bundles loosely with natural fibre or soft synthetic fibre (not polypropylene, which can cut the bark very easily). If the plants are going to be transported to the planting site within about seven days, they can be packed directly into plastic bags (see below). If there is going to be some delay before the plants are despatched, they must be temporarily stored. Bare-root plants can be heeled in (see below), or for shorter periods, kept outside in a moist, cool, sheltered, shaded place, with the roots covered with damp peat. Protect against damage by rodents. Alternatively, plants can be kept in an unheated shed for a week or more, out of the sun and with the roots covered with damp peat. If storage is needed for a few days only, put the plants in plastic bags left open at the top, and store upright in a cool shady position or shed.

Lifting larger trees

Trees over 90cm (36″) tall require more care than smaller transplants. Broadleaved trees may be planted bare-rooted but are more safely planted with a ball of earth around the roots. Conifers of this size should always be planted with a root ball.

The limiting factor when moving large trees is the size and weight of root ball required. For a tree of 38mm (1.5″) diameter at 150mm (6″) above ground level, the ball should be 450mm (18″) in diameter. A root ball this size weighs about 115kg (250lb), and this is about the maximum which volunteers should attempt to move.

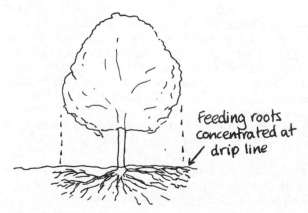

Feeding roots concentrated at drip line

A general rule of thumb when deciding on the size of the root ball is to dig around the tree at the drip line, under the outermost branches, where most of the feeding roots are concentrated.

Keep the following points in mind:

a   If the soil is so dry that the root ball is likely to crumble when lifted, water it thoroughly two days before lifting. If the soil is too wet, postpone the job! Extra water means extra weight.

b   Prune any limbs which may get in the way during lifting and transport, or wrap them in hessian and tie them to the main stem to keep them from rubbing.

c   If the tree has a large crown, prune it before moving to reduce the demands of the branches and leaves on the root system (p94). Evergreens may benefit from a spray of anti-dessicant eg S600 or Foliguard. These are non-toxic plastic materials which form a film on the foliage and reduce transpiration.

d   As with small trees, avoid lifting in hot sun or drying, windy weather.

Two people are needed. Follow this procedure:

1   If the ground is soft, score a deep circle around

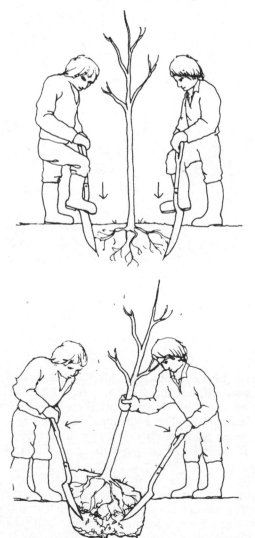

77

the tree at the diameter of the root ball to cut most of the lateral roots. Use a pointed spade. If the soil is hard or stony, dig a trench, using a mattock if necessary.

2 The two people should stand on either side of the circle. Push the spades as far under the rootball as possible to lever the tree up. Don't pull on the trunk or limbs to loosen the tree, since this may shatter the rootball.

If the tree remains anchored by long bottom roots, loop a winch cable around the roots and tighten to sever them.

3 When the tree and its rootball tear free of the earth, keep the spades underneath to hold up the ball. If the ball falls apart, quickly wrap the main roots in damp sacking or hessian to keep them moist. Use one piece of sacking on each major root. This way, if a piece comes loose only part of the root system dries out.

4 Lay a square of sacking or hessian, big enough to wrap around the root ball, to one side of the hole. Then gently manoeuvre the tree out of the hole, remove the spades and fasten the cloth tightly around the ball with rope.

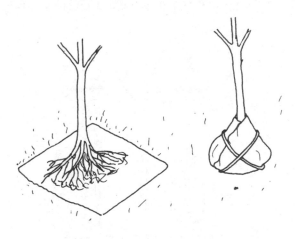

If the tree is to be loaded into a vehicle, push a stout round rod into the ball next to the stem before wrapping it up. The rod should project a few inches beyond the end of the stem to protect the tip.

Heling-in

Ideally, plants should be lifted, transported and replanted without interruption. Often, however, they need to be held for some weeks or even months before planting. The traditional storage method is to hele–in (customarily, though incorrectly spelt heel–in), and known as 'sheughing' in Scotland.

1 Dig a trench in good fresh moist soil which will not dry out or become waterlogged. Cultivated nursery ground is ideal. Dig the trench with a sloping back, deep enough so that the plants can be put in and their roots completely covered.

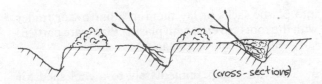
(cross-sections)

2 Trees in bundles should be separated and spaced along the trench, to keep the plants in the centres of the bundles from drying out or – in the case of evergreens – from heating up. It is convenient to place a marker stick every 50 or 100 plants to save counting later. Place the plants with their roots completely in the trench but with their tops mostly out.

3 If you anticipate having to lift the plants in very frosty weather, cover the roots in a thick layer of straw to prevent the soil freezing to them.

4 Throw soil over the roots to cover them and lightly firm the soil around the roots by treading.

Packing in bags

Where plants are going to be no more than about seven days from lifting to planting, they can be packed in polythene bags. Use bags of 250 gauge polythene, or 500 gauge if you want to re-use the bags.

If possible, try to sort and pack the plants so that the bags don't have to be opened or re-packed again before planting, as this will save a lot of time and trouble, and will also minimise drying of the roots.

For example, if you know that three teams are going to be planting mixed species in different areas of a site, bag up the plants accordingly in three lots, clearly labelled. It's easiest if you write out the labels beforehand, when you can sit at a desk with the planting plan in front of you if necessary. Remember you can only fit a certain number of plants per bag. You may want to label the species name, number of plants, planting team or code which refers to the planting plan. Use plastic plant labels or similar material (eg old plastic jerricans cut into strips) and waterproof pen. Get organised with a small team of workers so that the plants can be lifted, sorted, counted, bundled, bagged and labelled with the minimum of delay.

1 Pack all plants with their shoots in the same direction. Plants up to 45cm (18″) tall can be entirely enclosed in the bag, which should be tied at the top. Needles or leaves of evergreen plants should be dry when put into bags, otherwise they may rot. Thorny plants, and all plants over 45cm (18″) should have just the roots enclosed, with the bag securely tied around the stems. Plants 60cm (24″) and taller which may have roots too large to easily bag, should be kept moist and protected, by covering them with peat or straw, and wrapping them in plastic.

2 Squeeze the bags gently to expel excess air, and tie them with string. Attach label or mark the bags with indelible felt pen to avoid confusion.

3 Store bagged trees in a well ventilated shed or shelter, which should be below 5 degrees Celsius. Bags must not be stacked for more than a few hours or the trees may heat up. If they are stacked at all, it must be in such a way that air can get to at least one side of the bag. If stored for more than two or three days, bags should be opened and kept upright. Keep bagged plants out of direct sunlight at all times to prevent them heating up.

Transport

Bare-root plants should always be transported with at least their roots protected in plastic bags. Even if plants can be lifted directly from the nursery and transported, for example, on a trailer sheeted over with a tarpaulin, there is almost bound to be some delay before planting. Plants will dry out under the tarpaulin, or while they are being unloaded or sorted prior to planting. Even in the best organised schemes there will be a delay while work is explained, tools are fetched and so on, and a few minutes of exposure to wind or cold can damage the roots. Leave the plants in the bag until the moment you plant.

Keep the vehicle well ventilated and unheated. Place bagged plants no more than two layers deep, and if on an open wagon, cover them with opaque sheeting so they are shaded from sunlight.

Rootballed trees should be packed individually in peat moss or straw and secured in the vehicle by means of rope around the stems. Keep the root balls covered and moisten them if the trip is long or in hot weather. Evergreens can be protected from water loss during transport by wrapping the crowns in opaque sheeting secured with string or rope.

Pre-planting care

a If you buy plants from a nursery, inspect them on delivery. Notify the nursery of any damaged bags, as plants in torn bags are likely to be dry and, if the weather is cold, liable to frost damage. Soak any plants with dry-looking roots in a tank of water for a few hours before planting. If the plants themselves look dry and shrivelled, return them to the nursery.

b If you cannot plant the trees as soon as delivered, it is best to unpack them and hele them in, preferably in trenches dug in advance.

c If you receive the plants during a very cold period, wait until the frost ends to plant them. Place the unopened bundles in a dry, frost-free shed or cellar, where they will survive for two to three weeks if well covered with straw, bracken, sacking or newspapers.

If the frost seems likely to continue for longer than this, undo the bundles but leave the packing around the roots and hele the plants in a trench, if you can dig it in such weather!

PATTERNS, SPACINGS AND MIXTURES

Planting patterns

Trees may be planted in rows or in irregular clumps or random spacing. Row planting is best with transplants and small whips because it makes the trees easier to find later for weeding.

Of the various possible patterns, the simplest and most satisfactory is planting 'on the square', where the distance between rows is the same as the distance between trees in a row. In practice, this is never quite so uniform as might be expected, due to irregularities and obstacles on the ground. For planting on the square, the number of trees required is given by the formula: $2N = A/d$

where N is the number of trees required, A is the area to be planted (in square feet or square metres), and d is the distance between trees in the row (in feet or metres). Where the distance between rows is different from the distance between trees in a row, use the formula $N = dl$, where l is the distance between rows. Where you need to account for rides and other unplantable areas, subtract 15% from the total. Note that 1 acre = 43,560 square feet, and 1 hectare = 10,000 square metres.

Irregular patterns are more suitable for large, individually guarded trees which are planted at wider spacings and which can be seen easily for weeding. Here it is easier to take advantage of topographical variations. For example:

a On exposed, sites, plant trees on the north or east side of sheltering stumps, boulders and hummocks.

b On dry sites, or with moisture-loving trees, plant in dips, hollows and furrows.

c On damp sites, or where trees need good drainage, plant on hummocks, hillocks and ridges.

Spacings

Trees are usually spaced according to their size (see the table, page 74). Bear in mind the following points:

a Conifers for timber production are now usually spaced not less than 1.8m (6') apart and normally 2m (6½–7'). Broadleaved trees are sometimes planted at the traditional distance of 1.2–1.5m (4–5') but 1.8m (6') or wider is more common. On weedy sites, plant at the wider spacings to minimise costs, as the fewer trees to weed, the lower the cost. A few broadleaved timber trees are planted at much wider spacings, eg 7.5m (24') for poplars and 9m (30') for willows.

b Conservation and amenity trees can be planted at wider spacings, eg 3–3.5m (10–12'), where you expect the survival rate to be high and where you want the trees to develop spreading lower branches.

Wide spacing also allows a herbaceous layer and self-seeded wild trees to grow up.

c   Mature specimen trees, in parks, gardens or roadside situations, should be spaced widely so that they can develop a full crown. To prevent the site looking bare in early years, you can plant a variety of species that grow to different heights, or you can plant closely and thin later to give some of the trees sufficient room.

Broadleaved trees vary greatly in crown spread, but a total spread of about 40% of the mature height is usual. Crown spread of broadleaved trees can be increased in relation to height by lopping or pollarding, or restricted by fairly frequent pruning of side branches.

WORK RATES AND ORGANISATION

Work rates

Rates vary greatly depending on the size of trees planted and method used, the terrain and the experience and organisation of the planters. Rates for volunteers are about 80–100 notch-planted transplants (50–75 if in tree shelters), 15–20 pit-planted whips, or 4–5 pit-planted, staked and individually guarded standards, per person per day.

Organisation

The following points apply to mass plantings of small trees, where proper organisation can make a big difference to the work rate and the survival of trees:

a   Each volunteer should have a plastic sack, or a bag with a shoulder strap or a bucket or other container, lined with moist peat moss, earth or sawdust (p61). This is used to carry the trees.

b   Mark the line to be planted, using poles or stakes. For long lines, use at least three poles. It is usual to plant in echelon, with the leader setting the spacing along the sighted row, and the other following along adjacent rows a few plants back.

Use your planting tool, or stick cut to length, to measure the distances between plants, or pace the spacings.

c   It is often easiest for volunteers to work in pairs, with one person measuring the spacing and cutting the notch, while the other person plants.

d   On large tasks, one or more volunteers should act as couriers to keep the planters supplied with trees, stakes and guards as necessary. Provide extra containers so that some can be refilled while others are in use. It may be worth storing or heling-in the trees and stockpiling materials in several places around the site for convenience.

e   When planting mixtures, stake out the boundaries of the bands or groups in advance. Then let people plant the rows within the bands or groups as for single-species planting.

The following points apply to pit-planting tasks where larger trees are used:

a   When planting trees which do not need staking, work in teams of about six people, with four digging the holes and two planting the trees.

b   When planting trees which need staking and extra protection, minimise the number of tools required by working in a production line. For example, three teams of two people dig the holes, two people put in stakes, two people plant and two people fix rabbit guards and tree ties, water the trees and help the others as needed.

Planting Methods

GENERAL RULES

a   Keep fine root fibres moist at all times. If bare roots are exposed to the air on a hot, sunny or frosty, windy day the root fibres can be killed within a minute or so. Even on a rainy day the trees' survival chances are greatly reduced if bare roots are exposed for more than a few minutes.

b   Make planting holes big enough for the roots, otherwise trees grow poorly and develop weak root systems. Trim excessively long roots before planting or make the holes deeper.

c   Plant trees to the same depth at which they were growing in the nursery, shown by the soil mark on the stem at the root collar (see the diagram, p74). Trees planted too shallowly may dry out or be loosened by the wind. Those planted too deeply may rot.

d   Plant trees with the stems vertical, otherwise they tend to grow weak near the base and have poor form.

e   Firm the soil around the plants by treading in with the heel. This fills in any air pockets and firmly anchors the roots. Take care not to scrape the bark when treading in, and be sure the trees stay vertical. Test for firmness by tugging the stem: the tree should not shift.

Check the trees again for firmness at least once in the first weeks after planting, and more often if there are heavy frosts or high winds.

f Protect and care for the trees as necessary after planting (p86–94).

NOTCH PLANTING

Notch or slit planting is the quickest method but not the most reliable. It is generally suitable for the mass planting of bare-rooted transplants and whips under about 90cm (3′) high. It should not be used in wet soil or for large or expensive trees or where failures must be minimised.

The technique varies somewhat according to the tool used. The choice of tool depends on the ground conditions as well as on personal preference. A small garden spade (p61) is the usual tool in most conditions. A grubbing mattock is better in hard, stony, ploughed or steeply sloping ground or where much screefing is needed. A Schlich or Mansfield planting spade (p61) is stronger than a garden spade and may be better for T-notching, although some people dislike them, and they can make it harder to plant trees firmly. A dibber is useful when planting small trees in very light or sandy soil.

Basic procedure

Where there is a thick grassy mat, the first step – whatever the planting tool used – is to clear a bare patch about 450mm (18″) in diameter where the tree is to be planted by 'screefing' with a spade or mattock.

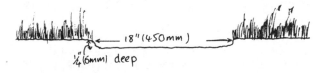

Use the following technique for planting with a garden spade:

1 Cut an L–, T– or H-shaped notch in the ground where the tree is to be planted. L-notching is usual but use whatever system seems best to you. Make the cuts 150mm (6″) deep or more, according to the length of the tree's roots. Make at least one of the cuts vertical so that the tree is held upright in the soil.

2 Lever the soil up with the spade to create a notch.

3 Take a tree from your bag or bucket and insert it in the notch a bit too deeply. Don't cram it in, but use a wiping motion to get the roots well in, and then pull upward a little to bring the root collar level with the soil surface, helping to straighten the roots. Don't pull too hard or you'll strip the roots.

4 Pull the spade out, taking care not to dislodge the tree, and tread in around the stem to firm the roots.

Variations

a When planting small trees in soft ground with a spade, make a notch simply by jamming the blade down and levering back or working the handle to and fro. Insert the tree, remove the spade and close the notch by treading.

b To L– or T–notch with a grubbing mattock, make the first cut with the tool's axe blade, and then make a cross-cut with its adze blade and lift.

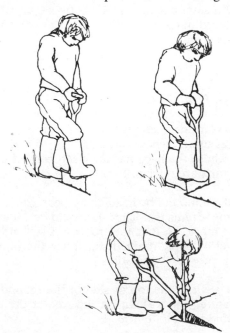

In suitable soil you can just jam the adze blade down and pull up on the handle to make a hole for planting. In very stony ground, you may need a pick-ended mattock to make a hole.

c To use a dibber, simply push the tool into the soil, work it around to make a conical hole and drop in the plant.

TURF PLANTING

This method is useful for planting small trees in wet ground, especially peaty soils, as it improves the drainage around the roots.

Planting in individual turfs

When you are cutting drains by hand, or where drainage has not been carried out, use the following method:

1 Cut turfs using a garden or planting spade. Cut them at least 300mm (12″) square, and 100–150mm (4–6″) and preferably 230mm (9″) thick. The bigger the turf, the better the tree growth. Cut the turfs from the lines of the drains or wherever convenient, and place them grass–side down where you want to plant the trees.

2 Cut a slit in the side of the turf from the middle outward. It is usually recommended that the slit be made in the side of the turf facing the prevailing wind, so that the wind pushes the tree against the uncut part of the turf. Edlin (1964, p45), however, suggests cutting on the opposite side, to prevent the wind drying the turf around the slit which may open and allow the roots of the plant to dry.

Cut through fairly thin turfs down to, but not below, ground level. With thick turfs cut 150mm (6″) or so into the turf, but not through it. When planting oak it is best to cut deeper so that the roots can go through the turf into the ground.

3 Insert the tree as shown below.

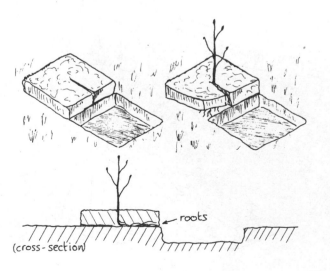

(cross-section) roots

4 Remove the spade and tread in around the tree to firm it.

Planting in ridges

Where a ridge has been created by ploughing, plant in the ridge. There are three methods:

a Using a garden or planting spade, cut a slit in the top of the ridge, insert the tree and firm it as when planting in individual turfs (above). If the ridge is more than about 230mm (9″) high, slice the top off it where you intend to plant and cut a slit in the platform.

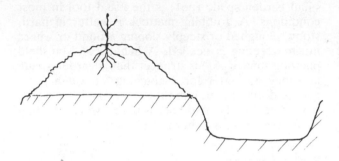

b Cut a V-shaped wedge of turf out of the side of the ridge away from the wind, with two strokes of the spade. Then place the tree in the notch and replace the wedge, trampling it down to make sure the roots are held firmly in the turf.

prevailing wind

c Use a semi-circular spade to twist out a plug in the ridge to make a suitable hole. Replace the plug after positioning the tree.

MOUND PLANTING

Mound planting is slower than turf planting but gives the trees extra inches above the wet soil. It is most useful where drainage has not been carried out and where turfs are difficult to cut.

1 Make a mound by heaping up peat, loose soil or spoil from drainage ditches. It should be 230mm (9″) high or more, so that the tree roots will be above the level of badly drained soil. Firm the mound as much as possible by treading.

2 Cut a slit in the top or side of the mound as for turf planting (above). Insert the tree at the correct depth and tread in to firm.

PIT PLANTING

Pit planting is the slowest method but one which ensures plenty of room for the roots. It is essential for trees over about 90cm (3') tall. It is also worth doing when you are planting only a few trees or where failures would be expensive or difficult to replace.

Treading in is most important when pit planting. Most failures are due to lack of firming. In heavy soils don't firm so much that the soil becomes compacted.

Small trees

Pit planting trees under about 1.5m (5'), or 1.2m (4') in exposed conditions, can be done without staking:

1 In grassland, cut a square of turf about 1½ spade widths wide. Lift the turf out and put it to one side.

2 Dig the soil out to the depth of the spade's blade (a 'spit'), to make a square sided hole. Place the spoil neatly in a heap nearby, or, for ease of retrieval, onto a plastic sheet. Keep the topsoil separate if it is noticeably better than the subsoil, and remove any big stones from the spoil. Loosen the soil in the bottom of the hole using a spade or fork, to make it easier for the roots to grow down.

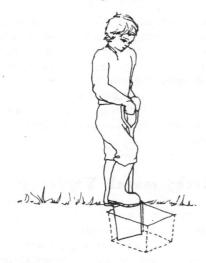

3 Hold the tree vertically in the centre of the hole, checking that the soil mark at the root collar is at

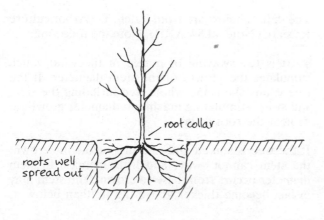

ground surface level. A cane or other straight stick held across the hole makes it easier to check. Shovel or push the best soil, usually the topsoil, around the roots. Work quickly so that the roots don't dry out, but do the job thoroughly to ensure no air pockets are left. Firm the soil with your hands or boot, taking care not to damage the roots or stem. Backfill with the remaining spoil, and then cut the turf in two, and put it upside down around the stem.

Larger trees

Trees over 1.5m (5') tall will normally need staking (see below). The bigger the tree, the more care is necessary in planting, but the method is essentially the same for all. The work is best done by two people, or more when planting large trees with heavy root balls.

1 Dig a hole large enough to comfortably take the roots when spread out, and deep enough for the soil mark to be at ground level. Roots should never be coiled or bent to fit the hole, but instead the hole should be enlarged. Put the turf, topsoil and subsoil in separate heaps beside the pit.

When planting on a slope, cut a level shelf before digging the hole.

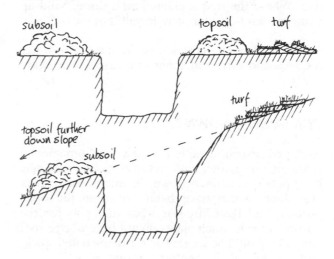

It is best not to dig the hole more than a few hours in advance of planting, as it may fill with water which will then need to be emptied before planting can be done. If the hole fills with water as you are digging it, the site is too wet and tree roots will 'drown'. Find an alternative site, unless such waterlogging is due to unusually rainy weather, in which case planting should be delayed until conditions improve.

2 Fork over the soil in the bottom of the hole to loosen it thoroughly. Where the soil is poor or very heavy, or where you want to give the tree the best possible conditions, dig a loam-leafmould mixture, compost, well-rotted manure or peat into the bottom of the pit, and mix some in with the soil for backfilling. Mound some of the planting mixture into a rough cone in the base of the pit.

3 Position the stake and drive it in (see below).

83

4 If the tree has a root ball, place it in the hole with the ball intact. Then loosen the wrapping if it is a material which quickly rots, or remove it if it is plastic or heavy canvas. Don't break up the root ball. If the tree is bare-rooted, one person should hold it while the other spreads the root crown over the cone of topsoil and works the soil in among the roots. It is a good idea to shake the tree gently up and down to help the earth settle between the roots as you lightly tamp the soil by hand.

5 Fill the hole in stages, starting with topsoil and adding subsoil nearer the top. Make sure the stem is vertical and the soil mark at ground level. Firm around the roots after adding the topsoil and again after placing the subsoil. Light soils need to be firmed much more strongly than heavy soils. Where practical, firm heavy soils minimally if wet at planting time, and then tread them in strongly when the soil is drier. Continue adding soil until the pit has been filled and slightly mounded at the level of the root collar.

Usually it is best to replace the turf grass–side down around the stem (see above), so that it rots down to provide a mulch around the tree. Where watering by hand is possible in dry soils, form a dam around the tree by putting the turfs upside down in a circle 600–900mm (2–3') out from the stem or at the drip line. Where the tree is planted on a slope, build up a higher, semi-circular dam downhill of the tree.

6 Tie the tree to the stake, position a guard, water the tree and carry out other aftercare as necessary (p92).

CONTAINER-GROWN TREES

Evergreens such as holly and yew, and ornamental trees such as garden cultivars of native species may be supplied container-grown. 'Containerised' stock are plants which have been grown in the open ground, and then lifted and put into pots for the purpose of sale. Such plants do not have a large root ball, and should be treated as for bare-rooted stock, and planted only in the dormant season.

The following points should be noted about container-grown trees and shrubs:

1 In theory, container-grown stock can be planted at any time when the soil is suitable (with the exception of evergreens which are best planted in late spring to avoid frost), including all through the growing season. In practice, planting in late spring or summer is risky unless provision is made for regular watering.

2 Container-grown trees often have a large amount of top growth for the size of the root ball. This is made possible by careful cultivation in the nursery.

To transplant successfully, the tree will normally need to be staked so that the roots have a chance to grow out of the rootball and into the surrounding soil. If this is not done, the rootball will be loosened. Until such rooting takes place, the tree will also need to be regularly watered during the growing season, in order to sustain the amount of top growth.

3 Container-grown trees and shrubs are normally grown in a peat-based compost, as this promotes rapid root growth. If the rootball is put direct into a heavy soil, the roots will have difficulty penetrating the soil and may simply continue to grow round the rootball, as if 'pot bound'. The tree may put on some growth, but then die as it is starved of water or nutrients, and even after several seasons in the ground may be found to have made no new growth beyond the original rootball. It is therefore very important when planting container-grown stock that the roots are weaned slowly into the surrounding soil. Do this by digging a planting hole twice the diameter of the pot and half as deep again, and backfilling it with a mixture of half soil to half peat or garden compost.

4 Container grown stock is more expensive than the same stock grown in the open ground, because of the extra work and materials involved in growing them, and in higher transport costs. Most species establish much faster from small, bare-rooted stock or container-grown seedlings (see below) than from larger container-grown stock.

Container-grown seedlings

A fairly new development is that of one year old container-grown seedlings, grown in Japanese paper pots. These do not suffer the problems outlined in points 2 and 3 above, because they have not had the time to develop the unnatural and unbalanced characteristics of older container-grown plants. They are proving to have a higher success rate than bare-root transplants on poor soils, and are ideal for using with tree shelters.

Staking and Tying

The recommendation for staking trees has changed in recent years, as a result of studies of the effect of wind sway on trees, and from experience of what happens to trees which are staked. Tying a tree just below the start of the crown using a tall stake is not now recommended.

The details below are from Patch, D (Arboriculture Research Note 40:84:ARB). Note the following:

a It is the swaying of a tree in the wind which stimulates the growth of the stem diameter. If the tree is unstaked, the whole tree including the stem will sway, stimulating maximum diameter growth at or near the root collar.

If the tree is staked and tied just below the crown, the stem cannot sway, and little increase in stem diameter occurs from base to crown. The stem may in fact become thicker above the tie than below it,

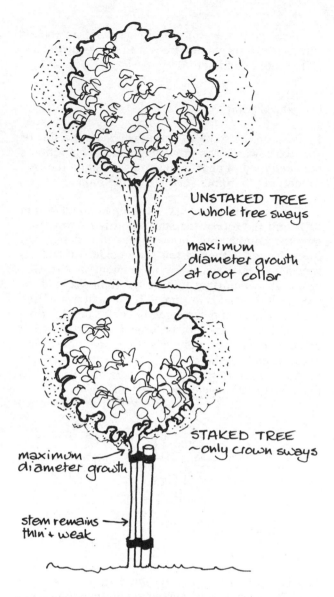

UNSTAKED TREE
~whole tree sways

maximum diameter growth at root collar

STAKED TREE
~only crown sways

maximum diameter growth

stem remains thin + weak

tree is increased by planting 'feathered' trees, rather than trees with clean pruned stems. Pruning can be done progressively over the following years as necessary.

g Stakes and ties cost money and need maintenance. It is usually much better to avoid the need for them altogether by using smaller trees.

Stakes

Where necessary, stake the tree sufficiently to anchor the rootball in the ground, but leave enough stem free to sway in the wind. The stake should extend no higher than a third of the way up the stem. Tie the tree with a single tie, preferably of a flexible material which allow some movement. Old inner tubes, tights and other materials are suitable though not particularly sightly (see below).

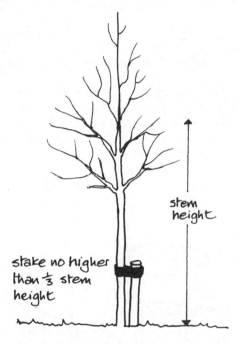

stem height

stake no higher than ⅓ stem height

because diameter growth increases in response to the movement of the crown.

An unsupported tree will be shorter, with an evenly tapering stem from base into the crown, making a stout and firm tree. A supported tree will initially gain height faster than the unsupported tree, but the stem will be thin and weak up to the tie, and then taper rapidly.

b An unsupported tree thus develops a structure which can flex under the force of wind or vandalism. A supported tree can flex only over the height of the crown, and is more likely to be snapped off.

c The diameter growth of roots at the root collar is increased by movement of the stem.

d When the stake is removed from a supported tree, the crown and lower stem may be out of balance, so that it may lean or bend right down to the ground.

e Ties are often not checked and maintained, and may cause abrasion and constriction to the stem.

f Stem diameter growth towards the base of the

Provided soil or weather conditions do not impede growth, sufficient root growth should have occurred to anchor the tree by the end of the growing season after planting. It is suggested that the stake be removed at the beginning of the second growing season.

Treatment of previously staked trees

The tree may need to be gradually weaned from its support, by lowering the tie successively for a few years at the start of each growing season. Cut off the extra piece of stake each time, in order to avoid it rubbing against the stem.

Ties

There are several types of commercial tree ties available, designed for different types of uses, sizes of tree and degree of exposure. They are generally much stronger, easier to adjust as the tree grows, and look more acceptable than any home made equivalent, therefore justifying the extra expense.

Prices vary from about 15p each for small chainlock ties to 50p and more for large buckle and collar ties.

Types include:

a Chainlock ties, which are threaded through and twisted to lock in place. Available in 25m rolls. Similar locking ties are available in packs of 5, each 450mm (18″) long.

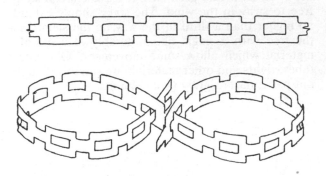

b Nail-on or buckle ties with collars or pads, which prevent the tree from chafing against the stake. Buckle ties can be loosened to adjust for the tree's growth or re-use. Nail-on ties can only be adjusted by removing and re-nailing.

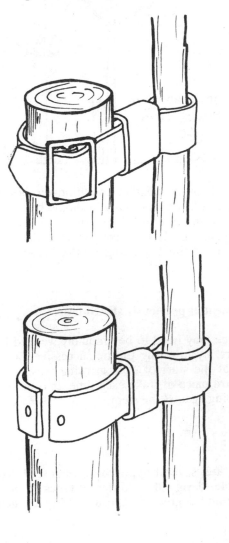

c Three-point ties, for use with guy wires to anchor extra–large transplanted trees with trunks of 100mm (4″) or more diameter.

Procedural points

1 Position the stake so that it will be on the side of the tree towards the prevailing wind. This reduces the likelihood of chafing in storms. Position the tree so that it is 25–50mm (1–2″) from the stake.

2 For ties with pads, first fix the pad about 75mm (3″) from the top of the stake by driving two tacks into the countersunk holes. Then thread the belt through, and either fasten the buckle, or tack as shown to leave space for adjustment as the tree grows. It is important to have the right size pad for tree, as if the pad is too small, it can split as the tree grows. When fitted correctly, the belt should form a loop as shown, and not be drawn in tightly by the pad to make a 'figure of eight'. Some pads have four slots instead of the normal two, so that they can be used on different sizes of tree. J. Toms Ltd manufacture a range of ties and pads.

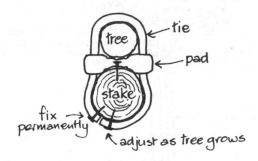

3 Ties with collars can be fitted to most sizes of tree. The tie should be tacked to the stake to prevent it slippping. Inspect trees twice a year to make sure they are secure and not chafed or constricted by the stakes and ties. Loosen ties as necessary to accommodate stem growth.

Tree Protection

Trees may need to be protected against damage by hares, rabbits, deer, livestock, machinery or vandalism. In group or woodland planting the perimeter fencing may protect against all or some of these factors, depending on the type of fence and the situation. Whether to use perimeter fencing or individual guards, or a combination of both, needs to be carefully weighed up. Tree shelters were designed originally to increase the rate of tree growth (see below), but also act as guards against deer, rabbits and hares. Special heavy duty shelters are available for protection against livestock.

The subject of tree guards is covered in Arboricultural Leaflet 10 'Individual Tree Protection' (Forestry Commission 1985).

Fences and tree guards are costly to build in terms of labour and materials. Needs must be assessed carefully, as failure can mean loss of the tree, as well as time and energy wasted in trying to maintain a badly designed system. Individual tree guards nearly always cost more than the tree itself, but it is never worth planting trees unless you can give them adequate protection.

Fences or guards?

The cost of individual tree protection increases directly with the number of trees protected, whereas the cost of fencing relates to the size and shape of land enclosed, irrespective of the number of trees. Long thin or complex shapes are the most uneconomic to fence, with squares and rectangles being the cheapest. The following formula is given in Arboricultural Leaflet 10, to calculate the 'Critical Area Index'. If the answer is greater than 1, then individual tree protection is cheaper. If the answer is less than 1, then a perimeter fence is cheaper.

$$\text{Critical Area Index} = \frac{F \times P}{N \times C}$$

where

F = fencing costs per linear metre
P = perimeter of area in metres (length of fence-line)
N = number of plants per hectare to be protected
C = cost of protecting individual trees

Factors to consider

When designing or choosing the type of tree protection, the following factors should be considered:

a   What are the threats to the tree? Are there rabbits or hares in the area? What type of livestock may have access around the tree?

b   For how long is protection required? Tree guards can be designed for a long, maintenance-free life, or to disintegrate after a few years. Some tree guards will themselves restrict and damage the tree if left in position too long.

c   Does the guard allow access to the tree for weeding, loosening of tree ties and so on?

d   Is the guard in a situation where its appearance is important?

e   Do you want the guard to be conspicuous, for example to aid weeding, or inconspicuous, to reduce vandalism?

Damage by animals

There are many ways in which wild animals and livestock can damage trees. Leaves can be browsed during the growing season, or buds and twigs chewed off during the winter. Horses, sheep, hares, rabbits, deer and voles can all damage trees by stripping the bark, normally during winter and spring, when other food is scarce. When snow covers the ground and covers fences and guards, this type of damage can occur at a height above the ground. Bark stripping can severely damage trees, and will kill the tree where bark is removed all the way round the stem. All sizes of tree may be vulnerable, and even mature thin-barked trees such as beech, hornbeam or sycamore may be damaged or killed. Note that squirrels are one of the worst culprits at bark stripping, especially of beech in mid-summer, but they are not controlled by any form of guard (see p101).

Deer may fray trees by rubbing their antlers against the stems during the build up to the rut. Cattle, horses and sheep can damage trees and guards by rubbing against them. Where livestock gather around trees, compaction and poaching of the ground can cause waterlogging and damage to tree roots.

The following tables give information on suitable dimensions to protect trees against different types of animals. Use of a herbicide on the grass within a tree guard will not only aid tree establishment and growth, but will mean there is less inducement for animals to lean through to graze.

For further information on identifying and controlling damage by wild animals, see the 'Wildlife Rangers Handbook' (Forestry Commission, 1985). For further information on fencing, see the BTCV handbook 'Fencing' (Agate, 1986).

TABLE 7A   *HEIGHT OF GUARD REQUIRED (metres)*

Horses	2.50	2.25	2.00	1.75	1.50	1.15	1.15	1.15	1.15	
Cattle	1.85	1.70	1.50	1.15	1.15	1.15	1.15	1.15	1.15	
Man	2.25	1.90	1.70	1.50	1.35	1.15	1.15	1.15	1.15	
Red Deer	2.10	1.75	1.45	1.20	1.20	1.20	1.20	1.50	1.80	zone A
Fallow Deer	1.80	1.60	1.25	1.10	1.10	1.10	1.35	1.80	1.80	
Goats	1.85	1.70	1.35	1.20	1.15	1.15	1.15	1.15	1.15	
Roe Deer	1.60	1.35	1.10	1.00	1.00	1.00	1.60	1.80	1.80	
Sheep	1.10	0.90	0.90	0.90	0.90	0.90	0.90	0.90	0.90	zone B
Hares	0.85	0.85	0.85	0.85	0.85	0.85	0.85	0.85	0.85	
Rabbits	0.75	0.85	0.85	0.85	0.85	0.85	0.85	0.85	0.85	

```
    0   0.25   0.5   0.75   1   1.25   1.5   1.75   2   2.25
              DISTANCE FROM TREE (metres)
```

Table 7a shows the height of the guard required against various animals, and the distance it should be from the tree. In zone A, the barrier must be of netting or timbers which are close enough to prevent the animal putting its head through and reaching the tree. In zone B, the barrier need only be sufficient to prevent the passage of the animal. The spacing of the horizontal and vertical members of netting or timber are shown in Table 7b. Note that in Table 7a the height of the barrier against deer increases as the distance from the tree increases. This is to prevent deer jumping into the exclosure.

TABLE 7B SPACING OF VERTICALS AND HORIZONTALS

	zone A	zone B
Horses	100	500
Cattle	100	500
Deer	75	225
Goats	75	225
Sheep	50	150
Hares	30	30
Rabbits	30	30
	vertical and horizontal spacing (mm)	horizontal spacing (mm)

Plastic spiral guards

These are designed to protect young trees against bark-stripping by rabbits and voles. They are easy to install, being simply wound around the stem of the tree, and are suitable for trees of between 10 and 40mm stem diameter. Trees smaller than this may bend over under the weight of the guard, and the space between the guard and the stem is large enough to give access to voles. A cane can be used inside the spiral to support the stem. Stems larger than 40mm diameter will not be properly protected as gaps will form in the spiral. Spiral guards are awkward to fit to strongly feathered or branching trees, nor are they suitable for multi-stemmed trees.

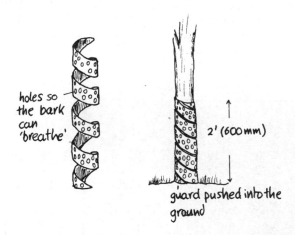

holes so the bark can 'breathe'

2' (600mm)

guard pushed into the ground

When fitting the guard, push the end into the ground around the base of the tree, to lessen the chance of the wind or animals dislodging it. Guards should be checked every year to make sure that they are still properly fitted, and that they are free to expand as the stem thickens. Any side shoots protruding through the holes in the guard should be freed or cut off, or they will prevent the guard expanding with tree growth.

Spiral guards give no protection against animals other than rabbits and voles, and are usually used in addition to a timber or other guard, or perimeter fence. They are available in white, green, grey or black. White is better not used where vandalism may occur, as it draws attention to the trees. This quality is useful however when weeding young trees. Spiral guards should last 5 years or more, but eventually become brittle.

Tubular plastic guards

These serve a similar purpose to spiral guards, but are made of a rigid plastic. They cannot be fitted to trees with side branches below the height of the guard. They are more durable than spiral guards, but also more expensive.

Plastic mesh guards

Use of these is fully described in Arboriculture Research Note 5.87.WILD 'Plastic mesh tree guards', available from the Forestry Commission.

'Netlon' plastic mesh guards are available in two types: pre-formed guards, 75mm diameter x 1.2m, and in rolls 450mm wide x 50m, for cutting as required.

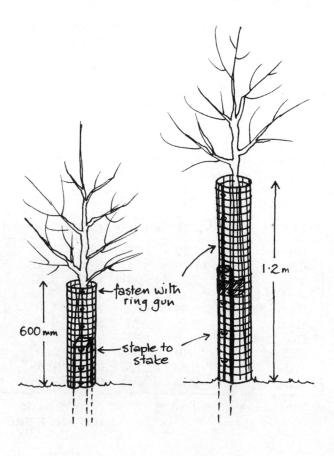

fasten with ring gun

600 mm

staple to stake

1.2m

The smaller guards can be used whole, to protect against roe deer, or cut in half to protect against rabbits and hares. When fitting to small transplants, make sure the guard is erected vertically with the tree in the centre, and fasten the guard to a supporting stake. The stake should be about 25 x 25mm (1 x 1″), and long enough to hold secure in the ground. It is only required for a few years until the tree is large enough to support the guard. Use a staple gun or small fencing staples to fix the guard to the stake.

For larger trees, the tree itself provides the necessary support so stakes are not needed. Fasten the guard with netting rings or wire ties. Check the guards occasionally to ensure they are still fitted correctly, and that the leading shoots are not growing out through the mesh. Undo and refasten as necessary. The guards are designed to degrade at between 5 to 10 years, so they do not need to be removed from the trees.

The larger guards can be used to protect amenity and parkland trees from browsing and fraying by deer, as well as to exclude rabbits and hares. Cut the required length (usually 1.2–1.5m) from the roll, and then form it into a tube of 150mm diameter. Fasten either to the tree stake, or to itself for established trees.

Wire mesh guards

These guards are durable but expensive, and are normally only necessary to prevent mechanical damage to high-value urban trees, or to protect established trees against horses or cattle. If used around young trees, side shoots which grow through the mesh must be cut off before they become entangled, or the wire will eventually 'strangle' the branches, and be difficult to remove.

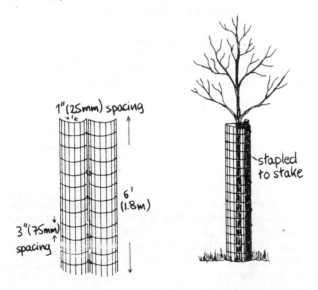

Timber guards

These are suitable for long–term protection of trees in parklands and pastures, to prevent cattle, sheep, horses and deer causing browsing damage to young trees, and bark damage throughout the tree's life. If properly built of preserved timber and maintained regularly, timber guards should have a life of at least 20 years. They are only worth doing well: poorly constructed guards or those of weak timber will soon be damaged by leaning and rubbing animals.

Note the following:

a Use the tables 7a and 7b to find the required dimension of the guard. It is difficult to upgrade the protection at a later date, so make sure that all likely damaging animals are taken into account.

b Unless vandalism is a problem, a section of climbable fence is useful for tending the tree.

c Use a mulch or herbicide within the tree guard to lessen the inducement for animals to reach in.

d It is not possible to build an exclosure simply of three or four posts with strained wire or netting, as sufficient strain to keep the wire taut will cause the posts to move. Horizontal rails, preferably rebated, must be included.

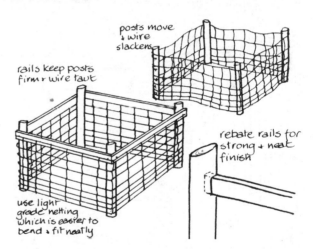

e It is not usually a good idea to increase the distance of the top rail from the tree by slanting the posts outwards, as this makes it difficult to fit netting neatly and securely.

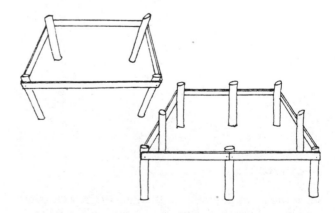

f Don't automatically top the exclosure with barbed wire, except against vandals, as this does not stop animals leaning over and makes it difficult to climb in to tend the tree.

Some designs for timber tree guards are shown below. These should be adapted, using the above tables, to fit the space and materials available. All guards can be made rabbit proof by fitting rabbit netting (900mm hexagonal mesh, 31mm gauge), with the bottom 150mm of netting turned out and pegged to the ground.

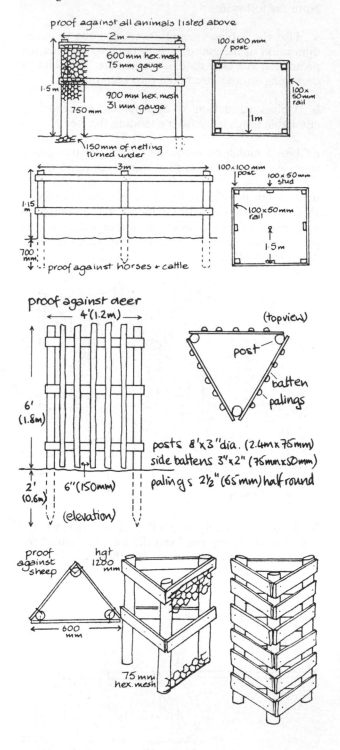

Tree shelters

Since their development in the late 1970s, well over 6 million of these shelters have been used in Britain and overseas. They are probably now the most common form of tree protection for plantings of less than a hectare, above which perimeter fencing against deer or rabbits usually becomes cheaper.

Tree shelters were designed to promote rapid growth by acting like a mini-greenhouse, and growth can be up to five times the normal rate in the first two years. They are also useful in other ways. The shelter protects the young tree against damage by animals (see below) and against spray or granular herbicide used around the base. Being readily visible, shelters make it easier to relocate newly planted trees for weeding and maintenance.

Shelters currently on the market are made of corrugated polypropylene, extruded polypropylene or PVC. The corrugated type are probably the most popular, being stronger than PVC, but having the advantage over the extruded type of being supplied flat-packed. Extruded tubes are very strong and only require a short stake, but are bulky to store and carry. Various colours are available including white, green and pale brown, and should be chosen according to whether the shelters need to be conspicuous or camouflaged.

Shelters are best used on transplants, 150–400mm tall, with a single strong leader. Any spreading side branches should be pruned at the time of planting, to enable the shelter to be fitted. Transplants with multiple stems or many side branches are not suitable. It is not worth using shelters on taller whips, as they will soon outgrow the shelter. The main benefits are gained by using transplants, which are cheap, transplant well, and are able to make the most of the improved growing conditions in the shelter.

The following sizes are recommended against various animals:

Shelter	Stake	Animals
600mm	800mm	Rabbits and hares
1.2m	1.2m	Sheep and roe deer
1.8m	1.8m	Fallow, sika and red deer
1.8m heavy duty		Cattle and horses

Where there is heavy pressure of deer or sheep, shelters may get damaged by animals rubbing against them. In a sheep paddock, this can be reduced by providing other posts for the animals to rub on.

Trees in fields grazed by cattle, horses or sheep will need protection for longer than the 5 year life of a shelter, and thin barked trees will be vulnerable to bark-stripping throughout their lives.

Most suppliers of shelters can also supply the stakes, as necessary. A square 25 x 25mm stake is suitable for the most commonly used 1.2m size shelter. Tanalised timber should not be necessary, and timber such as untreated larch, western red cedar or chestnut is sufficient for a 5 year life. Single chestnut pales can also be used. 1.8m shelters should have a thin quarter-sawn, split or round stake. Knotty or otherwise weak stakes should be rejected, as they will not last 5 years. Stakes must be long enough to be securely knocked into the ground, to hold the shelter firmly against wind and weather.

The method of fixing varies with the make of shelter.

Easy to use are those with an integral tie which can be quickly attached to the stake by hand. The design should be such that the tie is fixed to the shelter without encircling the tree. This means that when the shelter eventually disintegrates, the tie drops to the ground and is not left encircling the trunk. If shelters with encircling ties are used, the ties must be removed when the shelter falls apart. 'Tubex' shelters have ratchet-locking nylon straps which do not encircle the tree, but are threaded through a recess in the shelter to take the stake. Other types have non-encircling wire ties which are twisted to fasten, although problems have arisen with wires that break on being twisted, and also the wires causing the shelter itself to split and fail after only a couple of seasons.

Another feature to look for is the top edge of the shelter, as if this is sharp, it can cut into the emerging leader of the tree when blown about in the wind. The shelter should be made with a rounded edge or the top edge folded over to reduce this problem.

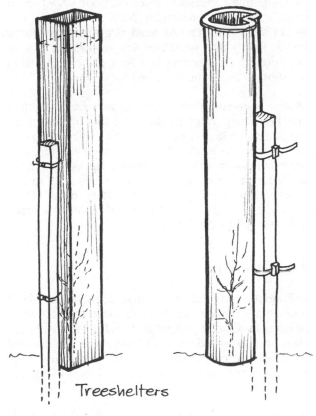

Treeshelters

Of the various shelters available (see p165), 'Correx plus' are widely used. They are made of corrugated polypropylene, with a folded top and non-encircling wire ties, and are supplied flat-packed. The 'Tubex Treeshelter', a twin-wall extruded shelter with nylon straps, is also shown here. It is best to shop around and find the best type to suit any particular requirements. Prices vary with make, and with the number ordered.

The procedure for erecting a shelter of the Correx type is as follows:

1   Plant the transplant, usually by the notch or T method (see p81). Cut the notch away from the side where you want to place the stake, so that the roots do not get damaged when the stake is knocked in. If possible the stake should be on the northern side, so it does not shade the transplant.

2   Prune off any spreading side branches.

3   Place the shelter over the transplant, with the folded edge to the top, wires towards the stake position and the plant central in the shelter. The bottom of the shelter should be pressed firmly into the soil to exclude voles, to prevent them eating the bark or taking advantage of the ideal nesting site which a shelter provides!

4   Place the stake flush against the shelter, and positioned correctly to take the wires. Then push the top of the shelter slightly away to give room to knock the stake in. Fitting the shelter first and then knocking in the stake makes it easier to get the stake in exactly the right position, square to the the shelter, and vertical. Use a small lump hammer on 25 x 25mm stakes. The stake should be knocked in far enough to leave about 50mm above the upper wire.

5   Fasten the wires around the stake, bending the ends in neatly as shown to avoid them snagging on people or animals.

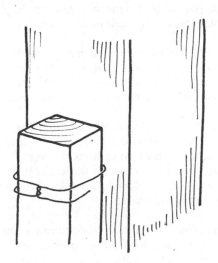

Tree shelters should last at least 5 years, and should be left to disintegrate, and not removed from around the protected tree. This is because the rapid growth will produce a slender stem that may not be strong enough to support the crown if conditions suddenly change.

Check the shelters regularly to make sure they have not come loose due to wind or animals, and replace any broken stakes. It is important to check early in the growing season that the shelter is not becoming choked with weeds. If necessary, remove the shelter to clear the weeds and then reposition. Granular herbicides used around the shelter will help control weeds within the shelter, or a mulching mat can be fitted at the time of planting.

Chemical repellants

Chemical repellants are available to protect young trees from winter browsing damage by mammals. They are relatively quick and easy to apply, and may be cheaper than tree guards or fencing for small, awkwardly shaped areas. They are contact chemicals, applied to the tree in the early winter, and last 2–3 months. They should not be used when trees are in active growth.

The Forestry Commission have found that 'AA Protect' and 'Dendrocol 17' are effective, and other products are currently being tested.

These repellants may be worth using on some sites against deer, and if repeated over several winters should give the trees a chance to get established. Normally though, fencing or shelters are more suitable.

Other deterrents

Other methods that have been used, particularly against deer, include tying rags soaked in creosote at entrances to small woods, paths, crossing points and so on. Tie the rags at deer head height (about 1m for roe and fallow, 1.2m for sika, 1.3m for red deer). Deer are also discouraged by brightly coloured strips of plastic tied near the vulnerable plantings, or at intervals along perimeter fencing.

Neither of these methods will give permanent protection, but may be successful for a few months over the winter. Swap around with different colours, siting and so on to keep the deer guessing!

Deer fences are described in 'Fencing' (BTCV, 1986). A single strand of electric fencing at deer head height on an existing stock fence is an effective deterrent, or fences of two or three electrified strands can be used. Low electric fences can also be used against rabbits and hares.

The only effective method of combining commercial timber production with a deer population is by deer management. This includes designing the forest to include deer glades, and clearing rides and paths to link up the areas where deer move so that culling can be efficiently carried out. Deer management is described in detail in the 'Wildlife Rangers Handbook' (Forestry Commission, 1985).

Feeding and Tending

FERTILISING

It is usually unnecessary to fertilise trees except in the situations described below. Other than on the poorest soils, tree failure is much more likely to be caused by bad planting, waterlogging or drought, rather than by lack of nutrients.

Forestry trees on poor soils

It may be essential to apply phosphate fertiliser to newly planted trees on very poor soils to ensure satisfactory growth. The usual dose is 60–80g (2–3oz) sprinkled around the base of each transplant, which is about one level handful per tree. Alders need another 60g (2oz) after six years. Fertilising should be done at the same time as planting. Planting bags equipped with compartments for fertiliser make the job simpler.

Occasionally, trees need phosphate at the pole stage or later, but this requires expert knowledge to determine. Very occasionally, trees show signs of potassium deficiency (eg uncharacteristic yellowing of the leaves), which can be corrected by an application of potash.

Specimen trees

Newly planted specimen trees on poor sites benefit from a dose of combined NPK fertiliser a few weeks after planting. At least 60g (2oz) should be forked lightly into weed-free soil around the base of the young tree, keeping it a foot or so away from the stem to avoid burning the roots.

Mature specimen trees which show signs of decline may be reinvigorated by the same sort of treatment, but at a much higher dose of up to 12.5kg (28lb) for a large tree. As a rule of thumb, use 1kg of fertiliser for every 50mm of stem girth (1lb for every 1″). To apply the fertiliser, dig small holes about 1.5m (5′) apart under the tree's crown, where most of the roots are. Put about 250g (8oz) of fertiliser in each hole and refill with earth.

Soil ameliorants

Soil ameliorants include a range of materials, some proprietary, which can be mixed into the soil when planting in difficult ground such as light sands, heavy clays and disturbed soils. The materials are claimed to enhance root growth and plant establishment by increasing soil water retention and improving soil structure.

As detailed in Arboriculture Research Note 69:87:SILS (Davies, RJ, 1987), the Forestry Commission have done trials of various ameliorants including 'Alginure', 'Broadleaf P4', 'Ficote 70', sedge peat, pulverised bark and farm-yard manure. These were tested on ash and small-leaved lime which were pit planted in heavily disturbed clay soil, and sycamore and Corsican pine in sandy soil overlying chalk.

After two seasons growth, none of the ameliorants were found to have been of any benefit to tree establishment, when compared to untreated trees.

However, proprietary ameliorants have been in use for several years by nurserymen on field-grown trees, with apparent benefit, and most gardeners will swear by farm-yard manure and other organic matter – so 'you pays your money and you takes your choice!'.

MULCHING

Mulching is a simple and effective way of suppressing weeds around trees, at the same time keeping the ground surface moist and cool. Organic granular mulches gradually improve the soil as the mulch breaks down. Mulching also aids trees in compacted or eroded soil.

Mulching is especially beneficial for trees of standard size and over, and is worthwhile for all newly planted specimen trees. Mulching is standard practice for poplars, but other forestry trees are not usually mulched. Turf-planted trees do not normally need mulching because the turf itself acts as a mulch, while pit-planted trees are mulched to some extent if the turf from the pit is replaced grass-side down around the tree.

Almost any bulky organic matter makes a suitable mulch. If you are planting in existing woodland, you can rake up leaf litter around the planted stems. Spoiled hay, which is excellent, may be available free from farms. Leaves and lawn clippings are sometimes available in large quantities from city parks departments or as a by-product of roadside verge mowing. Pulverised forest bark is reasonably cheap, and useful if available in bulk locally. Garden centres will also stock it by the sack, although this is more expensive. Woodchips are suitable, but sawdust is unpleasant to deal with and seriously lowers the nitrogen content of the soil as it rots. Miscellaneous agricultural and food processing wastes such as straw make good mulches where available. Proprietary mulching mats are also available (see below)

When mulching, keep the following points in mind:

a To mulch around a newly planted tree, simply spread a 100–150mm (4–6") deep layer of organic material around the stem in a circle of about 900mm (3') diameter. Keep the mulch away from the stem itself to avoid rot starting.

b Mulch around mature trees in the same way but spread the material over a wider area, especially around the drip line where the feeding roots are concentrated. If the soil is very compacted, fork over the top few inches first.

c Use sticks to weigh down hay or other lightweight material which may blow away.

d Avoid using inflammable mulch (eg dry sawdust, which can ignite spontaneously) in high fire-risk areas. Don't heap up the mulch too deeply since it may generate heat as it rots, which can damage the trees.

e One application of mulch is adequate, but trees benefit from mulching in later years if they grow where there is little natural build-up of plant litter.

f The mulch is best spread at the time of planting, during the winter. If this is not possible, spread in spring when the ground is moist. Do not spread after a period of drought, as this will only inhibit moisture from reaching the roots.

Mulching mats

Mulching mats of thick polythene, bitumen or woven polypropylene are available from various suppliers of forestry products (see p165). The mats are normally 600 x 600mm or 750 x 750mm square, with a slit to allow the mat to be fitted around the base of the tree. They have the advantage over loose mulching material of being much less bulky to transport, and are quick and easy to fit. The edges can either be pushed down into a slit to anchor, or soil can be overlapped around the edge. The mats are left in place and disintegrate after five years or so. Mats cost from 10–15 pence each, depending on the type and the number ordered.

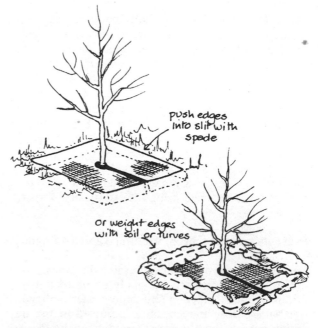

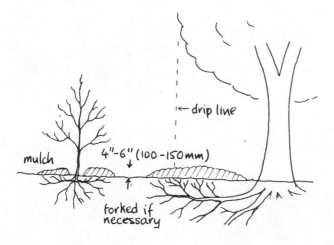

Mulching mats usually work out cheaper than two or more annual applications of herbicide, with none of the associated risks of using chemicals.

Old fertiliser sacks or other opaque polythene, roofing felt or old carpet can be used as a cheap alternative to proprietary mats.

WATERING

Most newly planted trees should not need watering, except in droughts, provided the roots are kept moist during the planting process and trees are mulched at planting. Too much watering can induce surface rooting, making the roots more susceptible to scorching in dry weather. With such trees, once watering begins it may have to be continued at every dry spell.

Watering may be essential in a few cases. Specimen-size trees, transplanted wild trees, and large trees which were container-grown should be well watered at planting time and during any periods of drought in the first growing season.

FIRMING UP

Check trees in the first weeks after planting, especially after storms or hard frosts. Frost can cause the ground to heave so loosening the roots. Also check in early spring before the leaves flush. Tread around any loose stems to keep the soil firm and the stems upright. Shelterbelt and other trees in exposed places are most likely to need repeated firming so check these often.

OTHER MEASURES

Weeding is covered in the next chapter.

Pruning

Transplanted wild trees usually need pruning when planted to reduce the amount of crown in relation to the root system. Prune weak and damaged branches and any limbs which cross or rub together. Cut back the side branches, by at least one third of their length. Do not cut the leader. For trees that grow in a spreading shape, make each pruning cut just above an outward facing bud. For upright or columnar trees, cut just above stem-facing buds. See the next chapter for more on pruning.

Shelterbelt trees occasionally need pruning to reduce their wind resistance during the establishment phase.

Prevention of sun scorch, windburn and frost damage

Specimen trees and transplanted wild trees which are moved from relatively shady or protected situations to more exposed sites may suffer damage to the bark before they become adjusted to the new conditions. Wrap the trunks and main limbs with tree-wrapping paper or hessian before or immediately after planting to prevent this. Wrap the material in overlappping spirals, tightly enough to stay in place, and tuck in the ends to hold.

Beating up

'Beating up', 'beeting' or 'filling up' is the replacement of any trees that fail. In a plantation, beating up is worth doing only if more than about 20% of the planted trees fail, assuming the failures are distributed evenly through the crop, or if more than 10–15% fail when the failures are concentrated in groups or when the original spacing was wide. A rule of thumb is to put in one replacement tree where three have failed together.

Beating up should be done in the autumn or winter after planting and, very rarely, again in the year after that. On sites where trees grow slowly, it may be worth waiting until the second year to do the beating up. Later than this, it is not worth replacing failures since the new trees cannot catch up with the main crop and are suppressed.

For plantings of specimen trees, and in hedges, screens and shelterbelts, beating up may be necessary even if failures are few, in order to preserve the required effect. Hedge and shelter trees may need replacing over as long a period as four or five years if growing conditions are difficult and the effects of gaps serious.

Use the best plants available as replacements, since they must catch up to the main crop. They should be at least as large as the originals or of a faster growing species. This is especially important when replacing hedge and screen plants after several years.

When beating up, check the surviving trees for firmness and tread them in as necessary.

Drain maintenance

It is important to maintain drains in plantations, since nearly all windblow problems, other than those caused by rare catastrophic storms, start in wet patches which may be caused by blocked drains.

A good time to check drains is just before the trees enter the thicket stage, and again just after thinning. Clean out debris, including brash, enlarge the channels as necessary and check and make good the outfalls.

8 Tree Maintenance

Weeding may be essential in woodland conservation work for three main reasons: to allow trees to establish successfully in the first few years after planting; to eliminate invasive exotic species such as rhododendron from woodlands where they are considered undesirable; and to maintain access rides and paths.

Weeding of Young Trees

Weeding is vital for the successful establishment of young trees. Lack of weeding, with resultant water stress on the young trees is a major cause of failure in tree planting schemes. Note the following points, which are based on information in Arboriculture Research Note 59.85.ARB, 'The Effects of Weed Competition on Tree Establishment', published by the Forestry Commission.

a Weeds compete for water, light and nutrients. All plants compete to some extent, but grasses and clover are particularly damaging.

b Grasses and other plants around the base of trees compete for water by taking it up from the soil and transpiring it through their leaves. This competes directly with the roots of young trees, which at this stage of growth rely on water supplies in the surface layer of soil. The rate of water loss by transpiration is much greater than the rate of evaporation from bare soil. In dry weather, a layer of dry soil will form at the surface of bare soil, and if undisturbed, will reduce further evaporation. By contrast, plants will continue to transpire, bringing up water from deeper in the soil.

c Tall weeds around young trees compete for light, can physically restrict and damage the tree when they fall, and harbour bark-gnawing rodents. However, tall weeds can be beneficial by protecting trees from drying winds, and also against damage from deer and vandalism. Tall lush grasses should certainly be removed in all situations, but other tall weeds such as brambles, nettles and many herbaceous plants which have fairly sparse growth can be left where they will give some shelter and protection. However, checks should be made to make sure that the young trees are not being physically restricted, particularly by bramble growth.

d Supplies of water and nutrients to trees are closely related, as nutrients are only available to the tree through the mechanism of water uptake. Thus the tree may appear to be suffering from a nutrient deficiency in the soil, where the real problem is the lack of water caused by weed competition. Fertiliser should not be applied where weeds are present, as this will only benefit the weeds. Instead, maintaining a weed-free area around the base of the tree will usually solve both water and nutrient deficiency.

e Avoid too heavy a weeding of woody and herbaceous growth since this often encourages grasses. Low herbaceous plants such as bluebells never harm trees.

f Maintaining a short sward of grass around young trees, either by scything or mowing, is the most counter-productive method of management. The repeated cutting stimulates grass growth, so that the grass is constantly using up nutrients and water from the soil. As cutting a turf from a lawn or meadow will prove, the grass 'tillers' and roots form a thick mat, effectively preventing rainfall from seeping into the ground below, which can become very dry in spring and summer.

g The best method of establishing young trees is to maintain an area of bare ground at least 1m diameter around the base of transplants, with larger areas for larger stock. The two main methods of doing this are by mulching (p93), or by chemical control, which is discussed below.

h The most critical months for water stress are usually April, May and June. During these months plant growth, both in trees and other plants is rapid. Soil moisture is usually in deficit from April, through until autumn, meaning that more water is lost from the soil by transpiration and evaporation than is gained by rainfall. Even one week's weed growth in April can be significant in reducing water availability right through until autumn. It is therefore vital to start weed-control early in the year, so that when trees start into growth they are completely free of competition, and the soil moisture level has not been depleted by weed growth.

Timing will vary with the season, the locality and the method of control. Some mulching materials for example are simply left in position from the time the tree is planted and give complete control for several years. Some herbicides work better at particular stages of weed growth, so application must be carefully timed. In general though, weed control measures should have been taken by the middle of March, and earlier in the south or in mild winters. Grass can grow at any time of year when the weather is mild enough.

i The number of years that weed-control will be needed will depend on the site, the species planted, the spacing of the plants and other factors. Usually control will be needed for at least three years from the time of planting. Single trees in open ground, or trees at the edges of planted areas where light levels are high will need weeding for longer than trees within woodlands, where grass growth in particular will be less. Where grass is absent, a woodland-type flora, that is less competitive, will develop more rapidly.

For good growth, trees planted in grassland should

have bare ground around them for perhaps five or more years. Trees that are cropped for fruit, in orchards and gardens, should be kept permanently in bare ground. Because both mowers and grazing animals can damage tree bark where they have access right up to a tree, it is anyway best to avoid a grass to tree-trunk interface.

PRE-PLANTING WEED CONTROL

It may be necessary or advisable to do some weed control before the trees are planted.

Woody growth, shrubs, brambles and so on will have to be controlled to allow planting to take place. This can be done by hand or machine clearance or by chemical control. It will not be sufficient to simply cut a small area for each tree, as cutting will stimulate growth, and where gaps are made by uprooting, surrounding shrubs will spread to fill the gap. What action is taken will depend on the species present, the type of site, and the object of planting. Existing shrubs, rhododendron excepted, are likely to have some wildlife value, and conservation may be best served by clearing areas and planting groups of trees. Where timber trees are being planted, complete clearance of existing vegetation may be necessary. This will be destructive of wildlife value, although ground disturbance will turn up buried seed which may be of benefit.

Where woody shrubs are cut and not uprooted, chemical treatment of stumps will be needed to prevent them re-sprouting. This technique is described below.

Grass and herbaceous growth can be killed chemically before tree planting is carried out, by treating an area of about 1m square for each tree. This is a useful technique, as it destroys the minimum necessary for good tree establishment. Suitable chemicals are described below. On some sites it may be possible to use farm animals to help clear areas for tree planting. Pigs are the most destructive, and will dig out roots as well as clearing top growth. Cattle, sheep or goats may also be useful, depending on the type of growth and the fencing. Beware that problems may arise if lack of grass forces animals to eat unusually large amounts of broadleaved plants and shrubs, as this can cause poisoning. Sheep find brambles appetising, but get badly entangled.

CHEMICAL CONTROL

Following the Food and Environment Protection Act 1985, regulations have been brought in covering all aspects of the development, advertisement, sale, supply, storage and use of pesticides.

From 1st January 1989, certificates of competence are required by contractors using pesticides approved for use in agriculture, horticulture and forestry, unless they are working under the direct and personal supervision of a certificate holder. The same certifi-cates are also required by all those under 25 on 1st January 1989 who are using the above pesticides anywhere, unless they are working under the direct and personal supervision of a certificate holder. The term 'contractor' includes anyone who applies a pesticide as a commercial service, or to land other than their own or their employer's. Volunteer groups would be classed as contractors, therefore need to meet the requirements.

With the exception of 'Tumbleweed' (see below), the chemicals described below are all in the restricted category. Therefore, anyone under 25 or anyone using them on a contractual basis must be certified. The process of being certified is like a driving test, in that there is no formal requirement for training, but you must pass a practical test (fee £25) and you must register for a certificate (fee £3.80). However, proper training is obviously essential, and is available for anyone through the Agricultural Training Board, who should be contacted for advice. The ATB also issue a list of other available courses which have been vetted by them. The certification is carried out by the National Proficiency Tests Council in England and Wales, and the Scottish Association of Young Farmers Clubs in Scotland, and will be included as part of any of the above courses.

Because of the requirement for certification, only outline information on herbicides is given below. This indicates which herbicides are suitable for use in non-commercial woodlands, for example where broadleaves and conifers are being grown for a variety of objectives, including conservation, amenity and so on. Their use, including storage, transport, mixing, safety precautions, protective clothing and other details are covered by the certificate of competence. Addresses of suppliers are given on page 165 of this handbook.

The subject of chemical control of weeds is comprehensively covered in the Forestry Commission Booklet 51 'The Use of Herbicides in the Forest' (revised 1986). This gives details of suitable treatments for control of grasses and grass/broadleaved mixtures, bracken, heather, woody weeds, gorse and broom, and rhododendron, both for coniferous plantations and mixed woodlands.

Atrazine with dalapon

This is available as Atlas Lignum, a granular herbicide, and is active against nearly all types of grasses. The atrazine acts on soft grasses, and the dalapon component on coarse grasses. It is not effective against bracken, brambles, docks and other broadleaved plants. The herbicide acts mainly through the soil, with grasses absorbing doses through their roots. Activity is dependent on the granules being dissolved into the soil by rainfall, and weeds treated during dry weather will not be controlled until rain falls. Atrazine is slow to break down in the soil, and remains active for up to six months. Dalapon remains active for up to three months.

Atlas Lignum can be applied either pre-planting, at the time of planting provided it is kept away from tree roots, or post-planting. If applied when trees are in leaf, it should not be used when the foliage is wet, to avoid granules sticking to and acting on the tree foliage.

Atlas Lignum is most effective if applied as soon as weed growth commences in spring, which may be from February to April. It is better to apply earlier rather than later, in case there is an early spring drought, which will both render the herbicide ineffective, and cause water stress on the trees. If more convenient, it can be applied at the time of planting, although effectiveness will be reduced if planting is done in November or December, as the dalapon will be inactive by the time spring comes.

Glyphosate

The formulation of glyphosate for commercial use is Roundup. It is also available as the garden chemical Tumbleweed, use of which is not restricted by the above regulations, but which is only economical for very small scale planting schemes.

Glyphosate is a liquid herbicide, which is mixed in water and then applied onto the weed vegetation by sprayer, drench gun or 'weedwiper' (see below). It is absorbed by the leaves, and translocated through to the roots, killing the plant. Glyphosate is effective against grasses, broadleaved plants, bracken, heather and woody weeds. It can also be used against rhododendron, if a wetting agent is added (see below). It can be used pre-planting up to three days before planting, or post-planting, if the following precautions are taken.

Broadleaved trees will be damaged if the herbicide is sprayed overall, so either a guard must be used to shield the tree, or the spray carefully directed to avoid contact. In winter, buds can be damaged, producing deformed leaves. Spraying should only be done in calm weather, and will be easier to do if young trees are in tree shelters, or if the weed vegetation is still fairly short. Tall weeds around small feathered trees cannot be safely sprayed. Use of a weedwiper avoids problems of spray drift. Glyphosate is best used in moist, humid conditions, but when heavy rain is not expected within 24 hours, as this will reduce absorption.

The weedwiper is a hand-held applicator that has a reservoir for holding the herbicide mixture and a wick to spread it directly onto the foliage. It is used by a sweeping action back and forth to brush both sides of the weed foliage. The tree must not be touched. The weedwiper can be used in a triangular pattern around the stem where the tree is higher than the weeds, or back and forth over the weeds where they are smothering the tree, leaving a 100mm clearance between wick and tree top.

Glyphosate can be applied at any time of year when the vegetation is actively growing, but is most effective from July to September. However, this is too late to benefit the tree for that year, and the height of the weed growth may make application difficult. Instead, it may be better to use Glyphosate in March or early April, once weeds are actively growing, to be effective through the critical April to June period. Another application can be made from July to September, as required. Depending on the site and the type of weeds, this may give sufficient control through to the end of the following spring growing period.

Remember that water for mixing will have to be transported to sites where water is not available. A red dye, available from Hortichem Ltd (p165) can be mixed with the solution to colour the treated vegetation and make thorough control easier to achieve. Glyphosate is useful because of the range of vegetation it kills, and because it works quickly, with treated plants yellowing within a few days. This speed of action can be significant if a spring drought threatens young trees, and its obvious effectiveness can be reassuring to the user!

Propyzamide

This is available as granules (Clanex or Kerb Granules), suspension concentrate (Clanex Liquid) or wettable powder (Kerb). It is a soil-acting herbicide which slowly volatilises in cold soil, and is taken up through the roots of existing weeds, particularly grasses, and by germinating weeds. It should be applied from October to December, or including January in upland Britain. Good control is dependent on persistent low temperatures following aplication. It remains active for three to six months.

Although propyzamide should not damage any of the commonly planted tree species, some users have experienced problems when used around trees in the winter of planting. To be on the safe side, it may be better to use it only in the second and following seasons. Propyzamide is not effective on peat soils.

Bracken control

Young trees surrounded by bracken suffer from lack of light in the latter part of the growing season, and the collapsing fronds can smother small trees at the end of the year. Chemical control should be used pre-planting if possible, as if used post-planting, the dead stems still need to be cleared by hand to avoid them smothering the young trees.

Bracken can be controlled by either asulam (Asulox) or glyphosate (Roundup). Asulam is specific to bracken, and gives better control, but glyphosate is useful where other weeds such as bramble need to be treated. In either case, bracken should be treated when the frond tips have unfurled, in July or August.

HAND WEEDING

Clearance of large trees and shrubs is covered in the next chapter.

As has been explained above, hand weeding of grasses by scything or mowing is counter-productive as a weeding method. It may be effective to scythe some types of herbaceous growth such as nettles or thistles, although this may only stimulate the growth of grass in the increased light, which will then need herbicide treatment. Where herbaceous growth needs controlling, only scythe an area large enough so that when the surrounding growth collapses it does not smother the tree. The cut growth should be left spread on the ground as a mulch to suppress further growth and conserve moisture.

As an alternative to scything, weak herbaceous growth such as nettles, creeping thistle or bracken can simply be trampled. This suppresses growth rather than stimulating it, but may need to be repeated a few times through the season.

Goose-grass (cleavers), a rapid-growing clambering annual, should be controlled before it smothers the tree or goes to seed, by pulling it away and compacting the unwanted growth into a heap. Persistent perennial climbers such as clematis (bindweed, old man's beard), honeysuckle and ivy should be cut back in late winter or early spring, and any young plants pulled or dug up. It may be necessary to treat bindweed with glyphosate, as this plant is very difficult to dig up, and grows very rapidly to smother young trees in a matter of weeks during the early summer.

Where the weed cover is mainly herbaceous plants, use a weeding hook or a scythe. Where there is up to a year's growth of climbers, brambles and other woody weeds, use a light brushing hook (curved slasher) or a bean hook. Where there is a heavy growth of woody weeds, use a heavy pattern slasher. Occasionally, a billhook may be necessary for heavy coppice regrowth (see page 61 for details of tools).

Procedural points

a If the trees are hard to see, mark out the row to be cut with poles stuck in the ground at intervals of 30m (30yds) or so. In the first year, clear lanes 600–900mm (2–3') wide along each row of trees, leaving the weeds between rows untouched unless they are likely to become tall enough to fall on the trees, in which case they should be topped. In the second and third years, just weed around each stem as necessary to keep the leader free from overarching growth.

Where deer are present, it is best to weed between the rows, to avoid vegetation overtopping the trees, but leave the weeds in the row uncut to help protect the trees.

b Be sure to find each tree before cutting around it. It is all too easy to decapitate tender stems.

c Keep well away from other workers when cutting. It is safest and easiest if each volunteer has a band of several rows to work on. Keep at least one row of trees between you and other workers. Take extra care where weeds are tall or the terrain difficult.

On moderate slopes work up and down hill. On steep slopes it is safest and easiest to work uphill only, so allow extra time for walking down to the bottom to begin each new row.

d Leave cut herbaceous growth where it falls, or if you have time, shift it into piles around each stem to act as a mulch. Keep major drains, footpaths and rides clear of cuttings. Where herbaceous growth is exceptionally heavy, pile the cuttings between the rows. Lay woody weeds and climbers between the rows.

e Tread in around any trees which seem to be loose or growing at a slant. When weeding around ash, prune off any double leaders to prevent forked growth.

MECHANICAL WEEDING

Mechanical weeding is less laborious than hand weeding where conditions are suitable, and may be suitable for sites where herbicides are not acceptable. However, it has several disadvantages, in addition to the high purchase cost of machinery.

It is necessary to design the planting layout and spacing with the type of weeding machine in mind, especially if a tractor-mounted machine is to be used. For efficiency and to prevent damage, the area should be cleared of large rocks and high stumps before planting. Access across drains must be prepared in advance.

Operators of weeding machinery, including portable brush cutters, must have proper training in safe use of machinery.

Supplementary hand weeding is usually required in inaccessible spots, on steep slopes or places missed by the machine.

Note that frequent mechanical weeding will result in grass cover forming, which as explained above, is the least suitable type of vegetation surround for young trees. Selective hand weeding of a site may be more appropriate than overall mechanical weeding, by maintaining the less competitive herbaceous growth, and allowing a woodland-type flora to establish instead of grass.

Types of machines include: portable brushcutters (scrub cutters or portable clearing saws); pedestrian-controlled motor scythes, rotating blade machines and flail mowers; and tractor-mounted blade mowers, chain mowers and flail mowers.

Portable brushcutters allow the operator to work standing up, out of the clutches of dense and thorny vegetation, and to weed in a more confined space than when using a larger machine. They are most suited for use on woody vegetation under 35mm ($1\frac{1}{2}''$) in diameter, although they may be used on larger material. Brushcutters are very fatiguing to use. It is essential for other workers to keep well away from the operator while the machine is going.

Pedestrian-controlled machines are designed for purposes other than forest weeding, so they tend to have too little clearance and to be hard on the operator in rough terrain. They are, however, useful where a machine is needed for clearing rides, paths and glades. Care is needed on slopes and where stumps and other obstacles may require extra manoeuvring. Motor scythes are best limited to use on grass, bracken and other herbaceous weeds. Flail mowers are rather easier to manoeuvre than the other types and tend to chop the material more finely.

Tractor-mounted machines are very efficient, provided the rows are wide enough and at least 90m (100yds) long, and clear of obstacles over about 100mm (4″) high. They cannot work where the ground is rutted or on heavy soils if the ground is wet. On hillsides, they should only be used up and down slope: side sloping is dangerous. Where trees are small, spot weeding by hand or herbicides should be carried out beforehand around the trees so that the tractor operator can see them.

Tractors can also be used to pull rollers to crush bracken and wood small-weed (*Calamogrostis epigejos*). For best effect, rolling should be done just as the weeds achieve maximum growth.

Woody weeds and rhododendron

It may be necessary to control unwanted or invasive species of shrubs and trees from woodlands. In commercial woodlands, this may include a whole range of native and non-native plants which are undesirable because they compete for space, light and nutrients and reduce the commercial value of the woodland. In woods managed for conservation and amenity, a wide range of native shrubs and trees is usually highly desirable, both for their own value, and for the variety of structure and cover which they provide.

However, even in non-commercial woods there is often a need to manage the cover of shrubs and trees. This may be to allow more desirable trees to thrive, to keep glades and rides open, to maintain the full range of woodland structure, to allow access for management and amenity, and to control invasive introduced species such as sycamore and rhododendron, and invasive natives such as wayfaring tree, birch and willow.

Methods of control include:

a Cutting by hand or chainsaw, and then removing the stump by hand or winch. Merely cutting encourages the plant to coppice strongly.

b Application of herbicide to foliage or to stem.

c Application of herbicide to the stump, after the tree has been cut and removed.

d Removal of seeding trees, and control of one-year old seedlings by pulling or by herbicide can be useful measures.

Techniques for cutting and stump removal are covered in the next chapter. The following section gives brief details of herbicides which may be useful in non-commercial woodlands. See p96 for general information on the restrictions on herbicide use and training requirements. Full details of the treatments are given in 'The Use of Herbicides in the Forest' (Forestry Commission Booklet 51).

HERBICIDES FOR WOODY WEEDS

Foliar treatment

This is the cheapest and easiest method to use on shrubs which are in leaf, and of a size which are accessible to spraying. However, it has several disadvantages which makes it generally unsuitable for conservation management, with the exception of rhododendron control (see below). Great care has to be taken to treat only the weed species, as desirable broadleaves will be damaged if sprayed. There is also likely to be damage to any ground flora beneath and around the weed plant. The treated plants will go brown and die, leaving unsightly dead growth, which can make access and future management difficult, as well as being a fire hazard.

Where foliar control is thought necessary, fosamine ammonium (Krenite) is effective on deciduous broadleaved woody weeds, or glyphosate (Roundup) on most woody weeds except for gorse and broom.

Stem treatment

This method involves applying herbicide to the stems of standing shrubs and trees, either by injection, or by applying the herbicide to a notch or frill cut around the stem. This technique is used on woody weeds which are too tall to spray, or where treatment has to be done in winter. Although avoiding damage to desirable species, this method still creates the problem of the standing dead trees.

Where treatment is thought appropriate, ammonium sulphamate (Amcide) can be used as a spray onto a frill cut around each stem, or the dry crystals can be placed into individual notches. Alternatively, glyphosate (Roundup) can be applied by injection to individual notches.

Cut stump treatment

This method involves applying the herbicide to the cut stump, to prevent regrowth. It can be a useful technique for non-commercial woodlands as it only affects the treated stump and there is no unsightly dead material left standing. It is labour intensive, in that clearance still has to be done first by hand or machine, and the cut material removed, stacked or burnt. Stump treatment avoids the ground disturbance caused by stump removal, although the cut stumps may be a hazard for machinery or for amenity use of the area. Suitable herbicides are ammonium sulphamate (Amcide), applied by watering can or spray, or placed as crystals, or glyphosate (Roundup) applied by paint brush, knapsack spray or clearing saw spray attachment.

Where Amcide crystals are used, the technique is to drill 25mm (1″) diameter holes, 50mm (2″) deep, and fill them with crystals. A 150mm (6″) diameter stump should have 4 holes. Cover the filled holes with stones to keep the rain out, or the crystals will become diluted and ineffective.

RHODODENDRON

Rhododendron is an introduced species which can spread rapidly on acid soils, particularly in the wetter western areas of Britain. It spreads mainly by seed, though also by stems which root where they touch the ground, and coppices vigorously. Its thick, dense foliage shades out virtually all other species, and fallen leaves rot slowly, leaving a thick, acid layer over the soil. Rhododendron itself can grow in dense shade. Seedlings grow slowly for the first five years, reaching only about 100mm (4″) height, but then can grow very rapidly. The mature leaves have a thick waxy cuticle which makes the foliage comparatively resistant to herbicide treatments. The young foliage is less resistant.

The following methods of control are recommended:

a Young isolated plants less than 2m tall should be sprayed thoroughly, with every leaf being sprayed to the point of run–off. The only suitable herbicides are Roundup plus Mixture B wetting agent, or Garlon 4 (triclopyr). The Mixture B wetting agent reacts with the waxy cuticle to improve uptake of herbicide, as detailed in Research Information Note 109:87:SILN (Forestry Commission, 1987). Glyphosate should be used in summer; Garlon 4 can be used diluted in water as a summer foliage spray, or diluted in diesel as a winter shoot spray.

b Mature plants, greater than 2m height, should be felled. The cut stump should either be treated immediately with herbicide, or the 1–2 year old regrowth can be sprayed as described above. Either Roundup plus Mixture B or Garlon 4 can be used, any time of year except spring. Another herbicide, Amcide, is effective as a cut stump treatment, but is more expensive than either Roundup or Garlon 4.

As an alternative to herbicide treatment, cut stumps can be winched out and burnt.

Pests and Diseases

The treatment of pests and diseases is, for the most part, outside the scope of this Handbook. The death of individual trees is an essential part of the woodland ecosystem, creating conditions for the survival of many insects, fungi and other forms of life. Natural checks and balances almost always keep pests and diseases under control. However, treatment of pests and diseases is very important in commercial forestry, and for the management and preservation of valuable amenity trees. The Forestry Commission publish detailed information on individual pests and diseases (see their current Catalogue of Publications).

PESTS

Insects

Insect pests can most easily be kept under control by ensuring that insect-eating birds have adequate nesting and feeding habitat. Provide nest boxes if necessary. Many insect outbreaks eventually collapse as a result of naturally occurring disease, or as parasites and predators reach effective population levels. Insect attack on mature trees is more often alarming than deadly, although it may slow their growth and reduce their timber value. Seedlings and young trees are more susceptible, particularly conifers.

The grubs of chafers (*Melolantha spp*), which feed on the roots of seedlings and transplants, may cause trouble in tree nurseries, especially those on agricultural soils. Control, other than by insecticides, includes soil cultivation and hand picking.

In conifer stands, forest hygiene can be used to reduce the incidence of several insect pests. General measures include regular thinning to remove all sickly and dying trees, prompt felling of trees damaged through fire, windblow etc, and the removal of all cut material within six weeks if felled during the period April–September.

Birds

In nurseries, netting of seedbeds may be needed to keep birds from eating the tree seeds.

The only species which may cause serious damage in woodlands is the starling. These birds roost communally, especially in winter, and they may cause the death of trees in the roost area due to the toxic effect of the droppings, although some roosts are occupied for many years with little damage. Winter roosts may contain up to 1½ million birds and cover 2 hectares (5 acres), though this is exceptional. Where necessary, the roosts can be dispersed by means of amplified distress-call apparatus and bird-scaring cartridges fired from shotguns or Verey pistols. See Curry, Elgy and Petty (1977) for details.

Rabbits

Rabbits, an anciently introduced species, became a serious forest pest in the 19th century. Myxomatosis killed off most rabbits in Britain during the mid-1950's, but a few areas were little affected by the disease, and in many others the rabbit populations have tended to build up in recent years almost to pre-myxomatosis levels.

Rabbits damage young trees of most species. Where they are present it is often necessary to fence the wood before planting (p75) and to exterminate the animals within the fenced area. Individual trees can be protected with guards or chemical repellants (p92). For further information see Forestry Commission Leaflet 67 'Rabbit Management in Woodlands' (Pepper, 1976).

Squirrels

Grey squirrel damage is one of the most serious problems in commercial timber growing, as trees are damaged at an advanced stage, and control is very difficult. Damage takes the form of bark stripping from trunks and branches of pole-stage trees, normally 10–40 years old. Damage can occur from ground level up to about 16m. On hardwoods the damage is concentrated around the base, and at the points where side branches meet the trunk, with both trunk and branches stripped. Damage to conifers can occur anywhere on the trunk, usually higher up in older trees. The most susceptible species are beech and sycamore, with pines, oaks, ash, larch and birch also badly affected. Bark stripping seriously weakens or kills trees.

Squirrels cannot be excluded from a woodland, and even if a population is killed, others will rapidly move into the area. Food and habitat is always in short supply, and is the main natural control on the survival of young animals. The only feasible method of management is to control the numbers by killing immediately before and during the damage period from April to July. If control is done at other times, numbers will only build up again by the following damage period. Although some species at certain stages are more vulnerable, in particular pole-stage beech, damage can occur unpredictably. It appears to be triggered by population stress, especially high numbers of males, with the food source of bark being a secondary factor. Risk of damage is greatest when populations are highest, which happens following mast years when food is plentiful, followed by mild winters and early springs.

The legal methods of control include cage-trapping, spring-trapping, hopper-poisoning with warfarin, and shooting. Cage-trapping and hopper-poisoning are the most efficient methods. Where both grey and red squirrels occur in the same area, such as

central Wales, live trapping should be used rather than poisoning, to avoid killing red squirrels. Control methods are described in the Forestry Commission publications 'Grey Squirrel Control' (Rowe, 1983) and the 'Wildlife Rangers Handbook' (1985).

Mice and voles

Mice and voles gnaw the bark of young trees and may cause damage in young plantations and nurseries, mainly those in areas of thick grassy sward. They are usually a problem only in certain years when populations peak. In such circumstances control may be necessary by laying poison, which should be placed in lengths of rainwater downpipe or tile drains, to prevent larger animals being poisoned. For details see the 'Wildlife Rangers Handbook' (Forestry Commission, 1985).

Deer

Deer, including the native red and roe deer and the introduced fallow and Sika deer, can cause damage by browsing young trees and branches, stripping bark and using the stems as fraying stocks. Fencing (p75), although expensive, is often the only practical way to keep deer from young plantations, coppice woodlands and other areas where damage may be significant. A successful, if untidy method for protecting newly cut coppice, is temporary 'psychological' fencing around groups of four to five stools. The fences, 900mm–1.2m (3–4') high, need not be long-lasting or of high quality, but need to be as conspicuous as possible. Red tape or strips of old fertiliser sacks can be tied on to make them more obvious. Deer dislike feeling restricted and tend to avoid these small enclosures. Temporary electric fencing can also be used (see p92). Individual coppice stools can be protected by making up rough wattle guards from felled coppice material, though this is rather labour intensive. Drive in stakes at about 1.8m (6') intervals and 1m (3') from the stool, and then weave cut branches between them, up to a height of about 1.2m (4') against roe or fallow deer.

A problem with fencing is that, if the deer are forced out of their natural woodland habitat, they may cause greater damage in surrounding agricultural areas and are more likely to be poached, hit by cars or killed by dogs. A better solution may be to control resident woodland herds by careful culling, while tolerating a continued low level of damage. Deer management is comprehensively covered in the 'Wildlife Rangers Handbook' (Forestry Commission, 1985).

Whatever steps may be taken to control deer populations, the Devon Trust for Nature Conservation (1970, p9) suggests a number of measures to ensure that the damage done by the accepted herd can be kept to a minimum:

a Retain natural browse, especially bramble and hazel, where possible.

b Limit weeding and clearing so that young trees are protected by a physical barrier of shrubs and herbs which also provide additional browse.

c Retain thickets where deer are known to shelter. This also aids control measures, since deer disperse if all their cover is suddenly removed.

d Leave roe deer rutting stands unplanted. These are hard to protect in any case, and if retained they can be used for observation and control.

e Provide 'lawns', either by leaving small areas unplanted or by seeding and fertilising stands of trees such as larch, in which there is often some growth of grass, to improve the grazing.

DISEASES

Tree diseases are often difficult to prevent or cure. The best or only solution to many serious diseases is to plant resistant types of trees in suitable sites.

A few of the most important diseases from a conservation point of view are described below. Watermark disease, poplar canker and fireblight are bacterial, whilst the others are caused by fungi.

Forest diseases and diseases of mature trees

Dutch elm disease is discussed separately below.

a Honey fungus (*Armillaria mellea*) attacks the roots of a wide range of tree species. It nearly always spreads from old infected stumps of broadleaved trees in the immediate vicinity, and is most serious where conifers are planted on old broadleaved sites, and in gardens and arboreta where it can harm valuable specimens. Members of the genus Rosacaea, which includes many fruit trees, are usually killed. Older trees of other genera can often live for long periods with the fungus, but conifers may develop root rot and become liable to windthrow.

You can't do much about honey fungus in woodlands. In gardens and arboreta you should grub up old stumps, to prevent them acting as sources of infection, and also remove and burn any infected trees with all their major roots. To prevent infection reaching a tree, cut a trench around the tree to the depth of the roots, and outside the drip line so that the roots are not harmed. Line it with heavy-gauge black polythene before backfilling.

b Beech bark disease is caused by the fungus *Nectria*, which gains access through wounds opened up by the scale insect *Cryptococcus fagi*. The disease is locally severe in southern England, mainly affecting vigorous trees aged 25 years or more growing in pure stands on good soils. The drought of 1976 seemed to increase its severity, although some trees were relatively resistant and selective breeding may provide a long-term solution. Often the disease causes only temporary set-back, with recovery within

10 years, but the stems of affected trees are liable to decay internally and snap. Affected trees should be felled promptly, if their timber is to be used, and newly infected trees and those which are markedly infested by the scale insect should be removed during plantation thinnings. On specimen trees, it is a good precaution to apply a tar-oil wash with a pressure sprayer to control the insect. Use 300ml (½ pint) of tar diluted in 6 litres (1.25 gallons) of water to cover the bole of a mature tree about 15m high. Spray between December and early February, taking care not to damage surrounding vegetation. You may have to repeat the treatment every three to five years.

c Sooty bark disease of sycamore, caused by the fungus *Cryptostroma corticale*, was first found in a London park in 1945 and since that time has spread to many parts of south and central England. There is no direct method of control, but due to its need for hot summer temperatures it is unlikely to spread north of the rivers Humber and Mersey. Within the region of occurrence it is likely to be held in check by normal relatively cool summers. In the area surrounding Greater London, where devastating outbreaks may occur, its effects can best be limited by assuring that any sycamores planted are intermixed with other tree species.

d Phytophthora root rot is a disease which attacks the roots of sweet chestnut (where it is known as ink disease), beech, common lime and horse chestnut as well as several conifers and ornamental cultivars. It is most likely to occur in trees on heavy or wet soils, which may include the patches of 'poached' ground which can occur where livestock gather under trees. It cannot be controlled, but risk of infection can be reduced by preventing wet conditions around the base of trees, for example by building a tree guard (p86).

e Watermark disease of cricket bat willow caused by *Erwinia salicis* bacteria, causes dieback and ruins the timber of this species. The spread of Watermark disease has been reduced by compulsory felling orders which apply to certain counties (p58), and by the planting of setts taken only from healthy trees or stool beds.

f Fireblight (*Erwinia amylovora*) is an extremely infectious bacterial disease which affects pears, apples, hawthorns, rowan, whitebeam and other species. Its main impact is in orchards and nurseries. Treatment of infected trees is not feasible. Attempts were made to control the spread of the disease by government regulations requiring the destruction of infected trees and plants in orchards and nurseries. However, these were not effective, and were dropped during 1987 for the area south of a line from Preston to Hull, where the disease is now widespread.

Preventative measures are best taken by not choosing susceptible species for group or mass planting, for example in landscaping schemes. Commonly planted ornamental stock including *Pyracantha* are a major source of infection. Where conservation projects are concerned, hawthorn hedges or other susceptible plantings should not be made near orchards.

g White pocket rot or butt rot of conifers (*Fomes annosus*), a bracket fungus, is the most serious disease in British conifer plantations, especially in pines on alkaline soils and former farmland and in western hemlock and western red cedar. To limit the spread of this disease, treat cut stumps with urea (available from forestry suppliers) immediately on felling. Even a delay of half an hour may allow infection.

Dutch elm disease

The current epidemic of this disease, caused by an aggressive form of the fungal pathogen *Ophiostoma ulmi*, reached its peak in the mid 1970s. The pathogen is carried by elm bark beetles (Scolytus sp.) which burrow into the tree, allowing the fungus to destroy the veining in the xylem layer. The disease is also carried by coppice shoots and suckers, which is the main method of elm regeneration. English elm rarely sets viable seed.

Suckers arise around living or dead trees, up to 50m from the original tree, and are very invasive. The elm hedgerows and hedgerow trees which were so prevalent in southern England were formed from coppice and sucker growth, and being linked by their root systems, were particularly susceptible to the disease.

The English elm was the first to be affected, with the wych and smooth leaved elm following on. By mid 1980 an estimated 18 million elms had died or been felled, mainly in the area south of a line from Chester to the Wash and in South Wales.

Where diseased and dead trees have been felled, coppice shoots and thick patches of suckers develop. Initially, much of this growth and particularly the coppice shoots is killed by the fungus still present in the root system. However, infected roots may also produce a flush of healthy suckers. Regeneration also occurs around dead standing trees, but is sparser than where the tree has been felled.

Beetle populations decline as the breeding habitat disappears, thus reducing this method of infection. However, new infection via the elm bark beetle can occur once twigs are two years or older.

The Forestry Commission has been monitoring the survival rate of regenerating elms since 1977, as detailed in Arboriculture Research Information Note 13/87/PATH. Amongst other findings, this has shown that the level of disease in regenerating elms is relatively low at present. Many groups or lines of suckers are now over 10m (32ft) tall, and are becoming significant features in the landscape. However, on many sites diseased suckers over 100mm (4″) in diameter are being colonised by elm bark beetles, and breeding is occurring, thus an upsurge in the disease is likely to follow. As the regenerating elms are genetically identical to the parent trees they will be liable to succumb rapidly. As has happened in Europe, where the disease is still active after 30 years or more, the elm population will thus be subject to periodic waves of infection.

For the next few decades it seems likely therefore that the elm will have a reduced role to play in the landscape, as a small suckering tree of the size of hawthorn or hazel. Hopefully the pathogen will eventually become less aggressive, or possibly be controlled by a virus-like disease of the fungus itself which has recently been discovered.

The recommendation at present is that there is little point in spending much time or effort in managing or encouraging elm regeneration, although it can provide useful shelter for young trees of other species where replanting is carried out.

Thinning and brashing

Thinning and brashing are techniques used to maximise the production of the woodland 'crop', usually with the aim of producing a uniform stand of even-aged, similar sized trees of good timber quality. Although mainly techniques of commercial forestry, thinning in particular is necessary for the management of many non-commercial woodlands.

THINNING

The main aim of thinning is to cut out poor, weak, diseased or over-crowded trees in order to leave room for the best specimens to grow vigorously to maturity. Thinning of saleable timber also provides an immediate financial return.

Whereas the commercial aim of thinning is to produce uniformity, conservation interests recommend that any thinning should diversify or maintain the existing age and size structure. Thus thinning of multi-use woodlands will require some compromise.

Note the following:

a A rule-of-thumb for commercial, even-aged stands is that over a whole rotation, the various thinnings should add up to about half of the total volume of production, with the other half being felled at rotation age ie the final felling.

b A second rule-of-thumb is that at early pole stage (see below), spacing between trees should be about one fifth of average tree height, and at late pole stage should be about one quarter of average height.

c The frequency of thinning will depend on many factors including the species, site conditions, rate of growth and object of management. Other variables such as current market conditions and availability of labour may also affect the timing.

Stage	Age	Mean Height (m)	Mean Diam. at Breast Height (cm)
Establishment	0–10	0–5	0–6
Thicket	5–20	2–10	4–12
Pole stage			
early thinnings (2–3 at 5 yr interval)	15–50	8–18	7–25
late thinnings (6–8 yr interval)	30–100+	15–30+	20–50+
Mature	40–150+	18–30+	30–60+

d Infrequent, heavy thinning produces a greater volume on each occasion, which may make marketing the thinnings more viable, as well as being efficient in terms of labour, access and ground disturbance. However, heavy thinning can cause problems including windblow, epicormic branching and variation in ring width (see below). It is usually more damaging to wildlife than frequent, light thinning.

e Windblow is caused when the removal of the shelter of surrounding growth exposes the remaining trees to the wind. They are particularly vulnerable immediately after thinning, as the root systems are not adapted to cope with the amount of movement, and the trees can easily be blown over. Gradually, in the increased light and space, the root systems expand to keep the tree wind-firm. Root growth is also stimulated by the swaying action of the tree in wind.

f Epicormic branches are those that arise directly from the trunk of the tree. They particularly occur on English oak, and where they persist for more than one year, form a knot in the wood. Such knots lessen the commercial value of the timber.

Epicormic branching usually occurs when increased light after heavy thinning stimulates dormant buds on the trunk. It can also arise from pruning scars. The result is a thicket of horizontal branches up the trunk, with weak epicormic shoots also developing on main side branches. Where they occur on potential high-value trunks the shoots should be pruned or rubbed off each year in mid-season.

g Variation in ring width is caused where heavy thinning results in a sudden rapid burst of growth. It affects the commercial value of the timber.

h It is important that mixtures of broadleaves and conifers are properly thinned, or the conifers will rapidly dominate the broadleaves. Pine and larch are especially light-demanding, and will suppress the growth of other species.

i Where thinning of broadleaves has been neglected, it is possible to save young stands for commercial use by doing about three light thinnings over about ten years. Older stands that have been neglected are more difficult to manage, as windthrow, epicormic branching, damage during extraction and other problems are much more likely to occur. Growth response

to thinning may be poor, especially in ash. Thinning should not be done where crowns are showing signs of dying back, or where trees are very spindly and drawn up with small, weak crowns. Such stands may have to be felled and replanted or allowed to regenerate.

Criteria for selection

Evans (1985, p53) gives the following criteria for the selection of broadleaved trees to favour in thinning. Selection should be done in winter, when the crown and upper stem can be easily seen.

Use the following criteria in order of priority:

1 Good stem form and freedom from defect on the lower 7m (23′) of stem.

2 Absence of deep forking in the crown.

3 Good vigour.

4 Freedom from defect in upper stem and crown.

5 Low incidence of epicormic branching.

6 Proximity of other selected trees. Even spacing should only be considered after other criteria are satisfied.

Normally two to four times the number of final crop trees are selected at the early thinnings, to allow for losses. Later thinnings should follow the same criteria, so gradually removing some of the originally selected trees.

Free growth of oak

This is a method of management which involves identifying potential crop trees at an early age, and then favouring these by heavy thinning of other growth. This thinning should leave the crowns of the selected oaks completely free of competition, with repeated thinning every five years to maintain this condition. The lack of competition allows the trees to grow more rapidly, with a greater diameter increment than trees grown in closed stands. The main problem with this method is that epicormic branching is encouraged. For more information on free growth see Jobling and Pearce (1977) and Evans (1984, p160).

Conservation considerations of thinning

The usual method of thinning involves the removal of smaller trees and shrubs from the understorey, which reduces the value of the woodland for birds, insects and other wildlife, as well as reducing the variety of woody species. In the 'Birds and Broadleaves Handbook' (1985) the RSPB make the following recommendations regarding thinning:

a Crown thinnings are preferable to low thinnings, especially if they diversify existing structure.

b Whatever method is chosen, thin early to avoid the development of a dense thicket stage which will suppress ground vegetation.

c Leave suppressed or dying trees which have no economic value and are not worth removing.

d Avoid the bird-breeding season from March to July.

e Avoid unnecessary 'tidiness'. Piles of brashings or prunings left in shaded positions can develop a rich insect fauna with associated bird life. Fallen and decaying timber rarely infects healthy standing timber.

BRASHING

Brashing is the removal of the lower branches of trees up to a height of about 1.8m (6'), carried out at 10 to 12 years after planting. The practice of brashing was developed for managing coniferous plantations, and is not necessary in broadleaved woodland. Brashing allows the crop to be more easily inspected prior to thinning, and reduces the fire risk by removing inflammable material near ground level. Because of the labour cost, brashing is now usually reduced to the clearance of occasional 'racks' for access. Shelterbelts should not be brashed, as this reduces their effectiveness. Brashing reduces the value of woodland for birds.

The usual brashing tool is a pruning saw (p62), with cuts made as close to the stem as possible to avoid the formation of dead knots in the wood. The work is done in winter, usually December.

Pruning, Pollarding and Wound Treatment

This section outlines basic aspects of tree surgery which volunteers may be required to carry out – most often on amenity trees. More complex operations, such as cavity treatment and wiring of limbs, require professional skills and may be hazardous for volunteers. The Arboricultural Association maintain a List of Recommended Contractors and Consultants.

PRUNING

Where trees are grown for timber, 'pruning' means the removal of branches for a considerable height up the stem in order to encourage the formation of knot-free high-quality timber. This treatment is mainly worth doing on potentially valuable broadleaved trees such as oak, ash, cricket bat willow, wild cherry, sweet chestnut and sycamore. Slow-grown Scots pine and a few other conifers grown for joinery

may also be pruned. Pruning is laborious, so it is important to treat only those trees which are to form the final crop or late thinnings.

It is important to start pruning early on in the life of a timber tree, to prevent the formation of knots and reduce the risk of disease. The stem should be pruned up to a height of 3m (10') before the first thinning, and up to 5–6m (16–20') before the second thinning. Pruning of the lower branches also reduces squirrel damage, by removing places where squirrels can perch.

Pruning of amenity trees involves crown management in one form or another. Pruning may be necessary to:

a Remove dead, diseased or damaged parts, in order to keep the tree in a safe condition, and to maintain the health of the tree as far as possible.

b Improve or maintain the tree's shape for its amenity value. Branches that cross through the tree or rub other branches should be removed, in order to avoid damage occurring.

c Reduce the overall size of the tree to keep it from overcrowding its living space.

General points

a The best time to prune is in the spring, before the period of leaf expansion. Callus growth, which protects the wound, is slowest during autumn and winter, so any wound made late in the summer will be open to infection for six months or more. The timing is less significant for large wounds on over-mature trees, on which the rate of callus growth is reduced to a very slow rate even in spring and summer. Species such as walnut, hornbeam, birch and maple, which tend to 'bleed' profusely if pruned in spring, are best treated in late July or August. Prune cherries and plums in early summer, by mid-July at the latest, to reduce the risk of silver leaf infection. Pruning live branches of conifers should be done in late spring as growth is beginning.

b Whenever possible, prune little and often rather than waiting until drastic measures are needed. Light pruning is relatively easy, requires less skill and is usually less hazardous than heavy pruning, and it involves little threat to the tree's health and powers of recovery. As trees age, they tend to respond less well to pruning, although species vary greatly. London plane and lime remain very tolerant. Beech, birch, cherry, sycamore and walnut, and sometimes oak and ash, must be treated very carefully after maturity. If drastic cutting is needed with these species, you must spread the work over two or three years.

c When planting, prune off damaged or broken roots and branches. For pruning of wild trees when planting, see details on page 94.

d Most trees can be adequately trained by regularly removing, from an early age, all surplus, dead, diseased, crossing or broken branches. Normally the leader should be retained and encouraged. For large trees, especially brittle species such as locust tree and elm, or those prone to producing forked leaders, such as Norway maple and sycamore, it is very important to cut off one of any pair of forked leaders as soon as possible.

Some ornamentals, such as flowering crab, cherry or hawthorn tend not to have strong leaders, and are best left to develop open crowns. Some of these trees are best pruned so as to maintain flower-producing spurs, as with fruit trees.

e If you have to limit the size of the tree, the best method is crown reduction ('drop crotching'). Trim back the crown to the main branch system, while maintaining a symmetrical crown.

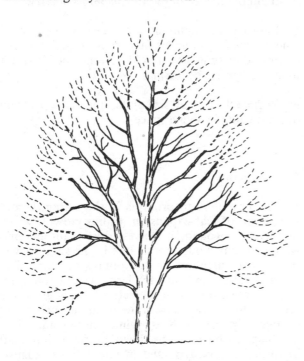

For quick recovery of the tree, reduce the crown before the tree achieves its maximum height. Repeat the job whenever regrowth reaches the previous limits, usually about every four or five years.

f 'Lifting' the crown may be necessary where you need to let people or vehicles pass beside the tree. Remove the bottom side branches but leave the

Before   After

upper crown untouched. Try to preserve the general shape of the tree.

Pruning techniques

See page 62 for tools which are used in pruning. Keep the following points in mind:

a All pruning cuts of live wood expose tissue to organisms which may cause decay. To minimise the chance of such decay, it is important that cuts are made at the optimum position on the stem or branch, as detailed below.

b Twigs and small branches under about 12mm ($\frac{1}{2}$″) diameter at their base which need pruning due to tip damage or to encourage further growth should be cut cleanly back, preferably to just above a node where they will resprout.

too long   too short   too slanted   right

c Larger branches will normally be cut back to the trunk or to the main branches. Recent work in the USA by Dr Alex Shigo has shown the importance of identifying the point where the tissues of the smaller branch separate from the major branch. This point is clearly visible on the bark by a raised ridge called the 'branch bark ridge'. The pruning cut should always to made to the outside of the branch bark ridge, and should be made as shown.

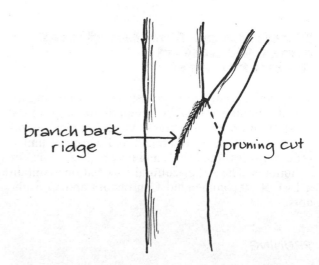

branch bark ridge   pruning cut

As side branches begin to age and lose vigour, the main branches or trunk start to form a protective layer of tissue around the base of the branch. This tissue is called the branch collar, and eventually forms a natural barrier against organisms which cause decay. Its position can be seen by looking at branches which have died back to the trunk.

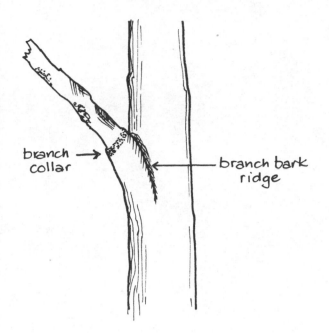

branch collar

branch bark ridge

When pruning live, dying or dead branches on hardwoods or conifers, always leave the branch collar intact. Any advice to 'prune flush' is outdated and should be ignored!

d Don't try to saw through branches over 12mm ($\frac{1}{2}''$) with one cut, since they are likely to break and pull off a strip of bark. This damages the tree. Cut such branches in three stages, as shown.

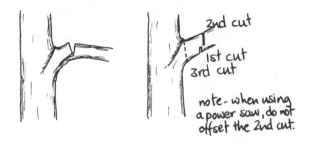

2nd cut

1st cut
3rd cut

note - when using a power saw, do not offset the 2nd cut.

Make the first cut about one third of the way through the branch from the bottom, but not so far that the saw binds. This prevents the bark tearing at the sides. Make the second cut from the top, parallel with and a little beyond the first cut. This severs the branch, leaving a projecting stub. Trim the stub with a third cut, from the top.

e Cut heavy branches in short sections, following the procedure given above.

The weight of a branch varies according to its length and diameter, and also according to the tree species. There is also considerable variation between trees within a species and even between branchwood and main stem, so it is not easy to predict the weight before cutting. A dense species such as oak or beech can weigh up to 20kg (50lb) for a section of branch 150mm (6") in diameter and 1.2m (4') long: the same weight is reached in a 300mm (1') diameter branch only 300mm (1') long.

Always be sure to err on the side of safety when cutting heavy branches. Normally the descent will

need to be controlled by 'slinging', which involves roping the section of branch to be cut. This procedure can be dangerous, and should only be undertaken by trained and experienced people.

POLLARDING

Garden and street trees are often left to grow tall and are then lopped back hard at the 3–5m (10–15') level, after which they are pollarded every few years to keep them in bounds. Such trees are often ugly, have poorly anchored branches which may be dangerous if left to grow large, and often become infected due to the large wounds produced. Poplars, planes and limes survive this treatment best, but even with these species it is far better to avoid the need to pollard by thinning the crowns earlier on.

Traditional pollarding of farm, waterside and woodbank trees begins when the trees are fairly young, before major branches have grown thick and heavy. It is repeated at five to twenty year intervals, in the same way as coppicing, depending on the size of poles required. Such trees often reach immense age and girth, and it is well worth maintaining pollard management even when the poles are no longer needed, to keep the crowns from collapsing under their own weight and to maintain the life of the tree.

When starting new pollards or maintaining existing ones, keep the following points in mind:

a New pollards are best started by the time the stem is 100–150mm (4–6") in diameter. Pollarding can be successfully initiated with trees up to 300mm (1') diameter, but this is tricky work and hazardous for the inexperienced.

b The height at which a new pollard is started is often determined by the height to which livestock can reach. Allow an extra 300mm (1') above their reach as regrowth may not be right from the top of the cut stem. Allow 1.8m (6') for fallow deer, 2.1m (7') for cattle, and 2.7–3m (9–10') for horses, assuming the tree is not fenced off.

c The safest tool to use when pollarding is a bow saw. Use standard felling techniques when cutting a new pollard (see next chapter), but take extra care to judge the size and direction of the sink in order to prevent the stem splitting. Be sure your feet, or the base of the ladder, are out of the way, since the butt end of the cut section of stem will drop abruptly when severed. When pollarding old trees with large branches, cut the branches in short sections using the cutting technique described in point 'd' above. It may be easiest to climb into the crown of an old pollard and saw branches off from above, but take great care when doing this.

WOUND TREATMENT

The standard advice until recently was that all cuts and wounds in trees should be treated with a wound paint which was claimed to seal the wound against fungal attack until the natural callus had formed. The value of this treatment has now been brought into question. For full details see P C Mercer (Forestry Commission, 1981).

a A treatment which forms a physical barrier must give long term 100% protection to be effective. Bituminous products have been found to give such protection for only one to two weeks after application, and may even encourage the growth of decay fungi. Latex paints, although lasting longer, also become badly infected with decay fungi.

b Proprietary sealants such as 'Arbrex' and 'Seal and Heal' appear to encourage beneficial callus growth, and remain effective for several seasons. However, their use on over-mature trees, where rapid callus growth would be of most value, appears to confer little benefit in improving the rate of healing, which is slowed by the tree's lack of vigour.

c Problems have also been found with fungicides, as systemic treatments tend to spread into the tree, which dilutes their effectiveness. Phytotoxic fungicides such as copper napthenate, copper oxine and phenols can discourage natural callus growth and break down the tree's natural defence compartments.

There has been some success with proprietary wound paints containing non-systemic non-phytotoxic fungicides. These include 'Santar' and 'Australian Arborseal', which appear to keep wounds free of micro-organisms for several months.

d The practice of trimming bark wounds to a neat oval or rounded shape is now no longer recommended, as this removes live tissue and increases the area which is left open to infection. Keep any reshaping of wounds to a minimum, and do not neaten them up merely for cosmetic reasons.

9 Tree Felling

Reasons for Felling

Tree felling may be done for several conservation and amenity purposes, including:

a To restore interesting habitats and traditional landscapes by clearing invasive scrub, reinstating coppice rotations or thinning overstocked and heavily shaded plantations.

b To diversify woodlands by creating paths, rides and glades, or by breaking up even-aged stands and admitting light for natural regeneration.

c To suppress exotic species such as rhododendron and sycamore where they are outcompeting native woodland plants.

d To supply material for estate uses, for sale, or for the promotion of woodland crafts.

e To improve amenity, remove hazards or restrict the spread of disease.

Factors to Consider

GENERAL POINTS

a Felling and clearance work is dangerous. Follow the safety precautions on page 59 and be sure to understand all procedures before starting work.

b Felling is only part of the task. Preliminary clearance, stump treatment and disposal of the cut material are equally important. Think out these and other aspects of work before starting. Take into account any restrictions which may be imposed if you plan to sell or use the cut material.

c Felling should be done in late autumn and winter (October–March). At this time the trees are less sappy and are easier to cut, handle and season than in spring or summer. Herbaceous undergrowth has died back, so visibility is good whilst wildlife disturbance is minimal. Decide on the area to be cleared in September, if this has not already been determined.

d Sort and stack any woodland produce as you go. Dispose of hazel for thatching and garden use in March or April at the latest. Other produce should be extracted to a central loading point as soon as the rides and woodland paths are dry and firm – usually by the end of May.

e On wet, badly drained sites you may have to work in late summer or autumn to minimise soil damage. If you plan to peel the bark (p133) after felling, this is easiest when the sap is up. Try, however, to avoid work during spring and early summer, the height of the nesting and flowering season.

WORK ORGANISATION

Organisation, including the sequence of operations and the division of labour, varies according to the situation. Use the following points as a general guideline:

a Most felling tasks consist of: 1) felling; 2) cutting up to size for 3) dragging; 4) cutting up to size again for 5) stacking or burning. On scrub clearance and some other tasks there may be also 6) stump treatment or removal. Divide up the work group so that all stages proceed together. Allow people to change jobs, within their capabilities and training, so that they do a variety of work.

A typical division of labour for coppicing and scrub clearance is to have three-person teams for the main felling work: for example one person with a saw, one with a billhook and one dragging. In addition you'll need one or two people stacking or burning, and one or two people treating or removing stumps. If felling large material by hand, you may need more people felling and fewer dragging cut material or minding the fire.

b Where the work area is not clearly defined, mark out its boundaries with blazes, bands round trees or stakes before starting to fell.

c Where felling may be impeded by the growth of brambles and other woody weeds, cut these out from around the base of trees and along routes used for access and dragging. Use an appropriate weeding tool (p61). Pull the cuttings into windrows where they can be collected for burning if necessary.

d Where material to be felled is of a wide range of sizes, it is best to fell and dispose of the lighter growth first before returning to clear larger material. This is especially important when felling coppice poles and standard trees in the same coupe. Any felling of large trees should only be done well away from where other volunteers are working.

e If a chainsaw is used, the operator should only fell trees which are too difficult for hand felling and should spend most of the time snedding or trimming high stumps. People get bored if they have to spend all their time following a chainsaw.

f Where coppice material is to be layered (p119), it is best to do the layering after clearance work is finished, so you don't trample on the layered stems during the course of work.

Basic Felling

This section deals with 'ideal' trees first – evenly tapering conifers with branches so small that they can be ignored. Basic felling procedures apply to this sort of tree. Broadleaved trees have additional requirements and trees weakened by disease, trees under stress or multiple-stemmed trees complicate the basic situation (p114). Think out all aspects of each felling situation before starting to cut.

Throughout these felling procedures, the 'front' of the tree refers to the side on which it is to fall. 'Front', 'back', 'left side' and 'right side' remain the same no matter which way the feller approaches the tree for a particular procedure.

Felling with a chainsaw is not described in this publication, on the grounds that a little knowledge is a dangerous thing. Anyone planning to use a chainsaw should get proper training through the BTCV, the Agricultural Training Board or an agricultural college. The best publication available on chainsaws is 'The Chainsaw – Use and Maintenance' by the National Board of Forestry, Sweden, and available in this country through Hyett Adams Ltd, distributors of Husqvarna chainsaws.

GENERAL PROCEDURES

a Choose the right tool for the job, depending on the size, form and position of the tree to be felled. See page 63.

b Wear a helmet when felling all but the smallest trees. Don't wear gloves when using edged tools, but have a pair available for handling thorny shrubs and heavy timber after felling.

c Before felling, PLAN YOUR ESCAPE ROUTE. This must be free of obstacles. Despite care, the tree may fall the wrong way. If this happens, get clear but never turn your back and run.

d Clear the danger zone of volunteers, other than your assistant if you are working as a two-person team. The danger zone is a minimum of two tree lengths in any direction. Make sure there are no hung-up trees within one tree length. Estimate the direction of fall – use ropes or a winch whenever in doubt. Less care is needed with coppice and shrubs, but don't take chances working near other people. If necessary, station somebody to watch the danger area to make sure nobody enters it.

Other volunteers working in an area where felling is taking place must be aware of the lines of fall and keep well out of the way. Remember, the fellers may not see or hear you, especially if they are using

power tools. Never approach a feller once he or she has commenced cutting – even to warn them. Watch out for hung-up trees – they are unsafe until fully felled.

e Try to choose a felling direction that lets the tree fall freely without getting hung up in the branches of neighbouring trees. Never fell a tree over an adjacent stump, boulder or another felled tree, as the tree can kick back dangerously and the stem may break.

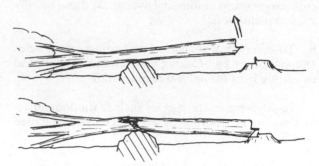

Never take chances when felling, especially near obstacles such as power lines, buildings or valuable specimen trees and shrubs. Don't fell within 15m (50′) of electricity cables. These can be disconnected if the Electricity Board is given advance warning. If you aren't certain you can make the tree fall where you want it to, call in someone with more experience.

f Prepare the cutting area. Remove debris, brambles and branches which might snag a saw or deflect an axe or billhook. Check the trees around you as well as the one you are working on. Clear dead wood to ensure a sound footing. Inspect the stem for embedded wires. Check out multiple or hollow boles for bottles, tins, stones and so on. If touched while cutting, these may damage the saw and cause injury.

Use a lopper to cut apart the tangled crowns of shrubs before felling them, otherwise you waste time trying to pull apart hung-up trees. A slasher can also be used, but this is more hazardous.

g Take a firm stance before starting to cut. Be especially wary on steep slopes.

h Wind conditions can affect felling safety. Assess the wind direction and force, and estimate how much it may deflect the tree as it fall. You can counteract this, if necessary, by cutting an uneven hinge (p115). Never fell in a strong wind, as you cannot predict the effects of sudden gusts.

i Unless otherwise directed, cut as low to the ground as possible, consistent with safety and efficiency. High cutting may impede later management, for example where sites cleared of scrub are to be maintained by mowing. Sometimes it may be quickest and safest to cut high first and then trim the stump as required. You should do this before moving on to another tree. High cutting is necessary to give adequate leverage if you plan to winch out stumps.

FELLING SMALL TREES WITH BOWSAW OR BILLHOOK

As a rough guide, you can fell trees under about 75mm (3″) in diameter at the base by cutting straight through, without the more complicated procedures needed for larger trees. Use your judgement, as you do not want the wood to split when the tree drops.

With a bowsaw

The bowsaw is the safest, most efficient and most versatile felling tool. Use it whenever possible.

1   Crouch or kneel to one side of the tree. You will be sawing through from the back.

Make the cut level or angled slightly downward in the direction of fall. Saw with easy relaxed strokes, using the full length of the blade. Use a slight rocking motion, cutting 'on the corner' as shown below, for greatest speed.

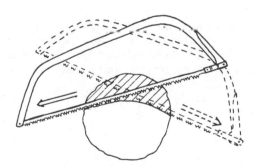

Place one hand on the end of the frame to power the stroke, and rest the other hand lightly on the back of the frame to keep it in line with the blade and ensure an equal force on push and pull strokes. This prevents the blade twisting in the cut. When necessary, you can use the smaller size saws, especially the triangular 530mm (21″) saw, one-handed.

2   With the larger, longer-bladed saws, the blade tends to vibrate if you exert more than a very slight pressure in the direction of the cut. With these saws, minimise vibration by just keeping the saw blade in contact with the stem and by pausing for an instant at the end of each stroke.

3   If the tree starts to settle back or twist, use one hand to push it in the direction of fall. Saw faster as the tree falls to minimise the risk of the stem splitting. Keep sawing to sever the stem.

With a billhook

As a felling tool, the billhook is best restricted to use on light coppice material and multi-stemmed shrubs where a bowsaw is awkward. When felling with a billhook:

1   Stand or kneel to the side of the tree, far enough back to achieve a full swing without endangering yourself. Standing is best for a powerful stroke, but kneeling may be more comfortable or necessary to avoid obstructions. Note that unless the tree is heavily leaning, you will be cutting into the front of the tree as shown.

Use the billhook one-handed, controlling the descent of the tree with the other hand, placed well up the stem for safety.

2   Do not try to cut directly across the grain, as the tool is not designed for this. For small stems, which can be severed with one blow, use a slightly upward sweeping stroke to sever the stem.

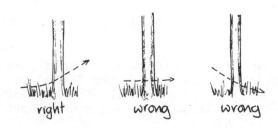

Avoid cutting downward, as you will drive the hook into the ground and dull or chip the edge.

3   Cut thicker stems by notching, as shown. Progressively enlarge the notch with downward and upward strokes until you can finish off with an upward stroke. Keep out of the way of the tree as it falls.

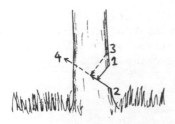

FELLING LARGER TREES WITH AXE AND SAW

Trees over about 75mm (3″) in stem diameter are difficult to fell accurately by straight-through cutting, and the stems tend to split badly as they fall unless you make an undercut first.

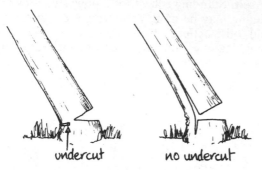

Even with an undercut, a limit is soon reached when the work becomes unsafe, and a 'sink' is necessary as described below.

Basic procedure

Follow the general points on page 110. In addition:

1 Cut away any large projections in the area of the felling cut. Buttresses must be cut down to a line below that of the intended felling cut.

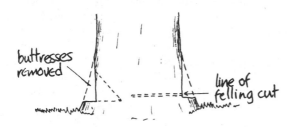

This 'rounding up' or 'laying in' is best done with an axe or a chainsaw.

2 Cut a 'sink' or 'bird's-mouth', by making a notch at the base of the front of the tree. The sink directs the tree's fall away from you as you make the felling cut. The sink should be one quarter to one third of the tree's diameter.

3 Sever the tree with a 'felling cut' or 'back cut', made from the back of the tree towards the sink. Leave a 'hinge' or 'hold', which is a piece of uncut wood between the sink and the felling cut, to control the rate and direction of fall.

The felling cut should be a little higher than the bottom of the sink: about 25mm (1″) higher for every

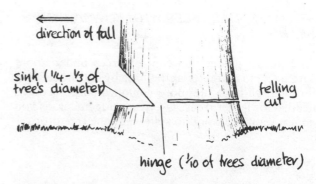

300mm (1′) of tree diameter. Normally the felling cut should be level, but if there is any danger of the tree settling back on you, start the felling cut a little higher and angle it down slightly towards the hinge.

Line up the felling cut very carefully and cut accurately. If you sever the hinge you lose control of the tree, which is dangerous. The hinge should be about one tenth of the stem's diameter in width. It helps to mark the point on the tree to which you plan to make the felling cut, in order to leave the hinge uncut.

Except in special circumstances, finish off the felling cut parallel to the sink so that the hinge is the same thickness throughout.

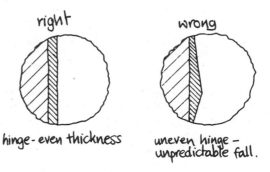

4 Keep sawing until the tree starts to move. You can use a breaking bar or wedges, driven in behind the saw blade, to keep the kerf (saw cut) open, and to allow you to control the timing of the fall.

Remember that the tree may rear upwards or kick backwards after felling, even in a harmless-looking situation, so stand well clear as it falls. When it goes, don't hesitate to use your voice! You never know when someone may be wandering through the danger zone. Try the North American lumberjacks' bellow, 'timberrrrrrrrrrrrrr!'.

5 Saw off the 'sloven', which is the thin strip of

wood torn out of the stump or stem when the hinge breaks, to tidy up.

6 If the tree is a conifer, paint the stump to prevent Fomes infection (p103) before moving on.

When using hand tools, the easiest and quickest method is to make the bottom cut of the sink with a saw, then cut out the top of the sink with an axe, and finally to make the felling cut with the saw.

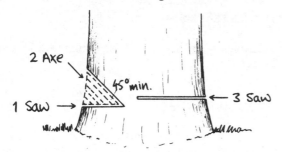

When using the axe, start small and open up the top of the sink as you cut deeper, as shown. If you are skilled with the axe you may find it easier to cut out the sink with the axe alone. If you don't have a good axe, use a bowsaw to cut both top and bottom of the sink. Make the top cut first, to reduce the likelihood of cutting into the hinge.

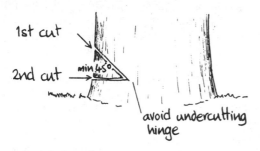

Cutting the sink with an axe

An axe is a dangerous tool in the hands of the inexperienced. Practise by cutting felled timber into lengths (p123) before using the axe for felling. Once you are sure of your basic technique, follow this procedure:

1 Stand to the side of the tree, far enough back for a full comfortable swing. You will be cutting into the front of the tree as shown.

2 In an upright position, swing the axe down at an angle to make the first top cut.

3 In a more crouched position, keeping the hands as low as possible, make the first bottom cut to split out a chip of wood from the tree.

4 Continue cutting from the top and bottom alternately, to enlarge the sink as shown.

Don't try to cut the sink at too narrow an angle, or you will only have to enlarge it as you get into the tree to keep the axe from glancing off the cut.

5 As you reach the side part of the stem, you may need to enlarge the cut around the sides before continuing to cut out the centre.

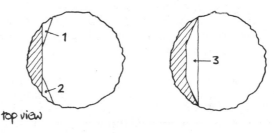

If the axe jams, don't twist it to free the head, as this may snap the haft. Loosen it by hitting the haft with the heel of your hand or a block of wood as shown.

113

Two person felling

On trees which are too big for a bowsaw, and where a chainsaw is unavailable, you need a two-man cross-cut saw for the felling cut and sometimes for the bottom cut of the sink. When using the large 910mm (36″) bowsaw it is also easiest to work with another person, as for a two-man saw. Keep the following points in mind:

1 The two fellers should crouch or kneel on opposite sides of the tree, in as comfortable positions as possible.

2 The secret of two-person sawing is to take it easy! Pull on the pull stroke, rest on the rest stroke (the other person's pull stroke). If you push the saw, it binds and you lose the rhythm of the stroke – and fray your partner's patience. Just hold the saw handle lightly when your partner pulls, to keep the blade in contact with the wood.

3 Get the saw started by making a few short cuts using the centre part of the blade. Then lengthen out the stroke so the whole blade is used each time. Don't pull too fast or jerk the saw, but aim for a steady, comfortable rhythm which gives each worker an instant at the end of the stroke to adjust from pulling to resting. Take care as you get towards the centre of the tree to shorten the stroke slightly, or you may scrape your partner's knuckles against the bark.

4 Keep the saw blade level or angled slightly downward, depending on the desired angle of the felling cut. If the blade binds, and neither of you is pushing when you should be resting, it means either you have changed the angle of cut, or the tree has settled back on the saw. The latter is only likely when you are most of the way through the tree. If it

has settled, stop sawing and knock in a couple of wedges behind the saw, to lift the stem off the saw. Use a mallet or maul to knock the wedges in, and not the back of the axe.

Tap in the wedges a bit farther if the saw continues to bind. When the tree starts to fall, don't bother trying to retrieve the saw or wedges. Get out of the way first – you can collect the tools afterwards.

Problems

See 'Coppicing and Layering' for felling multi-stemmed trees.

BROADLEAVED TREES

a Assess the weighting and lean of the tree carefully. Broadleaved trees normally have larger crowns than conifers, are more likely to be unevenly balanced, and in felling, are more likely to get caught or deflected by neighbouring trees. Take extreme care. When the tree hits the ground the butt end is likely to kick back far more than with conifers due to its large crown. Get well out of the way.

b Carefully note the species of tree to be felled. Some, such as ash, elm, sweet chestnut and willow, are particularly likely to twist or break off the stump, or to break up and shed limbs when being felled. Ash and sycamore may split during felling, causing a slab of trunk to spring back towards the feller. You can forestall this by fixing a chain or strong rope around the trunk about 1.2m (4′) from the ground before starting to fell the tree.

c Extra equipment is more necessary when felling broadleaved trees. Make sure you have an axe, a sledge hammer and wedges, a breaking bar, rope and if necessary a hand winch and cable ready for use, in addition to a saw. Saws are more likely to jam in broadleaved trees and especially in coppiced trees, due to the uneven weight distribution and twisted grain.

d Broadleaved trees may have buttresses which should be removed before felling (p112).

e Directional felling may be difficult due to the size of the tree and its crown. Make the sink one third of the stem diameter to aid control.

f If directional felling is required, you may have to lop unbalanced or awkward limbs. This is a difficult job. Use a ladder or a long-handled pruning saw for limbs which are too high to reach comfortably from the ground. Don't climb the tree unless you are specially trained and equipped.

LEANING AND WEIGHTED TREES

Few trees are in perfect balance. Most have at least a slight lean or imbalance in the weight of the crown,

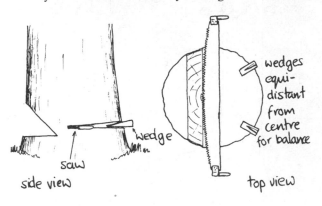

all too often in a different direction from the one in which you want the tree to fall. With a chainsaw, special techniques such as plunge cutting can be used in these situations, but this is highly skilled work which should only be done by experienced operators.

Methods for controlling the direction of fall when using hand tools are given below. These may also be useful for more 'ideal' trees if it is essential to fell them with great accuracy or where, because of the terrain or obstacles, you cannot make the sink and felling cuts in line with the needed direction of fall.

General points

a Where the tree is leaning or heavily weighted in the direction of felling, fix a chain or rope around it to limit splitting (point 'b' above). Make the sink and the felling cut as usual, but take great care to stand to one side when making the felling cut. Despite the chain, the tree is likely to split suddenly and fall. If you need the tree for its timber, it is best to use chainsaw techniques to prevent wastage.

b Where the tree is leaning or heavily weighted against the direction of felling, make the sink and the felling cut as usual, using a winch, ropes or progs to keep the tree from pinching the saw, and to overturn it against the lean (see below). If you haven't enough manpower for this, don't try to fell the tree.

c Where felling is an at angle to the lean, make the sink as usual but make the felling cut so as to leave an uneven hinge.

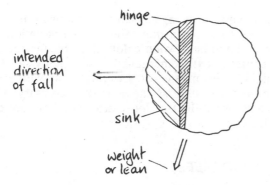

As the tree falls, it pivots on the thicker part of the hinge and swings around at an angle to the lean. It takes considerable skill and judgement to make the felling cut in this situation. Unless the lean or weighting is very slight, use a winch, rope or progs to give added control.

Use of winches, ropes and progs

Progs (p64) and ropes can be used to push or pull a tree against the direction of lean or weighting. Progs are generally simplest and best to use on small trees. Winches or ropes are safer on large trees. See page 160 for more on ropes and knots for tree work.

a Whether you pull with a rope or push with a prog, keep a fairly light, steady pressure on the tree in the early stages of felling. If you push or pull too hard too soon, you may split the stem. Exert more force when needed to keep the saw from binding. Then, when the tree starts to fall, give it all you've got, but be sure to keep well away from both the top and butt end. You never know how the tree may twist or bounce when it hits the ground.

b Never stand immediately in front or behind the tree when using a rope or a prog. Ropes should be sufficiently long that volunteers are out of the danger zone. Make sure everyone knows their escape routes. If you have to rope within the danger zone, use block and tackle around a tree to act as a pivot point, allowing expensive winches and volunteers to keep well out of the intended line of fall. If you have no block and tackle, use a carter's hitch (p161).

c Hold a prog with its fork as high up the tree as possible. Keep the prog to your side, not pushing against the chest. Two or three people each with a prog exert more force than one alone, but be sure to keep out of each other's way.

d Secure ropes before beginning to cut. Get them as high up the stem as possible. Some trees can safely be climbed (never once felling has begun) but often you have to lasso the tree by tying a weighted knot at one end and throwing this up and around the stem. Use a slip knot to secure the rope to the stem.

e Ropes work only when taut. Keep tension on the lines at all times. Only let go when the tree is falling the way you want. You can deflect the tree more strongly if you increase the tension as it falls.

Note that the effect is the same whether the rope is taken straight back or around a pivot. If you don't have a winch, the best way to control the rope is to tie its free end to a tree well outside the danger area, and to press downwards or sideways on the rope

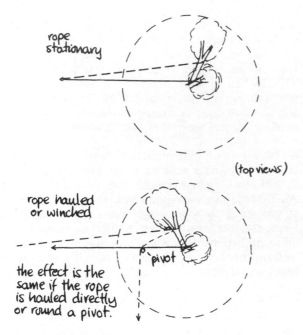

rope stationary

(top views)

rope hauled or winched

pivot

the effect is the same if the rope is hauled directly or round a pivot.

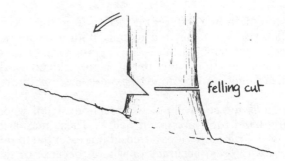

felling cut

near this anchorage. Merely sitting on the rope will often be enough. In this way, one or two volunteers can keep tension on a heavy tree without getting tired. This works better than pulling on the rope.

f With a winch, it may be possible to pull the tree right back on itself.

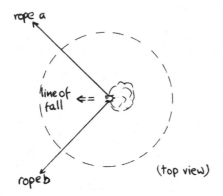

rope a

line of fall

rope b

(top view)

This is possible only if you can keep the saw from binding during the felling cut and the tree is not liable to fall to one side or the other.

TREES ON SLOPES

Trees on slopes require extra care. Be particularly sure of your footing and escape route. Keep the following points in mind:

a Where you are felling a number of trees, start from the bottom of the slope.

b Where there is no appreciable lean or weighting, or where the tree leans into the slope, fell it uphill. Although this leaves a high stump and the tree is quite likely to get hung up, this method is safest, and it is relatively easy to shift the butt end of the tree downhill to free it.

Take care to stand to the side when making the felling cut, since the tree may 'jump' badly or break

downslope when it hits the ground. Trim the stump to ground level afterwards if necessary.

Where it is not possible to fell uphill, fell across the slope.

DEAD OR DISEASED TREES

Dead trees are dangerous to fell because they may give way unexpectedly or shed limbs while you are cutting. Use ropes and winches to direct the fall. Dead trees of some species, such as elm and beech, can be frustrating to fell because the standing dead-wood may become much tougher, making it necessary to rest and sharpen tools more often.

Diseased trees may look normal on the outside, yet may have rotted a considerable distance up the stem or down from rotten limbs. This weakens the tree and makes it hazardous to fell. Always examine the sink after you've cut it. If there are signs of one-sided rot, make the felling cut with extra hinge thickness on that side (point 'c', p115), to counteract the weakness in this part of the stem.

Watch out for a change of sawdust colour from white to black (bearing in mind the normal variations in sapwood and heartwood colouration for the species concerned) or the emergence of soft pulpy sawdust or liquid. This means rot. Continue only with great care, and saw only as far as really necessary. Use ropes to break the tree loose after you have got out of the way.

HANGING TREES

Avoid hang-ups whenever possible. If one occurs, keep the following points in mind:

a Don't leave a tree hanging up. Hung up trees are unpredictable.

b Don't work immediately under a lodged tree.

c Don't climb a hanging tree to shake it free or to attach a rope.

d Don't saw sections off the base unless the tree is fairly small and you have a suitable prog (see below). If you saw sections from an unsupported tree you have no control over it.

e Don't try to fell the tree which is supporting the

hung-up tree. The stresses and imbalances make this highly dangerous.

The methods described below require a minimum of equipment and are suitable for volunteers.

Without mechanical aids

Small shrubs and trees which are light enough to be lifted safely are fairly easy to free without mechanical aids. Put your shoulder under the stem, lift the end (keeping your back straight and using your legs to lift) and walk briskly away from the tangled end so that the tree drops.

With a pole

To shift a hung-up tree with a pole, the ground must be level or sloping downhill in the direction in which the tree is to be levered, and the soil must be firm.

1   Cut a sound pole about 2m (6′) long with a minimum diameter of 100mm (4″).

2   Clear any obstructions from the path of the butt.

3   The stump must be level or slope downward in the direction of takedown, so if necessary cut a wedge off the stump.

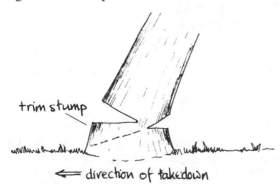

trim stump

← direction of takedown

4   Cut the hinge with an axe.

5   Place all tools well out of the danger zone.

6   Place the thick end of the pole under the tree, close to the butt. Stand behind the pole, grasp it with both hands and ease the butt forward. Reposition the lever frequently and move the butt only a small distance each time, so that you can stay out of the danger zone.

Where two people are needed to shift the tree, they can work from either side of the stem to free it. Use two poles as levers under the cut end of the stem to move it a few inches at a time. In some situations it may be easier to work from the same side, for example if the stem is firmly wedged against the stump.

With a winch or ropes

A hand winch allows you to move trees which are lodged firmly and which are too big to lever with a pole. Slope and ground requirements are the same as when using a pole. It is often easier to winch the butt sideways to avoid it digging into the ground.

1   Clear the takedown route.

2   Remove the hinge, using an axe.

3   Select a suitable anchor tree or stump as far as possible from the tree being felled, given the available length of winch cable.

Attach a strop to the anchor tree, being sure to pad the tree to protect it, and pull the loop as tight as possible. Then attach the winch safety hook to the strop.

4   Hook the winch cable around the lodged tree, making sure that the open side of the hook is behind the cable as shown.

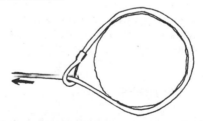

5   Thread the winch cable into the winch and take up the slack. Keep winching until the tree falls.

If you have to pull the butt down a steep slope, offset the winch so you can see and work from a safe position. Run the winch cable through a block fixed to a pivot tree.

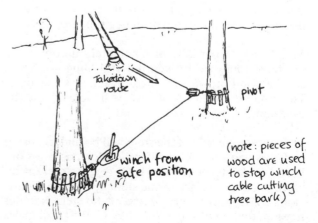

Takedown route

pivot

winch from safe position

(note: pieces of wood are used to stop winch cable cutting tree bark)

If you don't have a winch, use ropes instead (see notes on rope use on page 115).

a If the tree is fairly upright, use two ropes at 45 degrees to the line of fall to pull the top of the stem off the supporting tree. Lasso the tree to secure the ropes. Don't climb it.

b If the tree is lodged with too much lean to pull it backwards from the top, attach a rope near the bottom of the stem and pull the butt off the stump.

With progs

Where there is no way to shift the butt end of the stem away from the entanglement, you may be able to cut it in place. This is only possible where you have one or more strong progs which can support the weight of the remaining stem when a section is felled.

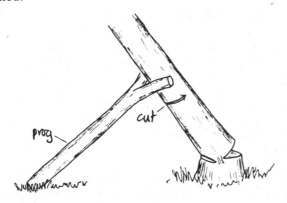

With the stem supported, make a cut just below the support by cutting upward from below. When the cut is almost through, knock out the prog with a sledgehammer and the tree should fall.

WINDBLOWN TREES

Hand tools are awkward, slow and dangerous to use on windblown trees, especially where you have to cut upwards from the bottom side of the stem. A chainsaw in the hands of an expert is the tool for the job. A few general points are given below.

a Windblown trees are very hazardous because they may be under considerable tension and are frequently in an unstable position. It is vital to assess the stresses on the tree before beginning to cut.

Trees may be partially or completely uprooted, or the trunks may be broken but still hung up. Trees can be windthrown and broken at the same time. The precise cutting sequence will depend on the situation.

In general, one side of the stem will be under tension and the opposite side will be under compression. Wood under tension may, however, be present on more than one surface of the stem at different points along it. Wherever the surface of the stem is under tension, that is the dangerous side. Cutting sequences

must be designed to reduce tension progressively and gradually.

b Always prepare an escape route and be ready for the unexpected.

c If there are large branches adding to the weight of the wood under stress, cut these off first (p121).

d Cut close to the butt if possible, as this is the area of least stress. Don't stand on the root plate while working, since this may suddenly give way as you sever the stem.

e Make the first severing cut in the wood under compression. Make the final cut in the wood under tension. Stagger the final cut at least 25mm (1″) closer to the root plate to minimise splitting of the stem.

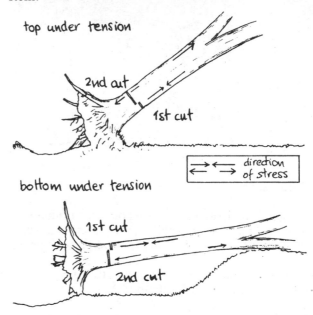

f Make the final cut standing on the safe (compression) side if there is side tension.

Coppicing and Layering

This section covers coppicing techniques. For details on stooling as a method of propagating coppice, see page 35. For use of coppice products, see page 157. A general description of coppice management is given on page 34.

Traditionally, coppice is cut from October to March, when the absence of leaves makes working easier, and there is a full season's growth ahead. However, it can be done at any time of year, except in August, when the shoots will not have time to harden off before the frosts.

COPPICING PROCEDURE

Depending on the size, age and condition of the coppice stems, you can use a billhook, bowsaw or axe. Trained operators can use a chainsaw. Billhooks are neatest and fastest on young regrowth, but on older coppice, saws are normally best. The 530mm (21″) triangular-framed bowsaw is especially useful on multiple-stemmed trees, provided the stems are not too large.

Follow the basic felling techniques described earlier in this chapter, keeping in mind these additional points:

a Take a close look before you begin cutting. Stones, glass or tin cans wedged amongst the stems can ruin saws and edged tools.

b Cut away all small, whippy growth from around the base of the stool, to avoid interference when cutting.

c Remove the stems one by one. Where the stems are all about the same size, cut from the outside of the coppice stool around and inwards, in a spiral pattern.

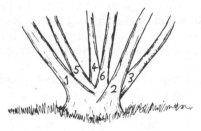

Where stems are of varying sizes, it is usually easiest to clear the smaller stems first to give access to the larger ones.

d Cut each stem upward towards the centre, to promote runoff of rainwater and help prevent rot.

In neglected coppice, where the stems lean outward and are heavy, the saw will jam unless a second worker helps by pushing the stem back off the saw while it is being cut. Even where you can cut from the back of the stem downwards, it helps to have someone support the stem to keep it from splitting.

e Cut stems as low as possible. Where this is difficult, it is often quicker and tidier to cut twice – a high cut to fell the stem and a second cut to remove the stub.

Don't try to remove the coppice all at once by cutting below the top of the stool, as the saw will jam.

right   wrong

Normally you should cut to the previous level, leaving the existing stool without reducing it.

If you have to cut the stool near ground level, do this only after all the stems are cut.

In some coppice woodlands, ash, and occasionally elm, are traditionally coppiced at 300–900mm (1–3′) high. Unless you have reasons against this, you should follow the evidence of past practice.

f If the coppice tree is very large, treat each stem as an individual tree and use the appropriate felling techniques.

g Clean up the stool after coppicing. Cut off any splinters or split wood, and brush dirt and sawdust off the cut surfaces. This reduces the chance of water collecting on the stool and causing rot. If water is lodging in the centre of the stool, cut the stool so it will drain.

LAYERING

Where the coppice growth is poor and spindly, or where there are large gaps between stools, you can propagate new plants by layering and pegging some of the coppice stems rather than cutting them off. Hazel and sweet chestnut respond particularly well to this treatment, but other species can also be layered successfully.

Layering procedure

1 Coppice the stool in the normal way, but leave one or two stems for layering.

2 Using a sharp billhook (or a saw if you are not skilled with a billhook), cut through the stem at a downward angle away from the stool. Cut in the direction in which you want to lay the stem, making the cut as shown.

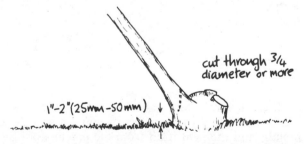

cut through 3/4 diameter or more

1″–2″(25mm–50mm)

If you cut too far, the stem may break off as it is lowered to the ground, or it may die after layering. If you don't cut far enough, the stem will split downward into the base as you lower it. When you near the point where you want the cut to stop, gently pull the stem down and to the left to open up the mouth of the cut. Then continue cutting and pulling at the same time until the stem can be eased down to the ground. This may be easier with someone else to guide the stem as you cut.

3 Trim the protruding stub, using a small bowsaw.

Begin the cut as low as possible and slope it upward toward the first cut, so that rain drains away.

4 Mark out the line of the stem along the ground using a spade or mattock. Follow any bends in the stem.

5 Move the stem aside and dig out a trench along the marked line. Dig it deep enough to ensure that bent or whippy stems don't spring out.

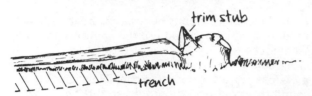

trim stub

trench

6 Some people recommend cutting off or fraying the bark on the underside of the stem where you want it to root, but others ignore this step. In either case, position the stem along the trench and peg it down (see below), choosing an 'elbow' or other point of juncture with the ground. Where the stem is very springy, use two pegs facing opposite ways. Knock in the pegs with a lump hammer.

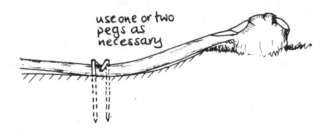

use one or two pegs as necessary

7 Cover the stem with earth, and preferably not with leaf mould, in the area where you want it to root. Cover it to a depth of 75–150mm (3–6"), and tread the earth firmly around the stem.

If you can't get the stem to lie along the ground, cut a notch in the upperside of the stem where it's closest to the ground, and then heap earth over the notched section.

8 If the layered stem 'takes', you can either leave it untouched to grow in place, or you can wait 7–12 months and then cut it off from the parent stool for transplanting.

Pegs for layering

To make pegs to secure layered stems:

1 Select hazel or other stems which have a strong side branch emerging at an acute angle. Cut these off with a saw or billhook, to form rough pegs at least 300mm (1') long, with crooks about 100mm (4") long.

2 Trim the pegs on a stump or chopping block (p126). Cut the points in line with the crook, as this makes them less likely to twist when you knock them in.

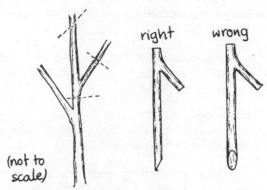

right   wrong

(not to scale)

Snedding

Snedding is the removal of branches from a felled tree. Snedding of conifers, which have many small radial branches, is most safely done by hand rather than with a chainsaw. On large broadleaves it may be best to clear away the small branches by hand and then use a chainsaw to sned the large limbs.

Use a light axe or billhook for most snedding. Most volunteers prefer billhooks, which are fine in many cases, but axes are better for cutting the tough, resinous branches of conifers, and are safer and easier to use on larger limbs. Saws can be easier to use on branches over about 25mm (1") in diameter, but are slower and more awkward than billhooks or axes and tend to snag on thin, whippy branches and twigs.

Trees should be snedded and the brushwood disposed of at the time of felling, and usually cross-cutting is best done at this time as well. This avoids a hazardous pile-up of stems and tangled branches.

BASIC SNEDDING

The following points apply to most conifers and to small hardwood trees.

With a light axe or billhook

a When possible, stand on the opposite side of the stem to the branches which you are cutting, so that the stem protects your legs and feet. This means you have to cross frequently from one side of the stem to the other to cut branches in different positions. Only try same-side snedding if you are very experienced, but take care as you are more likely to injure yourself.

b Never stand astride the tree to sned it. Always stand so the impact of the axe or billhook is made beyond your legs, so that you won't be hurt if the tool bounces from the cut. Always make sure there is a clear path for your swing, as even a small twig can deflect the tool and cause injury.

c Sned from the base of the tree towards the tip.

d A full swing is seldom necessary when snedding small branches. Hold an axe as shown below, with your hands part-way up the haft. You don't need to move your hands for the return stroke.

e For greatest control over the cut, swing the tool in a very shallow arc so that the side of the blade near its back edge glances against the stem just before the blade cuts into the branch. This prevents the cutting edge from digging in.

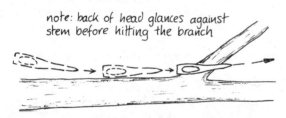

note: back of head glances against stem before hitting the branch

This swing is easy to exaggerate and requires some practice to master, but gives the best results.

f Sned flush to the main stem. Snags make the log difficult and dangerous to handle, and tear up the ground if the log is dragged away.

g To sned branches from the same side, lean over the tree so that your shoulders are above the cut. Hold an axe with your elbows bent and your left hand near its head.

It is hard to develop much power in this stroke, so use it only on small branches. Be sure that you are standing so that the tool will carry through well away from, and to the side of your legs. The stem gives no protection in this stroke.

h Clear away cut branches as you work, so that they don't get underfoot or in your way.

i When all branches except those supporting the stem are cut, place the tool out of the way. Roll the tree over from the tip, using the remaining branches as handles. If the tree is too heavy for this, lever it over with a pole. With a really heavy tree it is easiest to cut the stem in convenient pieces, using a chainsaw, and finish snedding the pieces. Otherwise, use a hand winch and cable. Turn the tree so that the remaining branches stick out to one side of the trunk, then sned these in the normal way.

PROBLEMS

Trees with branches under stress, large broadleaves and other problem trees require modifications to the basic snedding procedure.

a Ensure the tree is stable before you start, and that there are no bystanders.

b Remove the branches in conveniently disposable segments. Don't cut off more than can be handled by a clean-up crew.

c Sned from the outer branches into the main limbs, and from the lower limbs toward the limbs at the top. The idea is to lessen the weight of the limbs by removing the smaller branches first. Unless the limbs are to be used for timber, they can be cross-cut into handy lengths before severing them from the main stem. Use a bowsaw for large limbs.

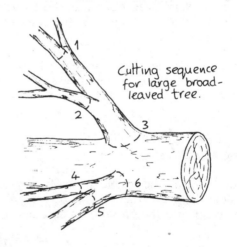

Cutting sequence for large broad-leaved tree.

d Estimate the stresses in large limbs. You may have to treat them as windblown trees (p118). Remember to make a small cut on the compression side first, before making the main cut on the tension side. Watch out, as the tree may move or the branch may spring back as you cut it. Tough springy wood such as yew is very prone to springing back.

e Large limbs projecting upward from the trunk should be treated as if they are standing trees. Fell and sned them separately.

f If you are faced with limbs which support the trunk but make it impossible to roll the trunk over, decide whether the limbs are safe to sned in place. Clear a line of retreat. Cut the limbs with an axe, and never work directly under the tree. Watch the tree carefully, and when it starts to shift, get out of the way and winch or roll the stem over to expose the remaining limbs.

The same procedure applies to trees which are held up too high by the branches to be safely snedded. In this case, reduce the length of the support branches progressively until the tree is in a suitable position to finish snedding in the usual way.

Cross-Cutting

Cross-cutting felled timber into shorter lengths is usually necessary, whether the material is to be extracted, stacked or burnt on site. Where the wood is to be utilised, cut it into lengths to suit the use (p138). If not, cut into whatever length is convenient. When cutting into specified lengths, mark out all the lengths with the log in the cutting position. Use a scribe, or notch the bark with a light axe or billhook.

Cross-cutting is normally done at the time of felling, after the branches have been snedded. If the timber is to be peeled (p133), this should be done before cross-cutting. Whether you choose to cross-cut at the stump or at the disposal point depends on the size and weight of the material. Try to minimise the amount of handling. For example, material which can be dragged or carried should be taken to the fire or stacking area before cross-cutting. Otherwise, cut at the stump, or at least cut into manageable lengths with final cutting at the disposal point. Do not cross-cut on very steep slopes, as short lengths are dangerous and hard to extract in this situation. (See also page 128.)

When cross-cutting, keep an eye out for useful pieces, such as forked poles to use as 'progs', or heavy branched ash or oak for chopping blocks (p126).

GENERAL POINTS

a   Get the log off the ground, if possible, by supporting it near the point where it is to be cut. Otherwise you may cut into the ground, or find that the tool

jams due to compression. Ideally, the log should be between knee and waist height. If necessary it can be levered up by two assistants.

b   Where you are cross-cutting a quantity of fairly small poles, it is worth making up a saw horse. A suitable design is shown on page 64. This gives a stable base for two-handed cutting with the bowsaw.

c   Stacked logs too large for a saw horse are best supported on the stack rather than across a single log.

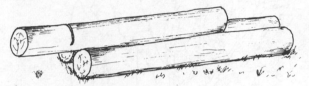

d   When cutting large logs on the ground, start from the lighter top end first. This makes it easier to lift the log onto a support. When cutting logs on a saw horse, cut from the butt end so that the pole does not overbalance.

e   Make as many cuts as possible with wood under tension, as in the diagram, so that the cut opens away from the saw.

f   Usually the final cut must be made with the log supported at both ends. In this situation the log is under compression, so the saw is likely to bind in the cut. Avoid this by inserting a small wedge in the cut, or support the log with one hand, lifting just enough to keep the cut open while you finish it. Logs too heavy for this should be rotated as soon as the saw starts to bind, so that you cut through from two or three places, each turned upwards in succession.

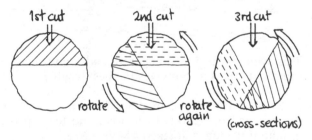

You may not be quite able to sever the log by cutting around it. Finish the job by giving the log a knock with a lump or sledge hammer, or by pushing it off the support onto the ground, where the impact usually breaks it.

g   Where there is too much tension, make an undercut first in the wood under compresssion, to reduce splitting. Make this further from the butt end.

TOOLS AND TECHNIQUES

Bowsaw

The bowsaw is the best tool for cross-cutting small logs. Use a saw of adequate size for the diameter of the logs (p63).

a Stand with your feet apart, both feet in line with the cut. Hold the saw with both hands as shown.

Don't use your thumb to guide the blade, as you would in carpentry.

b Use a more pronounced rocking motion than when felling, using your body as well as arms to power the stroke. Saw with fairly slow strokes. To speed up the work, increase pressure on the saw rather than the speed of the stroke. Cut easily on the push stroke and use more pressure and rocking motion on the pull stroke.

c When cross-cutting a log which is near the ground, use a half-kneeling position. You won't be able to rock the saw, so increase pressure instead. Don't push so hard that the blade starts to turn in the cut, this being a problem mainly with dull or damaged blades.

Axe

You should normally avoid using the axe for cross-cutting, since it is slow and hazardous and wastes a lot of wood if you are cutting timber lengths. Cross-cutting is, though, the best way to learn good axemanship, and is an essential technique to master before using an axe for felling or snedding. An axe may have to be used for cross-cutting where a log is difficult to move and obstacles prevent the use of saw.

a Clear any obstacles from the line of the swing. Obstacles at shoulder height are particularly dangerous, and may deflect the blade and cause injury. Make sure no one is standing behind you.

b Stand comfortably with your feet about shoulder-width apart. Check your distance from the log, as the axe head should meet the log solidly with your arms nearly straightened and knees slightly bent. It is better to over-swing than under-swing, ie fraying the axe haft rather than burying the blade in your foot. When cutting, always keep your eyes on the log, not on the tool.

c Always swing the axe 'from the shoulder', and never vertically downwards. The axe should strike the wood at an angle of about 45 degrees.

An angled swing is less likely to strike your legs. It

also cuts better, since the cut goes with the grain rather than directly across it. By swinging from opposite shoulders, alternately, you create a V-shaped cut. The axe bites out large chips of wood and keeps the cut clear. If you cut straight down you are likely to jam the axe.

d If you are right-handed, grip the haft near its lower end with your left hand, and lift the axe up with your right hand fairly near the axe head. Swing downward, sliding your right hand down the haft to meet the left hand.

If you are left-handed, reverse the position of the hands. Once you gain experience, it is useful to learn how to use the axe ambidextrously. Sometimes obstructions will mean it may be more efficient to use the axe 'wrong-handed'.

e Strokes should be controlled and relaxed. Accuracy is more important than strength, as with accurate cutting you remove the greatest amount of wood per stroke and you tire less easily. Try to keep the sides of the cut smooth and evenly tapered.

f It is usually best to cut half–way through the tree from one side, and then roll the log over to complete the cut from the other side. If you cut straight through from one side, you have to remove more wood and may dig the axe into the ground.

cut a wedge, rotate, then cut another wedge

Start the notch wide enough so that its sides will meet in the centre of the log when angled at about 45 degrees.

g If the axe jams, free it with a sharp blow up or down on the end of the haft, not with side-to-side twisting of the haft which may break it.

Two-man cross-cut saw

This is for use on logs too large for a bowsaw, and where a chainsaw is not being used. Follow the same method as when felling (p114), but stand or half-kneel as described above for the bowsaw.

Burning and Clearing Up

BURNING VERSUS OTHER METHODS

Carefully consider the advantages and disadvantages of various methods before choosing how to dispose of small roundwood, branches and other cut material.

Traditionally, all material cut in a wood was removed for use, including the tops, which were bundled as faggots for fuel. The flora and fauna of ancient woodlands are adapted to this practice, with losses of deadwood habitats, but gains in the form of a rich herbaceous ground flora, when compared to natural conditions. On some commons it is still a requirement that cuttings be stacked for firewood. Elsewhere, it may be possible to sell some cut material or to find use for it on other conservation tasks, such as erosion control. Extra time and care is needed to cut and stack according to use (p128), and transport cost must be weighed against the likely income if the material is removed for sale.

Burning has a number of practical advantages. Cuttings are completely removed, so that they do not interfere with plant growth by shading, obstructing the ground or altering the general soil conditions. Burning is quicker than cutting and stacking to size, especially where a task extends over several days, as the fire is easy to restart after the first day. Last but not least, a fire keeps volunteers warm and happy!

The disadvantages include the destruction of the woodland vegetation on the fire site itself. The soil becomes enriched with mineral ash so that the fire site usually gets colonised by rank invasive vegetation such as nettles, with only very slow if any recovery to 'natural' conditions. It is wasteful, in that burning removes a source of deadwood habitat and returns minerals to the soil in 'raw' form which are easily leached by rainfall.

Local erosion and soil compaction can occur if volunteers over-use just a few routes when dragging material to the fire. Sometimes it is unsafe to build fires, for example on steep slopes or where the canopy is very dense. Leases may have restrictions banning fires.

Soil enrichment can be reduced, though not prevented, by collecting the wood ash from the fire site. This material is high in potash, and can be used as a garden fertilizer. Collecting the ash also makes the site less attractive to rabbits, who often burrow in burned places and heavily browse the surrounding vegetation.

Keep the number of fires to a minimum to reduce damage. Mummery and Tabor (1978, p10) suggest that 20 per hectare (8 per acre) in coppiced woodland should suffice. Mark fire sites so that they can be re-used in later years, so localising the damage.

Where access is not required for several years after cutting, leave some tops scattered around to rot down. Tops piled around freshly-cut coppice stools can help protect them from deer damage.

Ranson (1978, p1) indicates that on some sites hazel, ash and maple tops can be walked over in three or four years, but Mummery and Tabor (1978, p10) caution that at Monks Wood, Cambridgeshire, oak tops are still present 50 years after cutting.

Where it is impractical to leave cut material scattered, you can pile it in stacks or windrows. Even where most material is to be burnt, a few 'habitat piles' provide useful shelter for birds, small mammals and invertebrates.

Take care to make stacks and windrows as compact as possible. Don't just heap up the cut material. Partly trim branches to reduce their bushiness before laying them in place.

Where you want to dispose of heavier material, you can pile brushwood around a log or uprooted stump, and then add the larger branches to hold this in place. This is better than putting the brushwood on top, if children are likely to try and pull the stack apart. Where there is too much material to dispose of in stacks, you can lay it in windrows. These can be spaced up to 20m apart, depending on the amount of material and the care you take in trimming and piling it. Make each windrow 2–3m wide at the base, and about 2m high. To prevent the sides collapsing, cut and drive in retaining stakes as necessary. On slopes, lay this 'drift' up and down hill, with the brushy ends downhill to prevent slippage. If you plan to utilise the cuttings, such as for pea sticks, lay them with the butt ends downhill to make later removal easier.

FIRES

Location

a Site fires where the vegetation is least valuable, such as on previous fire sites, heavily used tracks or where scrub vegetation has shaded out the ground vegetation. Where the site is of botanical interest, be sure you know where any patches of rare plants are located, and avoid these. The plants may not be visible at the time of working. When working at the edge of a wood, seek permission to burn in the adjacent field so that you don't need to harm the woodland flora at all.

b Site fires downhill of the worksite, if feasible, to make it easier to drag cuttings to them.

c Site fires downwind of the worksite, to keep the site less smoky and to reduce the likelihood of fires creeping towards coppice stools or standing trees.

d Sites fires well away from the boles and crowns of standing trees. The heat from a big fire reaches far beyond the visible flames. Overhanging branches may be killed even if they are high above the fire itself. Trees exposed to intense heat may appear unharmed at the time, but can lose their bark and die in a year or so. Smooth-barked trees such as beech, sycamore and ash are particularly susceptible to scorching.

e On wet sites, build fires in the driest place possible. Unless it is windy, choose a location a few feet higher than the surrounding terrain and away from obstructions, to maximise the draught. Avoid hollows. If the fire is on peat, the peat must be wet enough to resist catching light, otherwise the fire may smoulder underground for weeks and flare up unexpectedly, perhaps yards away.

f On sites with a high fire risk, such as heathland, pinewoods or woods on sandy soils, and on sites in view of main roads, it may be wise to alert the police and fire service in advance. On such sites it is a good idea to clear a firebreak and have water available if possible.

g In conifer plantations, do not site fires within the plantation itself since this favours the spread of Rhizina fungus.

Starting and tending

a Starting a fire can be frustrating and time consuming. Put one experienced person in charge of the fire, at least until it is going well. Ideally, the site manager should get a fire going the day before the felling task letting it burn for several hours to produce a bed of embers. This makes it easy to restart the next day. Where this is not done, it is best to get everyone on the task to collect dead wood to begin with. If the fire is too small or if live wood is put on too soon, the fire will never 'take off'. Any dead wood burned should be replaced by 'habitat piles'.

Once one fire is well started, additional fires can be lit by transferring embers on a shovel, taking care not to spill any, or in a bucket or other container.

b There are two ways to get a fire going: the clean heroic way and the foolproof polluting way.

The heroic method is most feasible in calm, dry conditions where you have plenty of dry material. Start with some kindling – loosely wadded paper, wood shavings or 'duff' from the inside of dry rotted logs, and dry twigs. Around this build a small 'log cabin' or 'tepee' of sticks. If it is windy, put a fairly large back-log on the upwind side of the kindling to shield it. If your courage falters, pour sump oil over the kindling before lighting.

Paraffin can be used instead of oil, but it is more

expensive and less effective because it is more volatile and burns too quickly. A solid fuel fire lighter is second-best for the same reasons. NEVER use petrol to start a fire.

The foolproof polluting method should only be used when absolutely necessary in very wet or windy conditions, or when dealing with difficult material such as hawthorn which is too springy and spiky to pile and burn efficiently. It requires using an old car tyre, which burns intensely and for a long time, but leaves persistent heavy metal residues in the soil which are not easy to clear up. Rather than using a tyre, try to get organised with a couple of sacks of dry kindling and timber which can be taken on site to start the fire in bad conditions.

If a tyre has to be used, then stuff it loosely with paper and pour used sump oil over the paper. Build a stack of wood at least 1m (3') high over the tyre to take advantage of the heat produced when you light it. The tyre will produce a cloud of noxious black smoke. At the end of the task when the fire is out, gather up all the wire reinforcing as this is a danger to animals. Then shovel up the ash and soil immediately beneath the fire site, to reduce the amount of pollutants left behind, and take it in sacks to an authorised dump.

c Start with a small fire and enlarge it gradually. Use thin, dry wood at first. Cut sticks into fairly short, straight lengths so that they pack close together at the base of the fire to form a bed of embers. Don't put on awkwardly branched wood or large timbers, as these can put the fire out by stopping fuel reaching the base.

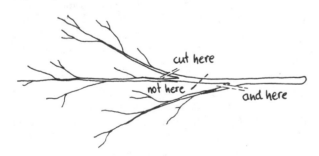

Be patient – don't put on green wood until you have a good hot base. Add more wood when flames appear above the sticks which are already placed.

d Always put branches on the fire with their butt ends to the wind. This ensures that the twigs lie in the hottest part of the fire, downwind, where they burn quickly. Otherwise, the fire can be completely obstructed by a tangle of unburned brush which prevents the free flow of air to the heart of the fire.

e Keep the fire tight, especially if it is sited in the woodland itself. With care you can limit it to an area no bigger than 1.2m x 1m (4' x 3') by cutting material to 1.2m (4') lengths and keeping the brushy ends well pushed down. There is no excuse for a big, sprawling fire or one which creeps downwind. This just causes excess damage to ground and trees.

Small fires need not be 'turned in', a requirement with larger fires. They are also easier to work near, as the fire tender can put cuttings directly on the fire from where he cuts them up, increasing speed and efficiency.

f Large material should be cross-cut before being brought down to the fire. Small material should be dragged to the fire area and cut up before being put on the fire. Use a sharp billhook, light axe or short-handled slasher. Cut on a block or stump, not on the ground, which damages the tools. The best chopping-block is made from a heavy forked branch of oak or ash, held in place by pegs.

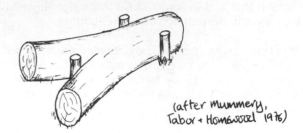

(after Mummery, Tabor + Homewood 1976)

Usually it is best to stack the material in a holding pile, butt ends together, so that the fire tender can trim it as necessary and add it to the fire as required. If everyone throws on their own material the result is likely to be chaos. Don't leave material heaped indiscriminately around the fire, as this just interferes with the work.

Where the group works well together you may not have to designate a fire tender – people can cut and add their own material once the fire is going well.

g Use a long-handled pitch fork or 1.8m (6') prog to push cuttings well down ito the fire. This keeps the fire compact and burning strongly. Fires which start to get a bit large should be thrown or turned in, by pushing the branches and embers in from the sides and the downwind end toward the centre. Do not stand downwind while doing this, as the fire may suddenly flare up. If the fire gets hollow, knock it into shape with a pole to keep it going. Once it is burning steadily with a good bed of embers, you should be able to burn all that is supplied by the fellers. But never overload the fire in an effort to keep pace, as the fire may be damped down or, worse, get out of control.

h Where there is any danger of the fire spreading, do not leave it at the end of the day until it has burned down to embers. On a windy day, it is wise to turn it in and cover it with mineral soil (not peat) before leaving.

i Never fell trees into the fire. This is extremely dangerous and the fire is likely to flare up or straggle and get out of hand.

Stump Treatment and Removal

Stumps can usually be left untreated after felling. Where it is necessary to suppress regrowth, herbicide treatment is often effective, if done at the time of felling or soon after (p100). Where herbicides are not being used, you can reduce the vigour of stumps and encourage rot by cutting gashes around them, through the cambium, and by notching the tops to retain rainwater.

In conifer plantations, special measures are essential to prevent Fomes infection (p103).

Where it is necessary to destroy stumps, this can be done in situ, or by removing the stump. 'Stump gobblers' are machines which reduce stumps to a pile of chips, and are operated by some forestry contractors. This service is expensive, but may be the only suitable method for stumps at roadsides or in amenity areas. Chemical destruction requires the use of oxidising agents which make the stump combustible. The chemicals are extremely toxic and are not suitable for use in woodlands, nor by untrained people.

STUMP REMOVAL

It is often quicker, easier and cheaper to remove stumps by hand or by mechanical excavation rather than trying to destroy them in place.

a Grubbing up trees and shrubs solves the stump problem without the use of chemicals. If whole trees can be removed and dragged away, it may be quicker than cutting followed by stump treatment.

b Grubbing up may be very difficult with large trees, on very boggy ground or at a distance from access and disposal points. In soft or wet earth it may leave 'craters' which make later management difficult. In peaty soil the craters gradually fill with soft peat and become masked by a mat of vegetation, presenting a hazard to man and animal. Depending on the soil, harrowing after tree removal can smooth the ground and encourage the quick regrowth of herbaceous plants. Machine mowing for several years will gradually even out the ground.

c Whatever the technique used, the basic method is to cut around and loosen the side roots which anchor the stump. Don't bother to attack the stump itself, as you will only waste your energy.

d Use a grubbing mattock on large shrubs and saplings. The grubbing mattock has a short axe blade to sever the roots and a longer mattock blade to lever them up. Cut all around the base with the mattock and lever the stump out with a crowbar. Don't use the mattock for levering, as the handle may break. Difficult stumps may require several people working together.

e If you haven't already felled the tree and it is small enough, you can try pulling it over without felling it. Secure two ropes at not less than 45 degrees to the line of fall, and of sufficient length that you can work from outside the danger zone. At first keep just enough tension on the ropes to help you cut the side roots, and then pull hard away to topple the tree. Stay away from the roots while this is happening as the tree may give suddenly.

f When dealing with trees which are too big to pull over unfelled, it is best to leave a stump at least 1m (3') high, or as high as can be safely cut, up to 1.5m (5'). This gives much more leverage than a very short stump.

Use a winch with a cable that hooks to chain about 2m (7') long. The chain should have small links for flexibility, and have a large eye at each end, of unequal size so that one fits through the other. Loop the chain around the stump, and then pull it tight and hook it to the winch cable. Both cable and chain must have safe working loads as great as the winch's hauling capacity.

The hand winch must be securely mounted to a fixed standfast, such as the base of a stout tree. Place pickets around the tree to protect it from damage. A tractor-mounted winch, necessary for really big stumps, usually has its own holdfast in the form of a metal bar that is lowered until it digs into the ground.

It is often best to winch one way and then the opposite to break the anchor roots. Don't work around the stump while the winch cable is under tension, as it may give suddenly. You can use a lever pole, as shown below, to help provide a lift to the haul.

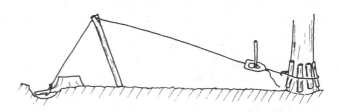

10 Extraction, Conversion and Marketing

Extraction, Stacking and Seasoning

This section considers the extraction, stacking and conversion of small size timbers, as produced at early thinnings. The harvesting of large timbers is a specialist job for contractors with the necessary equipment.

EXTRACTION

a Normally, timber should be handled as few times as possible, to save labour. Hand extraction is heavy work. The usual practice, where timber lengths are to be extracted, is to reduce poles to reasonable lengths of 3–5m (10-15'), and to leave large timber lengths lying where felled for later removal by tractor. Whenever possible, fell the trees so as to minimise the distance and effort of extraction. Plan the work so that the lightest material moves the farthest and the heaviest least far.

b Many conservation and amenity woodlands have rides suitable for access by a Land Rover and trailer, although often only at drier times of year. Rides can be reinforced to a certain extent for wet weather use by laying brash and other small material across them as a binder and filler. Tractors and Land Rovers can sometimes be used off the rides, along tracks prepared in advance, winding among standing trees and coppice stools. Beware of small sharp stumps which can pierce tyres.

c In general it is easier and safer to drag a pole along the ground, or to lift one end and drag it along using tongs or a similar aid, than it is to pick it up and carry it. Carrying may be necessary on easily disturbed soils. Take care whenever you lift and shift timber, always lifting with the knees bent and back straight. Lift logs one end at a time, and never use a 'dead lift' unless the material is very light. Move down or across a slope, not up it, if possible. Use other logs for moving and stacking, to avoid lifting. If you are struggling with the material, then it is too heavy – use a better method or get help. Fairly short lengths of timber and small-diameter cord wood can be shifted with a wheelbarrow, if the terrain is not too rough.

d Always wear gloves, preferably with armoured palms, and steel toe-capped boots or wellingtons, when handling timber.

e One of the simplest and most versatile tools for hand extraction is a 4–5m (12–16') length of 10mm ($\frac{1}{2}$") rope, spliced into a loop. Under normal conditions this is useful with fairly small trees, or larger trees if the poles are freshly peeled or the slope is favourable. A loop joined with a knot can also be used, though this is less secure than a splice.

To pull out a pole, simply pass a bight or rope around the end of the pole and loop the other end through to tighten.

Other aids to extracting and stacking logs include the sappie, hand tongs and pulphook (see p65). Other aids are described in Forestry Commission Leaflet 81 'Aid Tools for Timber Harvesting'.

STACKING

General points

a Clear the stacking site of all obstructions, choosing a level site if possible. When stacking across sloping ground, build the stack from the bottom upwards, supported to prevent rolling. Do not support stacks against live trees.

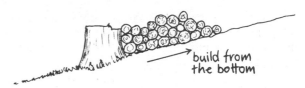

build from the bottom

b Stack large logs parallel to each other for stability. Stack smaller logs, which are to be cross-cut, as for cordwood, but don't bother stacking to standard cord dimensions.

c During coppicing, where there is a need to sort out useful material from lop and top which is to be burnt, it is usually best to make temporary stacks as you work. Make loose cords of the larger material, and windrows of small material for bean sticks and so on. Coppice material should be moved to point of conversion before the main growing season so it does not suppress ground vegetation.

d Shade the ends of newly stacked material from direct sun in summer, to keep them from splitting. This precaution is unnecessary once the material is partly seasoned.

e Never walk or climb over stacked wood unless absolutely essential, as you may collapse the stack. Grit from boots also collects on the timber and can damage tools which are later used on it.

f Always leave stacks in a safe, stable condition, especially where there is public access.

Cordwood

Poor-quality material and irregular branches, suitable for pulp, firewood or charcoal burning, should be cross-cut and stacked for storage and sale in cords. The normal cord has dimensions of 2.4 × 1.2 × 1.2m (8′ × 4′ × 4′) to give a nominal volume of 3.46 cubic metres (128 cubic feet). A cord of dimensions 1.8 x 1.2 × 1.6m (6′ × 4′ × 5′4) gives the same volume. Other cords in local use have dimensions which give volumes from 3.31 cubic metres (117 cubic feet) to 4.08 cubic metres (144 cubic feet). In all cases the cord is made up of material not more than 1.2m (4′) long.

The solid volume is actually much less than the nominal volume, since even a tightly stacked cord contains about 50% air space. A loosely stacked cord, containing much more air space, has far less sales value.

To make a cord:

1 Lay two poles, 50–75mm (2-3″) diameter and slightly longer than the cord on the ground, about 0.75m (2′6″) apart. If the ground is very uneven or the poles irregular, lay them on 'sleeper' poles to make a level base.

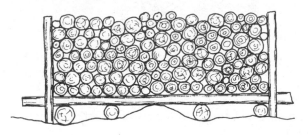

2 Provide end-stop stakes to keep the corded wood from rolling off the poles. Drive them well into the ground so that their tops are at least 1.2m (4′) above ground level. Place the stakes outside the poles to prevent the poles rolling apart.

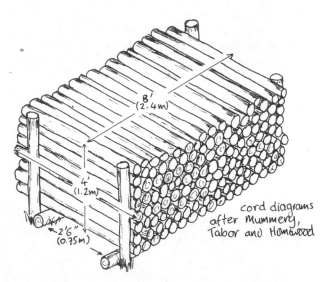

cord diagrams after Mummery, Tabor and Homewood

If more than one cord is to be stacked in a line using the same base poles, drive in stakes every 2.4m (8′) along the poles to help distribute the weight, and to make it easier to count the number of cords in the stack.

3 Stack the timber at right angles to the base poles,

being careful to centre the timber on the poles and to stack as tightly as possible.

Poles, fencing material and small produce

Stack poles and fencing materials as for cordwood, but stack each layer at right angles to the one below to aid drying. Normally no end-stops are needed, and the stack should be stable on its own.

Stack small produce, such as bean poles, pea sticks, packing rods and trees stakes, in alternating groups of layers, each group about 150mm (6″) thick.

SEASONING

On-site seasoning of roundwood is seldom necessary, apart from that which occurs naturally if the material is left in stacks until conversion. In some cases, where material is sold by weight (eg pulpwood), seasoning should be avoided. Such material should be sold as soon as possible after felling to minimise the loss of value due to drying. Material which is to be converted into products with the bark off, including all material which is going to be treated with preservative, should be barked at the time of felling (p133).

The time it takes for material to season depends on the type of timber and the weather. As an example, round softwood poles, 150mm (6″) in diameter, stacked in spring, should fully season in about six months.

On-Site Conversion

This section gives simple methods of bundling, pointing, hewing, cleaving, shaving and peeling bark, which can be applied to the conversion of many types of woodland products. For further details see Lambert (1977). For specifications on a number of woodland products, see the section on 'Marketing' later in this chapter.

BUNDLING AND TYING

Many coppice products, including thatching spars, willow rods and cleft chestnut spiles, are made up into bundles before being stored or sold.

Using a grip and cradle

To make up large bundles, such as willow rods:

1 Make a 'woodman's grip' of two poles 0.9–1.2m (3′-4′) long and 40–50mm (1½-2″) in diameter. Connect the poles with a rope, wire or chain, the length of which is about twice the circumference of the bundle to be tied. Attach one end to each pole about 300mm (1′) from the end of the pole.

2 Bolt a hook, made from strap iron, to a post driven into the ground. The hook should be of a size to hold the poles.

3 To use the grip, place the poles to either side of the material to be bundled so that the rope, wire or chain lies across the top of the material. Press one pole down and slip it under the hook. This frees one hand so that you can tie the bond while keeping a firm pressure on the other pole with the other hand.

To make up smaller bundles, such as cleft chestnut spiles:

1 Cut and attach two poles to make a woodman's grip, as in step 1 above.

2 Make up a cradle from two pairs of posts driven into the ground. Join each pair with a discarded bucket handle to form a curved support.

3 Place the material to be bundled on the cradle. Stand straddling it and position the grip around the material. As you press down on both poles to tighten your grip, squeeze the material with your knees to hold it firmly. This way you can let go of the poles and use both hands to tie the bond.

Tying bonds

Bundled material is held with a 'bond', 'tie' or 'rose', usually of wire, but sometimes of natural material (eg hazel or willow rods or brambles) to avoid damaging the material. Make rods more flexible before use by twisting them to open the fibres. Otherwise they are likely to split. If you use

brambles, 'shry' off the thorns by pulling the stems through your gloved hand.

To make a bond of natural material:

1 Pass the thicker end of the stem which you are using for the bond around the bundle, and then cross the thinner end over it.

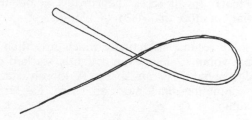

2 Loop the thin end (known as the 'running end') over the thick end. Pull the running end up tight and secure it by twisting it round itself a few times and tucking it in.

If the bond tends to slip using this method, and the stems used are sufficiently flexible, you can make a more secure bond by first looping the thick end of the stem around itself to form a noose. Pass the running end through this noose, tighten and secure as usual.

POINTING AND HEWING

Pointing stakes and removing surplus wood from items prior to final shaping is best done with a side-axe, although a froe can also be used (p66). If unavailable, use a light axe or billhook but take care – these tools tend to dig into the wood because their blades are bevelled on both sides. For pointing:

1 Hold the stake so that every stroke is vertical. Make a series of cuts up one side. Hold the tool near

its head and make light, controlled strokes. You can gain more control if you extend the forefinger to rest on the side of the blade.

2 Turn the stake one quarter of the way around and make a second series of cuts. Then trim the other two sides to complete the point.

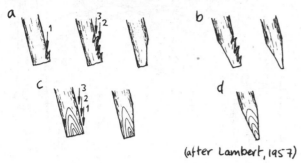

(after Lambert, 1957)

To square off small round poles by hewing, use the same technique as when pointing but hold the pole more nearly vertically so that the cuts do not run so deep. Larger poles are best scored before hewing, but cutting at regular intervals along the pole with a felling axe.

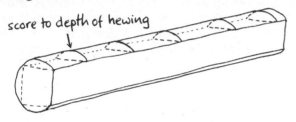

score to depth of hewing

Cleaving

Cleaving or splitting is the easiest and quickest way to separate wood along the grain. Cleft poles are stronger and more weather resistant than sawn ones since there are no cut ends of grain to splinter or trap moisture. Rip-sawing may be necessary, however, where exact dimensions are required or where the grain is too twisted or the poles too full of knots for cleaving. Cleaving small-diameter rods, such as for wattle hurdles, is skilled work and not safe for inexperienced workers.

Cleaving large poles with a sledge and wedges

Splitting large poles or logs, usually for firewood, is best done with a sledgehammer and wedges. Do not use an axe, as the head is not designed as a hammer. Do not use a mell either, as the cast iron head is for use on wood, and may shatter if used on metal wedges. Wear goggles to protect your eyes in case a wedge gets chipped. Avoid, if possible, trying to split logs with many knots or a twisted grain, as these do not split easily or cleanly. Inspect large logs carefully for cracks or checks, as you can take advantage of these when inserting the wedges.

To split a pole along its length:

1 Lay the pole on a hard surface. Two other poles

placed side by side make a good support because they keep the top one from rotating.

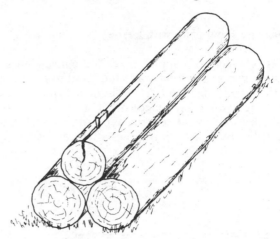

2 Tap in a wedge lightly, so that it stays in position, about a foot in from the end of the pole. Use a sledge or lump hammer. Then hammer the wedge in farther with the sledge to open up a split partway along the pole.

3 As soon as a split starts to open up, place a second wedge aligned with, but beyond the end of, the split. Hammer it in until the split extends well beyond the second wedge.

4 Continue to add wedges in line as necessary until the split extends to the far end of the pole.

5 Hammer the wedges in sequence to cleave the pole.

To split a short log:

1 Place the log upright, preferably on a stump or hard, flat surface.

2 For small-diameter logs, tap a wedge into the centre of the end of the log so that it holds. For large logs, tap in two wedges each on opposite sides of the log between the centre and circumference.

3 Hammer the wedge or wedges home. If this does not split the log, and the split has not yet spanned the end of the log, start another wedge to continue the split as necessary. If the split runs across the end of the log and the wedges are driven fully in, turn

the log on its side and continue the split along its length as when splitting a pole.

Cleaving small poles with a froe

Most cleaving of coppice poles for conversion into paling fences, gates, hay-rake tines and so on is done with a froe and mallet. To hold the pole during cleaving, you need to construct a cleaving-brake. The design depends on the type of material being cleft, but the illustration shows a typical design.

(after Lambert 1957)

1   Place the pole to be cleft upright in the brake so that it is held by the angle of the brake. Place the pole small-end up.

2   Cleave the pole through the centre. Place the froe across the end of the pole and strike the back of the froe blade with the mallet to open up a split.

3   Once the split is well started, change the position of the pole in the cleaving-brake as shown below.

Adjust the working height of the pole as necessary by moving it right or left between the tilted arms of the brake.

4   Continue the split by pushing down on the froe handle, using the froe as a combined wedge and lever. As the pole splits, pull the pole towards you.

If the split starts to move off-centre, turn the pole so that the larger section is underneath. Push down on this section with your left hand and push downwards with the froe to bring the split back to centre.

The split tends to travel towards those wood fibres which are under tension – in this case, those which are curved downward by the pressure of your hand.

By cleaving a pole in different ways you can produce timber of different sections. The diagrams show, from left to right, sections cleft for tent pegs or axe helves, for thin boards, and for rake tines. The numbers show the order in which the sections are cleft.

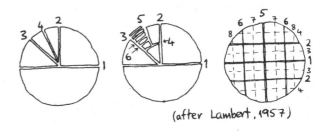

(after Lambert, 1957)

When cleaving short sections of pole into 12mm ($\frac{1}{2}''$) squares for hay-rake tines, wrap twine around the sections near their base to keep them from falling apart as they are split. Place the sections on a flat surface such as a log or stump to cleave them.

PEELING BARK

General points

a Where timber is converted into products which have the bark off, peeling is usually best done immediately after felling, before extraction and conversion. Once the sap dries in the felled trees, the bark holds more tightly and peeling becomes difficult. Timber with bark on is also more likely to be damaged by insects. And if you peel after instead of stacking, extra handling is required.

b Peeling of material felled in spring and summer, when the 'sap is up', is much easier than that felled in winter. Avoid peeling in hard frost, as water in the bark will be frozen, making work very difficult.

c Do not peel trees on steep slopes, as this is dangerous. Extract poles to level ground first.

d Occasionally, as when round ash poles are to be made into hay-rake handles, only some of the bark is peeled off to begin with. This slows down the rate of seasoning and reduces the chances of splitting.

e Note that in many parts of the country, it is illegal to move elm unless it is first barked and the bark burned, in order to prevent the spread of disease (p103).

f Waste bark left at the peeling site may enrich the soil as it decays. Take care to site peeling operations where they will not harm interesting woodland flora, or remove the bark for disposal elsewhere.

g Oak bark used for tanning requires special procedures. See page 140.

Large logs and poles

Use a Swedish peeling spade (p66). As a substitute you can use a worn spade with a well sharpened edge. Use the peeling spade with the large bevel upwards. The small bevel stops the blade digging into the wood and can be set to suit your own preferences. Sharpen and adjust the blade by using a hand carborundum stone on the small back bevel.

To peel a log:

1 Trim off larger branches cleanly, with a light axe, if this has not already been done. You can cut through small knots and irregularities with the peeler.

2 Support the pole on a horse or stand, if one is available, or on your axe driven into a stump. This reduces the strain on your back when peeling a lot of logs. Otherwise, peel the logs where they lie on the ground.

If the pole has a kink or curve, peel the bark with the pole in its unstable position first. It is much easier to steady the pole in this position before the bark on the other side has been removed.

3 Stand facing the pole about 1.8m (6') from its butt end. Hold the peeler in both hands with your knuckles on top.

6' (1.8m)

4 Make long, sweeping push strokes with the peeler, running the blade off the end of the pole at each stroke to remove the bark. Peel three quarters of the way around the circumference of the pole.

5 Turn and peel the stem in the other direction. If you have trouble using the tool ambidextrously, step over the pole to use it in a more comfortable position from the other side.

6 Continue peeling until you reach the tip of the pole. Turn the pole (the Swedish peeler has a hook to help in this) and work back toward the butt, taking off the remaining strip of bark.

Small poles and rods

A draw-knife (p66) is the easiest tool for shaving or 'rinding' fairly small-diameter timber. Use the knife with the bevel down, so that it digs into the wood less.

Support the pole on a shaving-brake or post–vice. A very simple shaving-brake can be made from local material.

133

Set the posts into the ground at a convenient height for working, and nail the diagonal braces to hold the posts rigid.

Pull the knife directly towards you, with the blade at right-angles or tilted to the work according to convenience.

Preservation

Timber exposed to the elements is liable to decay by fungi which feed on the timber, in the presence of moisture, oxygen and warmth. Some timbers are naturally durable against fungal attack, because they contain substances which are harmful or toxic to fungi. Treatment of non-durable timbers with a preservative produces the same effect.

Freshly felled timber may contain as much water as wood, and is then described as having a moisture content of 100%. Timber dried to below 20% will not decay as there is insufficient moisture for the fungi to live. However, dried timber that re-absorbs water through rainfall or other means becomes subject to attack. Timber totally immersed in water, or in an impermeable, heavy soil may avoid fungal attack due to lack of oxygen. Fungal growth is most active at around 20 degrees centigrade, and becomes dormant below 5 degrees.

The heartwood and sapwood of any timber differ in their durability, and also their suitability for treating with preservative.

The sapwood is the outer layer of wood, pale in colour and easy to recognise in species which have a dark heartwood, but more difficult to distinguish in pale timbers such as spruce. Sapwood of all species has a low resistance to decay, but is permeable and easy to treat with preservative. Heartwood is the central part of the trunk, and different species vary greatly in their qualities.

The table below shows the natural durability of the heartwood of British native and introduced species.

TABLE 10a BRITISH TIMBERS (HEARTWOOD)

	NATURAL DURABILITY				EASE OF PRESERVATION			
	Durable 15–25 yrs	Moderately durable 10–15 yrs	Non-durable 5–10 yrs	Perishable Less than 5 yrs	Extremely resistant	Resistant	Moderately resistant	Permeable
Alder				*				*
Ash			*				*	
Beech				*				*
Birch				*				*
Cedar, Western Red		*					*	
Douglas Fir			*				*	
Elm, Wych			*				*	
Fir, Grand			*				*	
Hemlock, Western			*					*
Hornbeam				*				*
Horse chestnut				*				*
Larch, European		*					*	
Larch, Japanese		*					*	
Lime				*				*
Oak, European	*				*			
Pine, Lodgepole			*				*	
Pine, Maritime		*					*	
Pine, Scots			*				*	
Poplar, Grey			*				*	
Spruce, European			*				*	
Spruce, Sitka			*				*	
Sweet chestnut	*				*			
Sycamore				*				*
Willow, white				*			*	
Willow, crack				*			*	
Yew	*						*	

The assessment is made by testing standard size posts 50 × 50mm square, partly buried in the ground, and tested over many years. In practice, durability will vary according to the site and weather conditions. Durability is also proportional to the size of the timber, and for example, a post of cross section 100 × 100mm would have twice the life of one 100 × 50mm.

The table also shows the permeability to preservative of different heartwoods. All sapwoods are in the category of either moderately resistant or permeable, and therefore can be effectively treated.

Timber must be dried to 25–30% moisture content before treatment. This is done either in the open air, or in a kiln.

TYPES OF PRESERVATIVE

Creosote

Creosote, a type of tar oil, is a long-established timber preservative treatment. It is very resistant to leaching, so is suitable for exterior timbers, especially those in contact with the ground or water. Creosote does not seriously corrode metals, and once thoroughly dried, treated timber is slightly more fire-resistant than untreated timber. Creosoted timber is unpleasant to handle, particularly in hot weather when it becomes sticky. It has a strong odour and tends to repel insects, birds, bats and some other mammals.

Creosote is available in various shades from light to dark brown, and different grades, according to the method of application. The heavy viscous grades (BS144) are only suitable for pressure treatment. Fluid grades (BS3051) are used for immersion and brush treatment.

Organic solvents

These contain various chemicals dissolved in an organic solvent similar to white spirit. The solvent, which is flammable, carries the preservative into the wood, and as it evaporates, leaves the preservative behind. Once evaporated, the flammability of the wood is not increased. Organic solvents do not contain water, and their use does not cause the wood to swell or distort. They are not suitable for wood in contact with the ground.

Organic solvents are best applied by double vaccuum, but can also be applied by immersion or by brush or spray. They are useful for treating small areas by brush, or where timbers are already fixed in position. Products available include Cuprinol, Celpruf, Solignum and Vacsol.

Waterborne copper chrome arsenate (CCA)

CCA preservatives are odourless, non-staining and non-flammable, and become resistant to leaching

within about a week of treatment. Treated timber has a clean finish of a pale greenish-grey colour, which can be painted or stained. These preservatives can only be applied by vaccuum pressure impregnation. Products include Tanalith, giving 'Tanalised' timber, or Celcure A, which gives 'Celcurised' timber.

APPLICATION METHODS

Commercial methods using pressure and heat are very much more effective than any 'DIY' method of treatment. However, immersion, brushing or spraying may be suitable where only medium-term durability is required, or where the saving in using home-grown and home-treated timber justifies using a less durable product.

Round timber, for example for fencing poles or tree stakes, is the most suitable type of timber for DIY treatment. The outer layer of sapwood is relatively permeable and easy to treat, so this forms a protective layer around the heartwood. Split timbers with non-durable heartwood are difficult to impregnate without pressure treatment.

Timber should be barked (p133), and then stacked for drying on a level, dry site. Cover the top against the rain with a sheet of corrugated iron or similar, well weighted down.

← base of larger logs

Drying time will vary according to the size of the timber, the weather and the time of year. As a guide, 150mm (6″) softwood poles, cut and stacked in autumn or winter, should dry in about 6 months. Wood felled in spring should season in 2–4 months in a dry summer.

The moisture content of the wood can be checked with a special meter that measures the electrical resistance across two steel pins which are pushed into the timber. Alternatively, an estimate can be made by weighing a few sample pieces before and after seasoning. The timber should lose a quarter to one third of its original weight.

Immersion

Immersion treatment can be done using either creosote or an organic solvent preservative. Any suitable tank can be used, according to the length of the timber. This could include old baths, galvanised tanks or oil drums. Arrange it so that the timber is not directly handled, but is lifted in and out of the tank by a hoist, that can transfer the timber to a stand for drying. Alternatively, use slings to move the timber.

Timber should be immersed for at least three minutes. Don't bundle the timber tightly or the flow of preservative will be inhibited. Timbers in a large tank may need pushing down and turning to ensure even coverage. Immersion only results in slight penetration of the timber, and is only suitable for permeable timber. Resistant timbers absorb little even after long periods of immersion.

Penetration of the timber can be increased by using heat. Because direct heating of preservative is dangerous, the method recommended (MAFF, 1977, Fixed Equipment of the Farm 17) is to heat the timber in a tank of water over a fire, to a temperature of 82–93 degrees C. Keep it at this temperature for 1–2 hours, and do not allow it to cool or water will be absorbed. Then quickly remove the timber to a tank of cold preservative, and leave it immersed for another 1–2 hours.

Brush or high pressure spray

These methods are the only way to treat timbers already in place, and can extend the life of less durable timbers by many years if treatment is repeated every few years. They are unsuitable for timbers in contact with the ground.

Keep in mind the following points:

a When ordering preservatives, specify formulations for brush or spray application.

b Treatment is best done during a spell of dry, warm weather.

c Brush or spray the preservative at the rate recommended by the manufacturer. Flood it on the end grain. Apply second and additional coats as soon as the previous coat has soaked in, to keep the preservative flowing into the timber.

d Wear protective gloves and clothing when brushing, and these plus protection for the face when spraying. Pressure sprayers of the type sold for garden use are suitable.

e Repeat the treatment every few years or as soon as the timber shows obvious signs of fading and surface weathering.

Commercial timber preservation

Some processors will treat customers' own timber. Contact local timber processors, listed under 'Timber Impregnation Plants' in the Yellow Pages, or consult the list of members available from the British Wood Preserving Association.

There are three main methods of commercial timber

preservation. The highest standard of protection is given by vaccuum pressure treatment, using either CCA preservative or creosote.

The double vaccuum method is similar, except that less pressure is used than in vaccuum pressure treatment, so the dimensions of the timber are not affected, and the method is therefore useful for accurately cut timbers. This method is only used for organic solvents, and is the best method for this type of preservative.

The hot and cold open tank process is only used for applying creosote. It should not be attempted without the proper facilities, because of the danger involved in heating creosote. The timber is immersed in an open tank of creosote, which is then heated to 90 degrees C, and kept at this temperature for one to three hours. The tank is then left to cool, and as the timber cools it draws in the creosote.

Timber treatment is strictly governed by British Standards and British Wood Preserving Association Standards. CCA and organic-solvent treated timber should always be dried at the processors after treatment, before being supplied to the customer. Organic-solvent treated timber is usually re-dried as part of the double vacuum process. CCA timber should be left to dry for at least 48 hours after treatment, and seven days should elapse before the timber is put where animals could come in contact with it.

Further information on timber preservation is available from the British Wood Preserving Association, including a series of free leaflets on different aspects of timber treatment. In conjunction with the Timber Research and Development Association they publish a booklet 'Timber Preservation'. Another useful booklet is 'The Treatment of Exterior Timber against Decay' (Information Sheet 13.1, Countryside Commission for Scotland, 1983).

Marketing

Marketing of timber is rarely a straightforward business, and requires consideration of many factors, as listed below. Many woodlands which have conservation or amenity value have limitations which make it difficult to harvest timber profitably, which is often the reason why they have remained 'unimproved' and thus ecologically valuable. However, as discussed in chapter 2, a large amount of broadleaved woodland at present unmanaged could be enhanced for conservation and amenity by being managed productively.

In the last few years there have been initiatives in Wales, the South West, East Sussex and other areas to make management of woods, and in particular small broadleaved woods, more viable. If they are not economically viable, the future of many small woods is in jeopardy, as without fencing and replanting regeneration is unlikely. These initiatives include looking at ways of using and marketing low-grade hardwood and small roundwood, which such woods can produce in quantity.

For detailed information on all aspects of marketing timber and underwood see 'A Guide to British Timber Prices and Forestry Costings' (Hart, C E). This contains details of current prices, market conditions, specifications for many products and addresses and requirements of mills and other buyers, plus much other useful information.

Note the following general points on marketing:

Type of material

The species, size and quality of the timber are the main determinants of its value. Large diameter butts of first quality hardwoods are usually marketable (though exceptional conditions such as the 1987 storm can produce a glut), and their value may make it worthwhile extracting them even where access is difficult. Further details are given below. Such quality timber is uncommon, especially in upland Britain, on poor soils or exposed sites, or where there has been no management.

Most timber is in the category of either low-grade sawlogs or small-size roundwood. The value is much lower than for first-quality timber, and whether it can be harvested profitably will depend on the other factors listed below. Many conservation and amenity woodlands, although not managed primarily for profit, need at least to cover costs on such operations as thinning, in order to get the work done at all. Although volunteer groups can do much to make such work viable, often the operation is too large, too skilled, or the time limits too short to make volunteer work possible.

Quantity of material

The quantity of timber becomes more important as the quality lessens. A single top quality butt may be worth selling, but low quality timber needs to be sold in reasonable quantity to make transport and other parts of the operation worth while. For pulp, the normal minimum load is 20 tonnes, or about 20 cubic metres of newly felled timber. As a rough guide, this might be produced by thinning about 0.4 hectare (1 acre) of outgrown coppice. It may be possible to make up a load by combining the harvest from two or more sites.

Alternatively, timber for fencing or firewood can be stockpiled on the site until sufficient quantity has been felled to interest a merchant. Where labour is limited, and the job has to be done over several years, this may be the most viable method of marketing the timber.

Site conditions and access

These are usually the most important factors in determining whether a timber harvest will be commercially viable.

Sloping sites are slower to work than level ground, and extraction is more difficult. Characteristically, small woods or those on sloping ground which have never been worth managing have no tracks or rides giving access within the wood. In contrast, woods with commercial potential have nearly all been exploited in the past, and so have some sort of access through the wood, although it may be very overgrown, blocked or badly drained and impassable.

Access from the wood to the roadside is also very important. If woods are isolated in farmland, it may only be possible to extract timber during dry spells of weather. The development of low-ground pressure vehicles has made it possible to extract timber from previously inaccessible sites, and also to work with the minimum of damage to the soil and woodland flora. However, these machines are only used by specialist contractors, and the cost is high.

Onward transport

Timber extracted to the roadside needs to be stacked in a loading area, preferably on a hard standing, where it will be reasonably secure if left for a short time, and where a lorry can load. Road access must be suitable for the size of lorry collecting the timber. Distance to the mill or other market is important, as profit margins will be reduced as distance increases.

Other considerations

If felling or extraction is limited by conservation or amenity interests, it may be important to do the work at a particular time of year, to avoid damage or disturbance to wildlife.

Timing

How urgent is the work? It may be better to delay thinning or harvesting of mature timber until markets improve or contractors are available to do the job. With windblown timber you may have to make the best of whatever marketing opportunities are available. Fallen pine should be moved immediately to prevent spread of insect pests in conifer plantations. Sycamore, poplar, beech, ash, lime, plane and birch should be moved as soon as possible, as staining and degradation will occur within a few months. Spruce, silver fir, Douglas fir and western hemlock follow in priority, while oaks, sweet chestnut and yew can be left up to five years without degrading.

Finding a buyer

Always do your market research before felling, as markets are constantly changing. Consult the current edition of Hart for market information and addresses of major buyers. Felled sawlogs and veneers must be moved quickly before they deteriorate, and some timber must be felled at particular times of year for best quality results.

A timber crop can be sold either standing, at stump, at rideside, at roadside or by load delivered to the mill. Normally the lower value coppice crops and thinnings are sold as a standing crop to a merchant or contractor, and higher value sawlogs are sold after felling at stump or roadside, where the buyer can inspect the timber in detail.

Selling a standing crop to a contractor means there is less control over the operation, and this may lead to problems on sites which are ecologically sensitive.

Self-sufficiency

There are many ways in which timber can be used within an estate or a land-managing organisation. Opportunity for this increases with larger operations, but this option is worth looking at even for small holdings of woodlands. Uses include large timbers for bridges and building construction, and other timber for fencing and fuel. Some organisations are now using home-produced woodchips as fuel for heating (see below).

QUALITY SAWLOGS

This is the best quality timber which is used for veneers, turnery, sports equipment and furniture. Normally the supplies from this country are very limited, as such timber can only be grown in the more fertile and sheltered areas. Very few quality sawlogs are felled in the timber-producing areas of Wales and Scotland, the main product being conifer sawlogs and thinnings. The storm of October 1987 produced a vast amount of quality timber, including exotic species from parks and gardens, occurring as it did over the heavily wooded south-east of England. However, much of this timber will not be utilised, because the sheer volume means that a lot of the timber will degrade before it can be moved, sawn and stacked. In the immediate aftermath, markets quickly became flooded.

Veneers

The most valuable timbers are cherry, walnut and oak, normally of diameter 40cm (16") and over. Highest prices are for butts over 3m (9'8") in length, but shorter lengths are still valuable. The timber must be free of any defects. Sycamore with 'ripple grain', only rarely found, is prized for musical instrument veneers.

Turnery

This is one of the best markets for small and medium-sized hardwood poles of good quality. Common alder, ash, beech, birch, cherry, hazel, lime and sycamore are the most in demand. Elm, maple, hornbeam, holly and other species may also be marketable.

Sizes required depend on the end use, ranging from pole lengths of 2–4m (6½-13'), usually with 15cm (6") minimum butt diameter, and from 7.5–18cm (3-7") top diameter. Markets include relatively large users for industrial purposes, for example, beech in 2m (6½') lengths and minimum butt diameter 20cm (8") may be marketable for paint and industrial brush handles. Small amounts can be sold to individual craftsmen.

For further information contact the British Wood Turners Association.

Sports equipment

Ash butts of diameter 20–40cm (8–16") and exceptional quality are marketable for hockey sticks, cricket stumps and other sports equipment. The timber must be winter-felled with the sap down, and sold quickly as it is liable to split.

Planking grade

The bulk of quality sawlogs are of this grade, and are used for furniture, joinery and flooring. Examples might include oak butts with occasional epicormics (side branches), but no shake or rot, and of minimum length 2m (6½') and minimum diameter 45cm (18"). Beech should be winter felled and moved, sawn and stacked quickly to avoid stain. Butts of minimum diameter 24cm (9") and random lengths are valuable. Sycamore similarly must be felled and moved quickly in order to keep the 'white' colour. Sweet chestnut is valuable when free of star and ring shake, the latter commonly occurring on trees older than 80 years old grown on soils that are liable to dry out. This effectively prevents the growing of commercial sweet chestnut to mature size in eastern Britain.

SECOND-GRADE SAWLOGS

Traditionally, second-grade hardwoods are used for fencing and mining timber, but both these markets are now changing. Chestnut and oak used to be the main fencing timbers, and although still used for high quality fencing, gates and gateposts, most stakes and rails are now of treated softwood. The National Coal Board has recently upgraded the specification for mining timber, which now has to conform to British Standard 5750, effectively putting much of the second-grade timber into the firewood and pulpwood grade.

Where oak is sold for fencing, the better quality is used for rails, and the rougher material for posts. The minimum diameter is 30cm (12"), in lengths as specified by the mill.

SMALL ROUNDWOOD AND LOW QUALITY TIMBER

This is the type of material which conservation and amenity woodlands are most likely to produce in any quantity. The main markets are for pulp and firewood, with chips for heating becoming more important. Transport costs become very important for this lower value material, and normally distance will dictate the particular end-use. Where woods are near urban areas, direct marketing of firewood is likely to be the most profitable option.

Pulp

Pulp mills require green, fresh–cut material in sizes which they specify; for example 1.22m (4'), 1.8m (6') and 2.3m (7½') lengths, of 5–40cm (2-16") diameter. Usually the minimum load is about 20 tonnes or one trailer-load. Mills may buy standing timber, at roadside or delivered to the mill, with regular supplies attracting premiums. The profit margins are slim, and if for example you are doing the felling and extraction yourself, it will only be profitable if you either have a very low labour charge, or the site conditions allow the work to be done quickly and efficiently by paid labour. If the mill does the cutting and extraction, they will take the working conditions into account when setting the price, and will be unlikely to work sites with slopes or poor access. For further information and details of mills contact the British Wood Pulp Association.

Firewood

The firewood market is not organised in any way, and is an uncertain basis on which to make decisions about long-term woodland management. Typically, firewood is the answer to getting rid of windblown timber, dead trees and 'waste' timber from other felling operations. Few woods are managed mainly to produce firewood. The arrangement whereby contractors come in and extract timber for firewood has tended to be regarded with suspicion, because of the difficulty of accurately measuring the quantity extracted, and of agreeing a price in the absence of any guidelines. Also, unless contractors regularly work the same pieces of woodland, there is little incentive for them to do the work carefully with minimal damage. A better arrangement is possibly where the contractor does the extraction as a no-cost remedial thinning, with the operation done to the standard specified by the owner.

The onset of Dutch Elm Disease and resulting glut of firewood encouraged the market in wood-burning stoves. This has improved the situation, as there is now a regular demand from stove-owners. However, as with the pulp market, profit margins are low, and an honest contractor dealing in firewood has to operate very efficiently to stay in business. Operators coming in and selling one-off loads can undercut a regular supplier.

Where owners do their own felling and extraction, firewood can be sold wholesale by the cord (p128) to fuel merchants and fencing contractors. With a roadside outlet or by local advertising, cut and split firewood can be sold direct to the public, or bagged and sold through garages, garden centres and so on. 'Rideside marketing' is another possibility where the right conditions exist, namely that of a suitable site fairly close to an urban area. The timber is extracted to the rideside and prepared either for firewood or other purposes, and is advertised for sale to the public by fixed price or auction on a particular day. Good prices can be obtained, but the site must be secure enough for material to be stored up to the advertised date and be suitable for numbers of vehicles, with transport to be arranged for larger quantities. The timber may either be sold by volume measure or 'as seen'.

Ash, beech, birch, hawthorn, hornbeam and oak are some of the best woods for fuel, with alder, poplar and willow the least efficient. What little dead elm now remains is mostly rotten and not worth burning. The species can affect the value if sold wholesale, but in practice few retail customers will bother to distinguish them. Where firewood is sold by weight, it is advantageous for the seller to sell as quickly as possible, to minimise weight loss due to seasoning. Contractors will normally have to cut, extract and sell immediately, both to save handling and storage and to speed their cash flow. Where firewood is sold by the cord or other volume measure, the weight loss is less significant for the seller, though the logistics of storing and handling as well as cash flow may still dictate a quick sale. Firewood burns more efficiently if left to season for a few months, so the wise stove-owner will purchase well in advance of need!

Woodchips

Woodchips can be made by putting any sort of timber, thinnings or 'lop and top' through a wood-chipping machine. The woodchips can be used for a variety of purposes including surfacing for paths and riding arenas, animal bedding, and increasingly as a fuel for special boilers. To save on handling, the chipper can either be towed out on site to convert material immediately after felling, or for example operated near a boiler to convert timber being brought in from various locations. The chipper has a chute which expels the chips direct into a high-sided trailer or hopper.

Chippers are being used increasingly by local authorities, as they are an efficient way of reducing bulky prunings and other waste from roadside trees, parks and other open spaces, which can then simply be moved as trailer-loads of woodchips. By installing suitable boilers, the woodchips can then be used as fuel for heating greenhouses and other buildings.

Woodchips can also be a useful way of combining woodland management with the need to heat large country houses. For example, West Dean College in Sussex has operated a woodchip system successfully for over seven years. Through the year about 1000 tonnes of wood produced in various sites around the estate is cut into 2m lengths. This is then extracted by a fowarder, loaded each day-end for its 'home run' to minimise transport costs. The lengths are then fed as required into the chipper which is kept by the boiler house, and expels the chips direct into the stoker bin. The chipping operation is estimated to take about 43 days per year for a 2 man gang, with much of this in winter during bad weather when other work is limited. As well as being cost-effective as a fuel, the woodchip system has the advantage of being a self-sufficent fuel supply, giving a guaranteed market for small thinnings, and encouraging proper woodland management. There are various chippers and boilers on the market, including some British-made, though most of the technology is Scandinavian.

Charcoal

Charcoal is formed by burning wood in conditions where there is insufficient air for efficient combustion. In order of preference, the best species for charcoal are beech, birch, hornbeam, oak, ash and elm. Earth kilns, portable or fixed kilns are used. Companies with portable kilns usually require at least 300 cords, which yields about 60 tons of charcoal, to set up in any area. In recent years production of charcoal in Britain has remained static, although demand has increased, partly through the popularity of charcoal-fuelled barbecues. Weight for weight, charcoal is substantially more efficient than coal, as well as being a renewable resource, and with large modern kilns, could be a viable industrial and domestic fuel. The 'Charcoal for Energy Project' run by Dr Young of Reading University is researching kiln design, as well as managing an area of woodland as a pilot production scheme. See also Driver, C (1985) for a discussion of charcoal production problems and costings.

Coppice products and greenwood crafts

See page 157 for a summary of the main coppice species, rotations and various uses. Coppice of appropriate size and quality can be used for many of the purposes discussed under other headings. Additional uses, for which coppice is especially suited, are listed below. The term 'greenwood crafts' encompasses various ways of using freshly cut, unseasoned wood such as hurdles, simple tools and furniture. The best way of learning these skills is by demonstration and practice. Several courses are run each year by the BTCV, who should be contacted for details.

a Crate rods, using hazel from 2–3.5m (7–12') or more in length, and 12–50mm ($\frac{1}{2}$–2") butt diameter.

b Hurdles. Wattle hurdles use hazel from 3–4.5m (10–15') in length and from 12–50mm ($\frac{1}{2}$–2") butt diameter, round or cleft. Gate hurdles use cleft poles of ash, sweet chestnut, oak or willow (and Douglas Fir – though not a coppice species).

c Thatching spars and other material (p158). In eastern counties, most thatchers prefer their material round, and of random lengths up to 50mm (2") butt diameter, from which they prepare their own spars, liggers and sways as required. In southern counties most thatchers prefer to buy their materials made up ready for use by underwood craftsmen.

d Baskets, using osier willow, hazel and oak.

e Hedging stakes and binders. Stakes can be made from any appropriate pole, but in the Midlands ash and hazel are preferred, 1.4–1.5m ($4\frac{1}{2}$–5') long and 40–50mm ($1\frac{1}{2}$–2") top diameter. Stakes should be made up into bundles of twenty for sale. Many hedgers prefer to cut their own stakes and binders, the latter being usually of hazel, 2.5–3m (8–10') long and about 25mm (1") in diameter at the base.

f Pea sticks (p159) and bean poles (p159). These can provide quite a good source of income, especially if sold direct to local allotment societies which can establish a regular order. Very often the pea sticks can be cut from the tops of the bean poles, with minimal waste. The only trouble is that derelict coppice tends to have large, umbrella-shaped tops and large bent poles so that it takes time to find suitable straight live poles with tops that have grown more or less in one plane. Once the coppice is restored, harvesting on a fairly short rotation should be easy.

g Stakes for tree planting.

Bark

Chipped or peeled bark of softwood species has a number of horticultural and estate uses, as mulch, potting and growing medium, and surfacing for paths. All these uses are increasing, particularly where bark can be used as a substitute for peat, supplies of which are dwindling. This market is only suitable for commercial softwoods, as large amounts are needed to make transport and treatment worthwhile. Bark should always be stacked and composted before being used as a mulch or surfacing material. For further details see Forestry Commission Forest Record 110 (1982).

Oak bark was traditionally the main source of tannin used by the leather industries. The best leather is still tanned with oak, although only two tanneries follow traditional methods. These are J & FJ Baker & Co Ltd, Colyton, Devon, and J Croggan & Son Ltd, Manor Tannery, Grampound, Cornwall. Tanbark is sold by the tonne, with better prices for dried than fresh bark. The bark should be harvested from April to early June, which is the only time it will peel freely. Most of the tannin is in the inner bast layers, so the thin bark of young stems (eg coppice poles and branchwood) is worth more than the bark of larger trees. The underside of the bark must be kept dry after harvesting to prevent leaching of the tannin. See Edlin (1973) for details.

Other uses

Other uses include such diverse products as faggots for coastal defence, lop and top for sand dune protection, poles for horse jumps, and wood ash, which is used by potteries. Wood ash is worth considering as it is easy to deal with, needing no treatment other than bagging to protect it from the rain, and its disposal helps to reduce unwanted soil enrichment on bonfire sites.

Additional minor uses include Christmas trees and foliage. Norway spruce is the most popular Christmas tree species, but the tops or small thinnings of Douglas fir, noble fir and other conifers can often be sold to garden centres and shops, or direct from the roadside. Sitka spruce should not be used because its prickly needles can be dangerous to children. Sprays of western red cedar, Lawson cypress, sallow, spindle, rowan, box, ivy and at Christmas, holly can be sold as foliage to local florists.

New initiatives

A major initiative into developing the uses of small roundwood is the development of The School for Woodland Industry at Hooke Park, near Beaminster in Dorset. This is part of the Parnham Trust, founded by the craftsman and designer John Makepeace. The School for Woodland Industry is developing ways of using small roundwood as the raw material for the design and manufacture of buildings, bridges, furniture, woodware and many other products. The aim is to bring new value to the large and greatly underused resource of small roundwood, and to improve woodland management by making thinning and coppicing viable operations. The School has been constructed using roundwood of 5–20cm diameter cut from the woodland within which it stands, with many new techniques developed during the construction phase. The first intake of students is in 1989, and both the School and the working woodland surrounding it are open to visitors at certain times.

TRADA (Timber Research and Development Association) are also looking at ways of utilising small roundwood, including EGAR (Edge Glue and Rip) and glue-lamination techniques, which allow greater use of small hardwood timbers.

Conservation and the Volunteer Worker

The British Trust for Conservation Volunteers aims to promote the use of volunteers on conservation tasks. In addition to organising work projects it is able, through its affiliation and group schemes, to offer advice and help with insurance cover, tool purchase and practical technical training.

To ensure the success of any conservation task it is important that the requesting person or agency, the volunteer and the leader all understand their particular responsibilities and roles. All voluntary work should be undertaken in the spirit of the Universal Charter of Volunteer Service, drawn up by the UNESCO Coordinating Committee for International Voluntary Service. Three of its most important points are:

1 'The work to be done should be a real need in its proper context and be directly related to a broad framework of development'. In terms of conservation, this means that tasks should be undertaken as integral parts of site management plans, not as isolated exercises. Work should never be undertaken solely for the benefit of the volunteer. Necessary follow-up work after tasks should be planned beforehand to ensure that volunteer effort is not wasted.

2 'The task should be a suitable assignment for a volunteer'. Volunteers cannot successfully tackle all types of work and they should be not be used where there is a risk of serious accident or injury, where a financial profit will be made from their labours, where the job is so large that their efforts will have little overall effect, where the skills required are beyond their capabilities so that a bad job results and they become dispirited, or where machines can do the same job more efficiently and for a lower cost.

3 'Voluntary service should not replace paid local labour'. It should complement such work, not supplant it. Employers should make sure in advance that the position of volunteers and paid workers is clear with respect to any relevant labour unions. Further advice may be found in 'Guidelines for the relationships between volunteers and paid non-professional workers', published by the Volunteer Centre, 29 Lower King's Road, Berkhamstead, Hertfordshire HP4 2AB.

Volunteers are rarely 'free labour'. Someone has to pay for transport, materials, tools, insurance, refreshments and any accommodation charges.

Before each party makes a commitment to a project it should be clear who is to pay for what. While volunteers may willingly fund their own work, 'user bodies' should be prepared to contribute and should not assume that all volunteers, who are already giving their time and effort, will be able to meet other expenses out of their own pockets. Several grant-aiding bodies may help pay the cost of environmental and conservation projects, notably the Nature Conservancy Council, the World Wildlife Fund and the Countryside Commissions. Details may be found in 'A guide to grants by the Department of the Environment and associated bodies for which voluntary organisations may be eligible', available from The Department of the Environment, Room C15/11, 2 Marsham Street, London SW1P 3EB.

It is important that volunteer workers be covered by some sort of public liability insurance for any damage or injury they may cause to property or to the public. Cover up to £250,000 is recommended. Volunteers should also be covered against personal accident.

The volunteer group organiser should visit the work site well before the task, to check that the project is suitable and that volunteers will not be exploited and to plan the best size of working party and the proper tools and equipment. Volunteers should be advised in advance on suitable clothing for the expected conditions. They should be physically fit and come prepared for work and they should genuinely want to volunteer – those 'pressganged' into service are likely to work poorly, may do more harm than good and may be put off a good cause for life! Young volunteers need more supervision and are best suited to less strenuous jobs where achievements are clearly visible, and it is recommended that where they are involved the task should emphasise education. Note that the Agriculture (Avoidance of Accidents to Children) Regulations, 1958, legally restrict the riding on and driving of agricultural machines, vehicles or implements by children under 13 years.

Volunteer group organisers and 'user bodies' both should keep records of the work undertaken: the date of the project, jobs done, techniques used, number of volunteers and details of any notable events including accidents, unusual 'finds', publicity etc. Such information makes it easier to handle problems or queries which may arise after the task. It also provides a background on the task site for future visits, supplies practical data by which the site management plan can be evaluated and allows an assessment to be made of the volunteer effort.

Stand Groups

This section gives descriptions of the 12 different 'stand groups' or types of semi-natural woodland as classified by George Peterken. An explanation of the classification and the key to identifying stand groups are given on page 22. For further information see 'Woodland Conservation and Management' (Peterken, 1981).

Group 1 Ash–wych elm woodland

These woods contain wych elm and usually contain ash, hazel and common hawthorn, the ash often being far more abundant than the elm. Alder, beech, hornbeam, Scots pine and suckering elms are always absent. Birch species are infrequent. Most of these woods have been coppiced.

1A Calcareous ash–wych elm woods. These are found on medium to heavy calcareous soils, and are especially characteristic of woods on carboniferous limestone in England and Wales. Elder is frequently found. Pedunculate oak is characteristic.

1B Wet ash–wych elm woods. Found on heavy, poorly-draining soils or medium-textured flushed soils, usually neutral, on flat sites. Pedunculate oak is characteristic.

1C Calcareous ash–wych elm woods on dry or heavy soils. This category is used for woods that don't fit in the above three categories.

1D Western valley ash–wych elm woods. On light to medium textured, free-draining, acid to neutral soils. Normally occur in the flushed zones along streams and at the bottom of slopes of birch–oak wood. Sessile oak is associated, holly and rowan are common. These woods are especially characteristic of the acid uplands of England and Wales.

Group 2 Ash–maple woodland

These stands always contain field maple and usually contain ash, common hawthorn, hazel and pedunculate oak. Alder, beech, elm, hornbeam, lime and pine are absent. Elder, blackthorn, midland hawthorn and honeysuckle are common, whilst birches are infrequent. Most of these woods have been managed as coppiced ash, hazel and maple, with pedunculate oak and, less often, ash standards. Ash and oak dominate the canopy of neglected coppices.

2A Wet ash–maple woods. Found on heavy, poorly-drained, mildly acid to alkaline soils. In a few woods ash is very rare.

2B Ash–maple woods on light soils. Most of these have heavy subsoils. Elder is abundant, midland hawthorn and rose are rare.

2C Dry ash–maple woods. These are found on medium to heavy free-draining soils, mainly on chalk and limestone. Spindle, ivy and holly are frequent, aspen, elder and midland hawthorn are rare.

Group 3 Hazel–ash woodland

These are stands containing ash, but not maple, alder, beech, elm, lime, hornbeam or Scots pine. Almost all stands contain hazel, which is often more abundant than ash. Most stands contain birch, common hawthorn, honeysuckle and oak.

3A Acid pedunculate oak–hazel–ash woods. These are found on strongly acid, heavy, poorly draining soils. Common hawthorn, birch and honeysuckle are common. Most stands have been managed as hazel–ash coppice with oak standards.

3B Southern calcareous hazel–ash woods. These are found on calcareous soils, with pedunculate oak associated.

3C Northern calcareous hazel–ash woods. These are found on calcareous soils, with sessile oak associated although uncommon. Birch, rowan and yew are often present.

3D Acid sessile oak–hazel–ash woods. Generally found on strongly acid flushes which are too base–poor for stand type 1D to develop. Blackthorn, elder and pedunculate oak are usually absent.

Group 4 Ash–lime woodland

Stands containing lime and ash, almost always containing birch, common hawthorn, hazel, honeysuckle and oak, with roses frequent. Alder, beech, elm, hornbeam and Scots pine are absent.

4A Acid birch–ash–lime woods. These stands occur on poorly-draining, acid soils. Most tree and shrub species are absent or rare apart from birch, common hawthorn, hazel, honeysuckle and pedunculate oak. Birch has appeared with the neglect of coppicing.

4B Maple–ash–lime woods. These are similar to type 4A, except that field maple is present and the soil is neutral or alkaline.

4C Sessile oak–ash–lime woods. These are tree-species rich communities found on very dry sites over limestone.

Group 5 Oak–lime woodland

Stands of lime, very frequently containing birch, hazel, honeysuckle and oak, but without alder, ash, beech, elm, hornbeam, maple or Scots pine. They occur on strongly acid medium-light textured soils.

5A Acid pedunculate oak–lime woods. These contain little or no sessile oak. Most stands have been managed as lime, hazel and birch coppice, with oak and rarely, lime or birch standards. They mainly grow on plateaux or in valleys where a free-draining light topsoil overlies a heavy subsoil.

5B Acid sessile oak–lime woods. These contain little or no pedunculate oak. They have generally been managed as lime, hazel and oak coppice with oak standards. They mainly grow on free-draining, light, acid soils. Ivy, holly, wild service tree and yew are characteristic.

Group 6 Birch-oak woodland

These are stands that contain one or both native oak species and, usually, birch. Holly, rowan and honeysuckle are commonly found. Alder, ash, beech, maple, elm, lime, hornbeam and Scots pine are absent, although beech and Scots pine are often found because of planting. Birch–oak woods may develop out of oak–beech woods because of beech's lack of vigour when coppiced. In other places they may have developed where lime has failed to recolonise after the disturbance of primeval oak–lime woods. They occur on strongly acid, light to medium-textured soils, mostly free-draining. Most birch–oak woods have been managed as coppice. Those with hazel coppice usually have oak standards, but many of the oak coppices of the North and West lack standards.

6A Upland sessile oakwoods. Birch-oakwoods in upland Britain, containing sessile but not pedunculate oak. Birch, holly, honeysuckle and rowan usually present.

6B Upland pedunculate oakwoods. Birch–oakwoods containing pedunculate oak, though sessile oak may also be present. Birch, honeysuckle and rowan are usually present, but holly is less frequent than in type 6A.

6C Lowland sessile oakwoods. Birch–oakwoods containing sessile oak, but pedunculate oak may also be present. Birch and holly are usually present, and wild cherry is recorded only in this type. Many stands which would naturally conform to this type have been converted to sweet chestnut coppice, especially in Kent.

6D Lowland pedunculate oakwoods. Birch–oak woodland in lowland Britain containing pedunculate oak, but not sessile oak. Birch is usually present, with holly infrequent.

Group 7 Alder woodland

The alder grows throughout Britain on sites that are permanently or seasonally wet but not stagnant. This group consists of all woods that contain alder. Most stands contain ash and hazel.

7A Valley alderwoods on mineral soils. Stands usually contain hairy birch, hazel and pedunculate oak. Alder is generally in the minority. The soils are light to medium textured, but can be from strongly acid through to alkaline.

7B Wet valley alderwoods. These grow where the water table is high and therefore the alder is dominant and other species, except grey willow, grow poorly or not at all. The soil is usually neutral to alkaline.

7C Plateau alderwoods. These are on flat plateau positions, generally with a seasonally high water table and strongly acid to alkaline soils. Ash, hairy birch, pedunculate oak and grey willow are present in most stands.

7D Slope alderwoods. These are found mainly in the North and West on moist, flushed slopes with medium-textured, acid soils. Most examples contain ash and hazel, while ivy, honeysuckle and grey willow are rare.

7E Bird cherry–alder woods. Valley alderwoods containing bird cherry.

Group 8 Beech woodland

Within its native range beech occurs on both acid and calcareous soils, mostly light to medium textured. It is rare on neutral soils. It is usually associated with holly and oak. The occurrence of beech has been strongly affected by management, being suppressed by coppicing, but favoured by pasture-woodland and often planted for timber.

8A Acid sessile oak–beech woods. Birch, ivy, holly, honeysuckle and rowan are common. Ash is absent and other species are rare or absent. They are confined to light, free-draining, strongly acid soils with deep humus.

8B Acid pedunculate oak–beech woods. These are similar to 8A, except that sessile oak is absent and ivy is rare.

8C Calcareous pedunculate oak–ash–beech woods. These are found on free-draining soils, especially chalk and limestone slopes. Honeysuckle is infrequent.

8D Acid pedunculate oak–ash–beech woods. On heavy, mildly acid to neutral soils, usually on plateaux over chalk.

8E Sessile oak–ash–beech woods. Occur mainly in South Wales on light, free-draining soils, both acid and calcareous. Birch and honeysuckle are common. Rowan is absent.

Group 9 Hornbeam woodland

This group includes all woodlands containing hornbeam. The main associated species are hairy birch, hazel, honeysuckle and oak. Hornbeam coppices vigorously, but casts such dense shade that it is infrequently grown as a standard. The coppice has little field layer. It grows mainly on poorly drained soils.

9A Pedunculate oak–hornbeam woods. These are found mainly on medium to heavy textured, acid soils. Hairy birch, hazel and honeysuckle are found in most stands, ash and maple in some, particularly on heavier and less acid soils. Sessile oak is absent. ·

9B Sessile oak–hornbeam woods. These woods are found either on strongly acid or alkaline soils, but rarely on intermediate ones. Hairy birch is common, along with hazel, honeysuckle and ivy.

Group 10 Suckering elm woodlands

Suckering elms, which includes English and smooth-leaved elms, but not wych elm, rarely reproduce by seed, but they have been widely planted and have spread into many woods by suckering. They are generally found on moist, medium to heavy, nutrient-rich soils.

10A Invasive elm woods. A broad category including most suckering elm woods.

10B Valley elm woods. A category based on one wood in this country although it is common in Europe. It is a mixture of elm forms, not just a few clones, which have not recently invaded. Reproduction is by seed as well as sucker.

Group 11 Pine woodland

Stands containing Scots pine as a long established native species. Birch is usually present and rowan and juniper are common. Pine is generally found on light, free-draining, strongly acid soils, although it can thrive on calcareous soils. They are natural only in the Scottish highlands.

11A Acid birch–pine woods. These occur on coarse-textured acid podsolic soils. Oak is absent.

11B Acid oak–pine woods. These are found on thin, coarse-textured acid soils.

Birch woodland

This group includes all woods containing birch, but none of the species characteristic of other groups. They are widespread, particularly on free-draining sands or peat. They occur as seral woodland over most of Britain, but form climax stands in the north beyond the range of other species.

Species Tables

Common and Scientific Names

The table which follows lists the common and scientific names of all tree and shrub species mentioned in the Handbook. An asterisk (*) before the name indicates an introduced species.

Common name	Scientific name
Alder, common or black	*Alnus glutinosa*
*Alder, grey	*Alnus incana*
Alder buckthorn	*Frangula alnus*
Ash	*Fraxinus excelsior*
Aspen	*Populus tremula*
Beech	*Fagus sylvatica*
Birch, dwarf	*Betula nana*
Birch, hairy; white or downy	*Betula pubescens*
Birch, silver or warty	*Betula pendula*
Bittersweet	*Solanum dulcamara*
Blackthorn (Sloe)	*Prunus spinosa*
Bog myrtle (Sweet gale)	*Myrica gale*
Box	*Buxus sempervirens*
Bramble	*Rubus fruticosus* agg
Broom	*Sarothamnus scoparius (Cytisus scoparius)*
Buckthorn, purging	*Rhamnus cathartica*
Buckthorn, sea	*Hippophae rhamnoides*
*Cedar, western red	*Thuja plicata*
*Cedar of Lebanon	*Cedrus libani*
Cherry, bird	*Prunus padus*
Cherry, wild (Gean)	*Prunus avium*
*Cherry laurel	*Prunus laurocerasus*
*Chestnut, horse	*Aesculus hippocastanum*
*Chestnut, sweet or Spanish	*Castanea sativa*
Clematis (Old man's beard; Traveller's joy)	*Clematis vitalba*
Crab apple	*Malus sylvestris*
Currant, red	*Ribes rubra (R sylvestra)*
*Cypress, Lawson	*Chamaecyparis lawsoniana*
Dogwood	*Cornus sanguinea*
Elder	*Sambucus nigra*
Elm, common; field or English	*Ulmus procera*
*Elm, Cornish	*Ulmus carpinifolia* var *cornubiensis*
*Elm, smooth-leaved	*Ulmus carpinifolia*
Elm, wych	*Ulmus glabra*
*Fir, Douglas	*Pseudotsuga menzeisii*
*Fir, grand or giant silver	*Abies grandis*
*Fir, noble	*Abies procera*
Gorse (Furze; Whin)	*Ulex europaeus*
Guelder-rose	*Viburnum opulus*
Hawthorn, common	*Crataegus monogyna*
Hawthron, Midland or woodland	*Crataegus oxyacanthoides (C laevigata)*
Hazel	*Corylus avellana*
Heather (Ling)	*Calluna vulgaris*
*Hemlock, western	*Tsuga heterophylla*
Holly	*Ilex aquifolium*
Honeysuckle	*Lonicera periclymenum*
Hornbeam	*Carpinus betulus*
Ivy	*Hedera helix*

Common name	Scientific name
Juniper	Juniperus communis
*Larch, European	Larix decidua
*Leycesteria	Leycesteria spp
*Lime, common	Tilia x europaea (T vulgaris)
Lime, large-leaved	Tilia platyphyllos
Lime, small-leaved	Tilia cordata
*Locust (False acacia; Robinia)	Robinia pseudoacacia
Maple, field or common	Acer campestre
*Maple, Norway	Acer platanoides
*Oak, holm or evergreen	Quercus ilex
Oak, pedunculate or English	Quercus robur
Oak, sessile or durmast	Quercus petraea
*Oak, Turkey	Quercus cerris
*Pear, wild	Pyrus pyraster (P communis)
*Pine, Austrian	Pinus nigra nigra (P n austriaca)
*Pine, Corsican	Pinus nigra maritima (P n calabrica)
*Pine, lodgepole or shore	Pinus contorta
Pine, Scots	Pinus sylvestris
*Pine, stone	Pinus pinea
*Plane, London	Platanus x hispanica
*Plum	Prunus cerasifera
Poplar, black	Populus nigra var betulifolia
*Poplar, grey	Populus canescens
*Poplar, white	Populus alba
Privet, common	Ligustrum vulgare
*Rhododendron	Rhododendron ponticum
Rose, dog	Rosa canina
Rose, field	Rosa arvensis
Rowan (Mountain ash)	Sorbus aucuparia
*Sequoia (California or coast redwood)	Sequoia sempervirens
Service tree, wild	Sorbus torminalis
*Snowberry	Symphoricarpus spp
Spindle	Euonymus europaeus
*Spruce, Norway	Picea abies
*Spruce, Sitka	Picea sitchensis
Spurge laurel	Daphne laureola
*Sycamore	Acer pseudoplatanus
*Walnut	Juglans spp
Wayfaring tree	Viburnum lantana
*Wellingtonia	Sequoiadendron giganteum
Whitebeam	Sorbus aria
Willow, bay	Salix pentandra
Willow, crack	Salix fragilis
Willow, creeping	Salix repens
*Willow, cricket bat	Salix alba var coerulea
Willow, goat or pussy (Sallow)	Salix caprea
Willow, grey (Sallow)	Salix cinerea
Willow, osier	Salix viminalis
Willow, white	Salix alba
Yew	Taxus baccata

Native Trees and Shrubs

The table on the following pages includes commonly managed native species of trees and shrubs over 5' (1.5m) tall, excluding climbers. Some species have been included which, though rarely planted, have considerable habitat value and should be encouraged when possible. Information is from a variety of sources, written and verbal, relying where possible on the experience of conservation land managers.

NOTES FOR TABLE HEADINGS

Size and growth Size = normal maximum height in Britain (+) = fast grower in good conditions, (−) = slow grower.

Tolerance C = tolerates cutting, D = tolerates or prefers damp soil (usually with some flow of soil water), E = tolerates exposure, F = tolerates spring frosts, O = tolerates sea wind, P = tolerates smoke or air pollution, S = tolerates or prefers shade, V = grows in a wide variety of soils, I = infertile dry soil.

Preferred conditions L = light demanding, T = frost tender (damaged by late spring frosts), W = wind firm.

Management notes A = availability, A1 – freely in a range of sizes, A2 – in a restricted range of sizes, A3 – from some nurseries, A4 – from specialist growers only, A5 – may be in short supply; B = attractive bark; C = varieties, cultivars or related species available in columnar (fastigiate) form; E = suitable for elm replacement; F = showy flowers or fruit; f = showy autumn foliage; H = suitable for use in livestock hedges; I = invasive; P = easily propagated, c – by cuttings, l – layering, s – seeds, x – by suckers or stooling; S = suitable for use in shelterbelts or amenity hedges; T = major timber use in Britain; t = limited or specialised timber use in Britain; U = suitable for urban use (eg in confined spaces, near buidings, along streets or in polluted conditions); W = varieties, cultivars or related species available in weeping (pendulous) form.

Comments The abbreviations 'N', 'S', 'SE' etc refer to general regions of Britain, but distributions cannot be indicated precisely in the limited space. See Perring and Walters (1962) for details.

NOTES FOR TABLE

1 Do not plant poplars near buildings due to damage by roots.

2 Evergreen or semi-evergreen broadleaved species.

3 This species is replaced by smooth-leaved elm as the common hedgerow and woodland elm in East Anglia and East Kent, and by the Cornish elm in parts of the West. Wee Jobling and Mitchell (1974) for identification of elm species.

4 This species, *Pyrus pyraster*, is probably feral rather than truly wild. The wild pear, *P cordata*, is one of Britain's rarest native trees.

5 'Summer' willow, bearing flowers during or after coming into leaf.

6 'Spring' willow, bearing flowers before the leaves appear. An important early spring food source for bees and other pollinating insects.

Name	Size & growth	Tolerance	Preferred conditions	Management notes	Comments
Conifers					
Juniper	20′ (6m)	O	Chalk, limestone, brown earths, acid or dry soils	(C, Pcs, U) Bird, insect food (fruit), nest cover, deer browse	Mainly SE, N Eng + Scot birch & pine woods. Poor regeneration. Berries flavour gin.
Pine, Scots	80′ (24m) (−)	EFIV	(LW) Light or sandy soil or acid peat if drained, low rain; tolerant	(A1, B, Ps, S, T, U) Best conifer for wildlife	Useful nurse. Often regenerates naturally where protected from grazing, but susceptible to exposure to sea wind.
Yew	45′ (14m) (−)	EPSV	Mainly chalk, limestone but tolerates all but very acid soil	(C, Pcs, S, U, W) Bird food (fruit), nest sites, deer browse	Good windbreak or clipped hedge, but poisonous to stock. Best planted small. Casts dense shade.
Broadleaved					
Alder, common	73′ (22m) (+)	CDEPSV	Hardy. Any damp soil (best if flushed) except very acid	(A1, E, I, Ps, S, t, U) Bird food (seed), nests, insect habitat	Often coppiced. Stands flooding, helps stabilise banks. Fixes nitrogen, improves soil. Voles eat bark.
Alder buckthorn	20′ (6m)	CD	Damp peats to acid sands in lowland fens & woods	(Ps, t) Bird and small mammal food (fruit)	Brimstone butterfly food. Once widely copiced for fuse charcoal.
Ash	90′ (28m) (+)	CDEOPSV	(LTW) Best in deep calcareous loams	(A1, E, Ps, T, U, W) Bird & small mammal food (seeds)	Profitable but difficult as timber tree. Good coppice. Avoid in gardens, cultivated areas because surface rooting and freely naturally regenerating. Good deadwood.
Aspen	80′ (24m) (+)	DEOPS	(L) Hardy. Heavy clay, damp fertile soils	(A3, I, Pcx, S, t, U, W) Good gen wildlife value, deer browse	Pioneer or nurse for upland shelterbelts but timber seldom good in Britain. Bushy on poor soil. Suckers freely[1].
Beech	90′ (28m)	CEPS	(TW) Any soil but peat, heavy clay	(A15, C, E, f, H, Ps, S, T, U, W) Bird and small mammal food (seeds)	Good for underplanting. Needs nurse on exposed sites. Bark disease and grey squirrel damage serious in some areas. Good park tree.
Birch, hairy	60′ (18m) (+)	CDEPV	Tolerant but especially on poorly drained peat and heath soils	(A1, Ps) Invertebrate habitat; bird food (seeds)	Good nurse. Best in groups. Major fen, heath, felled-wood invader but sometimes hard to establish on sites which have not carried trees.

Name	Size & growth	Tolerance	Preferred conditions	Management notes	Comments
Birch, silver	60' (18m) (+)	CDEFIPV	(LW) Prefers light soils in drier parts of country but very tolerant	(A1, B, C, f, I, Ps, S, t, U, W) As for hairy birch	As for hairy birch.
Blackthorn	10' (3m) (+)	EOPV	Calcareous to neutral soil	(I, H, Plsx, S) Insect food esp butterflies	Good for hedges but suckers invasively. Important scrub coloniser.
Box[2]	18' (5.5m)	O	Chalk, limestone or neutral soil	(F, Pcs, S, t) Bird nest cover	Local native but widely planted in S. Cover for game.
Broom	6' (2m)	E	(L) Neutral to acid sandy	(F, Ps, S) Insects esp butterflies	Useful nurse for conifers and to bind unstable slopes and improve poor soil.
Buckthorn, purging	15' (4.5m)	D	Calcareous, mainly damp but also drier sites	(A4, Pcls) Butterfly food plant	
Buckthorn, sea	20' (6m)	DEIO	Poor sandy soil near coast & deep soil over chalk	(I, Psx, S) Winter bird food (berries)	Good seaside hedge mixed with blackthorn but often very invasive. See Ranwell (1972).
Cherry, bird	45' (14m)	P	OK on clay; best on shallow soil over chalk, neutral to acid well-drained loams	(E, F, Plsx, U, W) Insects. Bird food (fruit)	Mainly N, in field margins and open woods. Good mixer when planted in thin woodlands.
Cherry, wild	50' (15m) (+)	PV	Fertile woodland soils esp on chalk; also clay, deep acid soils. Tolerant	(A1, C, E, F, f, Plsx, S, t, U, W) Bird food (fruit)	Mainly S. Tolerates same shade, suitable for shelterbelt margins or mixed with oak or beech.
Crab apple	20' (6m)	PV	Any soil, incl calcareous	(C, F, Psx, W) Insects. Birds, small mammal food (fruit)	Throughout, but less common in C, N Scot. Edible fruit (jam).
Dogwood	10' (3m)	CS	Calcareous or neutral soils, lowland woods	(A1, I, Pclsx) Bird nest cover	Mainly Eng, W Wales but also S Scot. Invasive in downlands.
Elder	20' (6m)	CEO	Lowland woods, scrub, disturbed phosphatic calcareous to neutral loams	(C, F, I, Pcs) Insects (flowers), bird food (fruit), early nests	Invasive in hedges. Edible berries (jam, wine).
Elm, common	110' (33m)	CEFOPV	(L) Any ordinary soil, esp fertile free-draining deep loams	(A3, C, f, Px, S, t) Bird nest cover. Insects, esp butterflies	Mainly Midlands and S, in hedgerows. Much reduced by Dutch elm disease. Branches liable to fall without warning[3].

Species	Height	Code	Soil	Wildlife/uses	Notes
Elm, wych	100′ (30m) (+)	COPS	(W) As for common elm	(A3, C, Ps, S, t, U, W) As for common elm	Thrives in woods, hilly country and near water, esp N & W valleys. Slightly less disease-prone than common elm. Non-suckering.
Gorse	8′ (2.5m) (−)	EIO	(L) Dry sandy, neutral or acid soils, lowland scrub	(A3, F, I, Ps) Insects, bird nesting cover. Burns readily	Stands extreme wind, salt spray. Useful fodder. _U galii_ and _U minor_ similar but dwarf and limited to W.
Guelder-rose	15′ (4.5m)	CDE	Lowland woods, hedges on neutral to calcareous damp fertile clay & loam	(F, f, Pcs) Insects (flowers). Bird and mouse food (fruit)	Mainly England.
Hawthorn, common	30′ (9m)	CDEOPV	Very tolerant, all but very wet or acid soils	(A1, C, F, H, I, Ps, S, U, W) Flowers attract insects. Bird and mammal food (seeds), bird nest cover	Hardy, thorny. Important hedge shrub, scrub pioneer. Good natural regeneration.
Hawthorn, Midland	30′ (9m)	CDPSV	As native, mainly in woods on clays and heavy loams	As for common hawthorn	Native in SE, C Eng. In hedges, often indicates relict woodland. Hybrids with common hawthorn frequent.
Hazel	20′ (6m)	CSV	Tolerant, especially calcareous to slightly acid loams & clays, in woods	(A1, t, F, Plsx, S) Bird & mammal food (nuts) & insect habitat	Mainly lowlands but also upland oakwoods. Important traditional coppice species (wattles etc). Edible nut.
Holly[2]	50′ (15m) (−)	CDEOPSV	Dry soil, deep soil over chalk	(A1, F, H, Pcs, S, U, W) Bird food (berries), nests; deer browse	Woodland subcanopy tree useful in hedges and shelterbelts. Holly blue butterfly food plant. Plant May or Sept only, if bare rooted.
Hornbeam	70′ (20m) (−)	CEFPSV	Tolerant but best on silt, gravel over heavy subsoil	(A2, C, E, f, Ps, S, t, U) Bird food (fruit)	Mainly SE lowland mixed woods, often coppiced.
Lime, common	135′ (40m)	P	(W) Fertile soils, clay	(t, U, W) Insects (flowers), bird food and nests	Doubtfully native hybrid, widely planted. Creates honey-dew (drip). Often lopped or pollarded in towns.
Lime, large-leaved	100′ (30m)	P	(W) Fertile soils, clay	(E, Psx, S, t, U, W) As for common lime	Rare, local native. Good for parks. Creates honey-dew.
Lime, small-leaved	60′ (18m)	CPS	(W) Fertile soils, clay	(A2, E, Psx, S, t, U, W) As for common lime	Native in Eng, Wales. Important constituent of mixed woods. Creates honey-dew.

Name	Size & growth	Tolerance	Preferred conditions	Management notes	Comments
Maple, field	36' (10m)	CPSV	Any soil, esp calcareous clays & loams. Very hardy	(A2, C, f, Ps, S, U, W) Flowers for insects, mammal food (seeds)	Common coppiced tree in England. Best autumn colour on heavy soil.
Oak, pedunculate	100' (30m) (−)	COV	(LTW) Best on well-aerated deep fertile loams, but very tolerant	(A25, E, Ps, T, U) Very good gen wildlife value. Avoid shallow, poorly drained or peaty soils, exposure, frost hollows	Important for timber; traditionally for coppice, tanbark. Scrubby on sandy soils.
Oak, sessile	100' (30m) (−)	COV	(LTW) As for pedunculate oak, but tolerates poorer more acid soils & more shade and frost	(A2, C, Ps, T) As for pedunculate oak	As for pedunculate oak. Less subject to insect, mildew attack and keeps better form as forest tree.
Pear, wild	30' (9m)	DV	(L) Wood margins, hedges, parks; shelter	(F, Psx, W) Avoid very acid soils	Doubtfully native, mainly S, as isolated trees and thickets of suckers. Edible fruit[4].
Poplar, black	100' (30m)	D	River and stream flood-plains rather than woods	(Px) Good gen wildlife value	Native relic, E Anglia and Midlands, now mainly displaced by quick-growing hybrids[1].
Poplar, grey	100' (30m) (+)	CDOPSV	Tolerant but best on light loam	(A5, I, Px, S, t) Good gen wildlife value	Hybrid between white poplar and aspen. Very free suckering, good for windbreaks[1].
Poplar, white	65' (20m) (+)	DOPV	Damp or dry, on clay or over sand, gravel, chalk	(C, Px, S)	Doubtfully native. Good for coastal windbreaks. Drops branches[1].
Privet[2]	10' (3m)	V	Tolerant, esp calcareous loams & clays in lowland wood & scrub	(I, Pcs, S) Some insects. Bird food (fruit)	Native mainly S. Semi-evergreen. Good game cover but can spread to form thick tangles.
Rose, dog	10' (3m)	CEOV	Lowland hedges, woodland fringe on calcareous to neutral clays, loams	(F, Pcsx) Food for birds (fruit), insects (flowers)	Root stocks for rose cultivars. Hips for jam.
Rowan	30' (9m)	DEOPV	(L) Esp lighter soils, sandy, peat, well-drained acid loams	(A1, C, F, Ps, S, U) Bird & insect food (fruit). Avoid lime	Useful for streets, grass verges. Edible berries (jam). Tolerates exposed sites. Susceptible to browsing.
Service tree, wild	70' (22m)	CS	Heavy soils in lowland woods	(E, Psx, U) Insects (flowers), bird food (fruit)	Local but widespread S, Midlands. Indicates ancient woodland on native sites. Edible fruit (jam).

Name	Height	Code	Wildlife value	Soil	Notes
Spindle	25' (7.5m)	C	(F, f, Ps, U) Flowers attract insects. Bird food (fruit)	Calcareous to neutral loams, in lowland woods	Mainly S. Attractive shrub. Alternate host for bean aphis (*Aphis fabae*).
Wayfaring tree	20' (6m)	CI	(F, f, I, Pcs) Insects (flowers), bird food (fruit)	Lowland wood, scrub and hedges on calcareous loam	Mainly SE. Invasive on deserted downland pasture.
Whitebeam	40' (12m)	CPS	(A2, C, F, Ps, S, U) Bird & insect food (fruit)	Chalk or limestone	Native mainly S but widely planted.
Willow, bay[5]	40' (12m) (+)	CDOP	(A4, I, Pc) Moth and butterfly food, bird nesting, roe & fallow deer fraying stocks	Fertile loam, fen peat, clay, deep acid soils	Stands flooding, helps stabilise banks. Coppice useful for wattles.
Willow, crack[5]	80' (25m) (+)	CDOP	(A4, I, Pc, S) As for bay willow	Fertile loam, deep acid soils, river banks	As for bay willow. Older trees often shed limbs.
Willow, goat[6]	30' (10m) (+)	CDOPV	(A2, I, Pc, S, W) As for bay willow	As for bay willow, and dry soil over sand or gravel	As for bay willow. Competes, so limit shelter use to waterlogged peat or exposed coastal areas.
Willow, grey[6]	30' (10m) (+)	CDOP	(A3, I, Pc) As for bay willow	Wet sites, esp rather acid in lowland woods	As for bay willow. Major fen carr species.
Willow, osier[6]	20' (6m) (+)	CDOP	(Pc, S) As for bay willow	Fertile loam or peat, deep acid soils	As for bay willow. Cultivars grown for basketry, wattles.
Willow, white[5]	80' (25m)	CDEOP	(Pc, S) As for bay willow	As for bay willow	As for bay willow. Many cultivars, incl cricket bat willow. Often pollarded.

Grants

Woodland Grant Scheme

The Woodland Grant Scheme was introduced in April 1988, and succeeds both the Forestry Grant Scheme and the Broadleaved Woodland Grant Scheme which were closed to new applications in March 1988. Obligations to existing participants under these and the Dedication Schemes, also now closed, will be fulfilled.

The Woodland Grant Scheme offers grants for new planting and restocking, with a single scale of grants for broadleaves, whether planted on their own or in mixture. There is also a supplement of £200 per hectare for planting on existing arable or improved grassland where a Farm Woodland Scheme annual payment (see below) is not being claimed.

Applications can be made by the owner(s) of the land, or by a tenant, provided that all the parties concerned are joined in the application.

Grants are available for individual areas of 0.25 hectares and over. It is not acceptable for individual areas of less than 0.25 hectares to be aggregated except where, with the Forestry Commission's agreement, restocking is to be undertaken by planting very small groups of trees with the object of infilling an uneven-aged wood.

The objectives of the Woodland Grant Scheme are as follows:

a   to encourage timber production

b   to provide jobs in and increase the economic potential of rural areas with declining agricultural employment and few alternative sources of economic activity

c   to provide an alternative to agricultural production and thereby assist in the reduction of agricultural surpluses

d   to enhance the landscape, to create new wildlife habitats and to provide for recreation and sporting uses in the longer term

e   to encourage the conservation and regeneration of existing forests and woodlands

In order to comply with statutory requirements, the production of utilisable timber must be one of the objectives, although it will not necessarily be the principal objective. The scheme applies to the establishment of conifer, broadleaved and mixed woodlands whether by means of planting or by natural regeneration.

There are various provisions which applicants must observe relating to the broadleaved component of existing woods, ancient woodland sites, native pinewood sites, ancient monuments and other matters. Planting consisting of mainly one species of conifer must incorporate other conifers or broadleaves, preferably through the retention of existing trees.

The planting of broadleaves where sites are suitable, either on their own or in mixture with conifers, is encouraged by attracting a higher rate of grant. Grants are paid at the appropriate rates in proportion to the area occupied by conifers and broadleaves respectively. Rates of grant are subject to review. The current rates for planting, restocking and natural regeneration are shown below.

Area approved for planting or regeneration (ha)	RATE OF GRANT	
	Conifer (£ per ha)	Broadleaved (£ per ha)
0.25–0.9	1005	1575
1.0 –2.9	880	1375
3.0 –9.9	795	1175
10 and over	615	975

The grant band is determined by the total area of planting, restocking or natural regeneration covered by the application. The grants are paid in instalments. Existing natural regeneration under 20 years of age or neglected woodlands under 20 years of age which have not previously been grant aided may qualify for partial grant.

The maximum tree spacings normally acceptable are 2.1m for conifers and 3m for broadleaves.

Applicants will be required to work in accordance with a five year Plan of Operations approved by the Forestry Commission.

Further details and application forms are available from the local Forestry Commission Conservancy Office (see p163).

Farm Woodland Scheme

This scheme is due to come into force during autumn 1988, and will be administered by the Forestry Commission together with the Ministry of Agriculture, Fisheries and Food.

The aims of the proposed scheme are

a   to divert land from agricultural production and assist the reduction of agricultural surpluses;

b   to enhance the landscape, create new wildlife habitats, encourage recreational use, including sport, and expand tourist interest;

c   to contribute to supporting farm income and rural employment;

d to encourage greater interest in timber production from farms and, in the longer term, to contribute to the nation's timber requirements.

Farmers who plant trees on land previously in agricultural production will be eligible for annual payments, the first of which will be made one year after planting and which will continue for 20 to 40 years, depending on the choice of species. The continuing annual payments will be in addition to one–off planting grants administered by the Forestry Commission as at present, and will help bridge the gap between planting and first income, eg from thinning.

The Farm Woodland Scheme is for an initial period of three years, with an overall planting target, and limit, of 36,000 hectares over that period. The Scheme is aimed primarily at arable land and grassland improved within the last 10 years, to help ensure that savings in agricultural support costs are achieved, and to avoid the planting of marginal land and other areas of possible conservation value.

The minimum area of planting per holding will be 3 hectares (1 hectare in Northern Ireland, where holdings are smaller), with a maximum of 40 hectares. Each block of woodland must be a minimum of 1 hectare, to ensure that real reductions in surplus production are achieved.

The rates of annual payment will vary according to land category, reflecting existing productivity.

1. Arable land and grassland improved within the last 10 years: a) Lowlands (ie non LFA): £190 per hectare per year b) Less Favoured Areas (LFA): £150 per hectare per year in disadvantaged areas, and £100 per hectare per year in severely disadvantaged areas

2. Unimproved land in Less Favoured Areas: £30 per hectare per year

The basic payment period will be 20 years. Woodland containing more that 50% broadleaves will attract payments for 30 years, and crops comprising only oak and beech for 40 years. The planting of traditional coppice stands will be eligible for payments for 10 years.

The rates of aid will be reviewed in 1991.

MINISTRY OF AGRICULTURE, FISHERIES AND FOOD

Grants for shelter belts, trees to shade stock, hedgerow trees and hedges may be available for established agricultural and horticultural businesses. The rules for eligibility of the business are based on the hours per annum worked on the holding.

Grants for shelter belts or shelter hedges to protect crops or livestock can include drainage work to aid establishment, preparatory cultivations and treatments, rabbit guards, temporary fencing, plants and

weeding. The costs of replacement tree plantings and weeding in the first three years after planting are also eligible.

The grants for trees for shading stock are for trees planted singly, and include the cost of the trees, planting and protection.

Eligible hedging work includes planting new hedges, replanting gappy hedges, hedge laying and temporary protective fencing. Routine maintenance is not included.

Grants are paid as a percentage of the total cost of the work, which can either be the 'actual costs' incurred, or based on 'standard costs' which are set by the ministry for all the various operations involved.

All work must be done to a specified standard.

Current rates of grant are shown below. 'Less Favoured Areas' (LFA), which have natural limitations of climate, soil, altitude etc, receive a higher rate of grant.

	Standard (%)	LFA (%)
Hedges (including hedgerow trees)	30	60
Shelterbelts, with 50% or more broadleaved	30	60
Other shelterbelts	15	60

Further details are available from your local MAFF office.

Farm Woodland Scheme

See above.

COUNTRYSIDE COMMISSION FOR ENGLAND AND WALES

Landscape Conservation Grants

In conjunction with the local authority, the Countryside Commission can provide grant aid for planting amenity trees and small woods of 0.25 ha or less. Other woodlands larger than 0.25 ha may also qualify for grant aid if managed primarily for amenity or recreation. Grants can be up to 50% of the cost of the scheme, which can include protective fencing and other establishment work. Details are available from the Countryside Commission, or from the relevant local authority, which is normally the County Council.

LOCAL AUTHORITIES

Many County Councils and other local authorities can give various types of help with tree planting. This may include grants, free trees, or direct help with planting and maintenance. Many local authorities employ tree officers who can give advice both on their own schemes and on the other grant schemes listed in this appendix, as well as useful local advice.

TREE COUNCIL

The Tree Council can provide limited financial help to projects by local groups to carry out tree planting schemes. Applications for grant, which is limited to 50% of total tree-planting costs, should be made by 31st July for autumn plantings and by 31st December for spring plantings. Application forms are available from the Tree Council.

NATURE CONSERVANCY COUNCIL

The NCC may give grants for the planting and management of small woods of particular wildlife interest. For details contact your regional NCC office.

WOODLAND TRUST

The Woodland Trust operate a licensing scheme, under which agreements are made with landowners for the Trust to plant and manage areas of half hectare or more, using only native trees. The landowner is expected to contribute to the cost of any new fencing required. The agreement lasts 25 years, after which period the trees become the property of the owner unless the licence is extended by mutual agreement.

Uses for Coppice Produce

COPPICE SPECIES AND THEIR USES

The table below summarises the main coppice species and some of the products they furnished at least into the post-war period. Many of these uses are now obsolete, but not all are beyond recovery. Cleft chestnut fencing, and firewood and pulpwood (a relatively new use) are on the increase. The willows listed are not woodland species but are included for interest.

Coppice rotations vary according to the site and use. General ranges are as follows: A = up to 12 years (eg wands for baskets, faggoting, woven hurdles, pea sticks, bean poles, thatching spars), B = 12–15 years (eg poles for fencing, cleaving, small turnery, firewood), C = 15–30+ years (eg large turnery, large cleft products, firewood, pulpwood). Long rotations may require progressive thinning of shoots.

Species	Rotation	Uses
Alder	A	River protection work
	B	Brush heads, clog soles
Ash	B	Hurdles
	C	Horse jumps, tent pegs, baskets, barrel hoops & rims, scythe & tool handles, hay rakes
Birch	A	Besoms, garden rustic work, bobbins, spools, reels, darning mushrooms
	B	Brush heads
Chestnut, sweet	A	Walking sticks, hop poles
	B	Fencing spiles, rails, hurdles, ladder rungs
	C	Hop 'king' poles, stakes
Elm	C	Beetle heads, turnery, pit wood, firewood
Hazel	A	Wattle hurdles, thatching spars, sheep cribs, hedging stakes & binders, garden rustic work, pottery crate rods, many other traditional uses
	B	Firewood
Hornbeam	C	Firewood, pulpwood
Maple	B, C	Firewood
Oak	B, C	Fence posts, spale baskets, tanbark
Willow, osier	A	Wattle hurdles, river protection works. Cultivars for basketry
Willow, white	A	Gate hurdles, trug baskets (usually pollarded)
Mixed	A	Pea sticks, bean poles, stakes
	B, C	Firewood, pulpwood

DISPOSAL OF COPPICE PRODUCE

The table on the following pages indicates potential uses for coppice material. Some uses are limited to one or a few coppiced species, but in many cases almost any species will do. The companies listed under 'Potential customers' are by way of example. For outlets which may exist in your area, contact the Rural Development Commission and the Forestry Commission District Office. Further addresses and other details of marketing are given in Hart (1987). Always check on demand and current prices before deciding on whether and how best to market coppice material, and before starting the year's cutting programme.

Product	Specifications	Potential customers and comments	Price
Standing coppice	Sold as such to contractor	Contractor – but get 2 or 3 quotes. The cost/price will depend on his outlets. He will take what he wants and dispose of the rest as you direct	Depends on quality and quantity of poles, the proportion of useless wood, ease of access and distance to consumer Sweet chestnut in Kent and Sussex, for cleft fencing and hop poles: £750–1500/ha Sweet chestnut elsewhere, for stakes and pulpwood: £350–750/ha Mixed broadleaves for turnery and refinery poles: £200–300/ha Mixed broadleaves for stakes, pulpwood and fuelwood: £150–250/ha
Underwood, 6–10 year rotations	Hazel and other mixed broadleaves, for pea and bean sticks, hedge-stakes, wattle hurdles and thatching spars		Hazel may be worth £50–70/ha standing in parts of the south east, but elsewhere may not be saleable
Unsorted poles as cut	Piles in cords for loading onto lorry	Firewood or pulpwood merchant (for addresses of merchants see Hart, 1987)	Price depends on location and other factors Firewood: £10–15 per cord Pulpwood: £17–20 tonne, delivered to mill
Sorted poles: straight, more or less free from knots	3.5m × at least 150mm base diameter. Any species, but straight ash, birch, oak and chestnut preferred	Rake heads: Whelnetham Woodwork, Little Whelnetham, Bury St Edmunds, Suffolk	
	1m × at least 150mm diameter (ash) or 1.2m or more (ash and oak)	Local sawmills for planking and turning. Also specialised outlets such as sports goods and handles for small tools	Prices variable – see Hart for details
	5.5m × 110mm average diameter; birch, alder, sycamore, lime. Also 2m × 75mm minimum diameter	CWS Brush Factory, Wymondham, Norfolk	
	3m × 150mm butt × 50mm top diameter; birch, alder, sycamore, lime	Kent Woodware, Hawkhurst, Kent	£5 per tonne standing £25 per tonne delivered
	2.2m × 200mm; alder, ash, beech, birch, sycamore	L G Harris and Co Ltd, Stoke Prior, Bromsgrove, Worcs	£33 per tonne delivered
	3m × 150mm; oak, sweet chestnut, alder	For use as piles, for river and coastal work. Regional Water Authorities	
Fairly straight, knot-free small poles	Selected for scythe, rake and tool handles. 2m × 12–90mm, of any species except lime, hornbeam, maple	Whelnetham Woodwork Ltd, (address as above)	

	Small stakes, 1.2–1.8m × 12–40mm, preferably treated with preservative	Individual gardeners, allotment societies, garden centres	30–50p each
	Bean poles; 2m × 25mm approx, ash or hazel best, but any species will do	As above	£1–1.25 per bundles of 25
	For thatching broachers/spits; 660mm × 12–50mm, hazel only, in bundles of 30–35 rods for riving	Individual thatchers. NB. It is difficult to rive hazel more than 4–6 weeks after cutting, but keeping the wood damp by covering it extends its usefulness by several weeks	
	For thatching spars; 1.8m × 12–40mm rods, bundles of 20 for riving		
	Hedge stakes, about 1.5m long in bundles of 20	Individual hedgers	£2–3.00 per bundle
Tops	Pea sticks. Branching, fan-like 1.5m hazel or birch. Bundles of 20	Individual gardeners, allotment societies, garden centres	60–70p per bundle
	Horse jumps. Birch, 1.5–2m, in bundles of 20	Hunts and race courses	£1.50 delivered
	Besoms. A handle with bundle of birch tops about 600mm long	Garden centres	£3–4
	Faggots. Birch, hazel, lime, alder, hornbeam; 150mm, 20 to the bundle. Used for coastal defence and reclamation work	Regional Water Authorities	
Wood ash	From any wood; dry, sifted. Yield is about 5% of wood burnt	Local or national potters for glaze	£14 per 50kg

Ropes and Knots for Tree Work

Suitable ropes are available from suppliers of forestry and tree nursery equipment. The most popular types are of polypropylene, which are much stronger than ropes of natural fibre, and need no special care after use in wet weather. A 'Nelson' rope is a particular type of polypropylene rope. Natural fibre ropes of sisal or manila are still available. Ropes should have a breaking strain of at least six times the weight being lowered.

Nylon ropes are used for tree climbing only, and are not suitable for working ropes as they have too much stretch.

Note the following basic points, which are intended only as a supplement to practical training. See also pages 115 and 128.

Knots for tree work must be reliable when under great tension, yet must be easy to untie after being under tension.

Timber hitch or killock hitch

Used when towing or lifting a log. The killock hitch is more secure than the timber hitch.

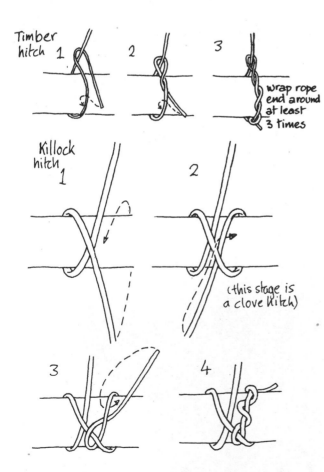

When hoisting, make a half hitch towards the upper end as shown.

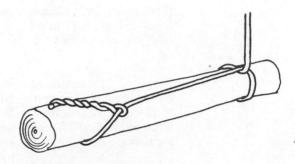

Weighted end or monkey knot

When throwing a rope over a high branch, it is safer to make a weighted end or monkey knot, rather than to try attaching a weight, which can come free. Even so, the procedure is still hazardous, as branches can be dislodged, and the rope itself is heavy. The operator should wear a safety helmet, and other people should move to safe positions.

The weighted end is tied as shown.

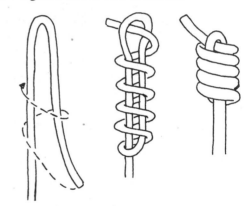

Alternatively, a monkey knot can be used, which should unwind as it passes over the branch.

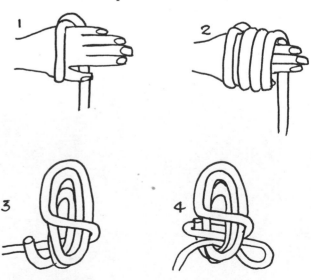

Running bowline

This is the best way of tying a slip knot in the end of a line, as it is simple and strong, and does not slip or jam. It is used for fastening a rope to control a tree in felling.

Pass the rope around the tree and over itself as shown. Then with a flip of the right wrist, make a loop through which the end is then passed as shown.

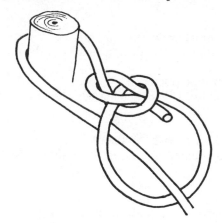

Carter's hitch

This can be used to give a mechanical advantage when pulling, where a winch and block are unavailable. When using artificial fibre ropes, clip a karabiner through the loop and run the hauling rope through the karabiner. This avoids rope to rope friction which could melt the rope.

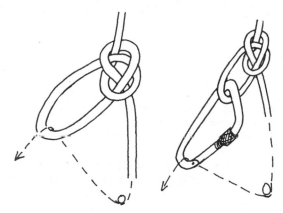

Bowline bend

Used to temporarily join two ropes, by making two interlocking bowlines. Although somewhat bulky, it is entirely reliable.

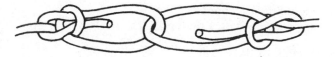

Relevant Organisations

Conservation and Amenity

Biological Records Centre
Monks Wood Experimental Station, Abbots Ripton, Cambridgeshire PE17 2LS   04873 381

Botanical Society of the British Isles
c/o Zoological Society of London, Regents Park, London NW1 4RY

British Ecological Society
Burlington House, Piccadilly, London W1V 0LQ

British Herpetological Society
20 Queensberry Place, London SW7 2EB 01 581 2657

British Trust for Conservation Volunteers
Headquarters: 36 St Mary's Street, Wallingford, Oxon OX10 0EU   0491 39766

North East: Springwell Conservation Centre, Springwell Road, Wrekenton, Gateshead, Tyne and Wear NE9 7AD   091 482 0111

North West: 40 Cannon Street, Preston, Lancashire PR1 3NT   0772 50286

Yorkshire and Humberside: Conservation Volunteers Training Centre, Balby Road, Doncaster, S. Yorkshire DN4 0RH   0302 859522

East Midlands: Conservation Volunteers Training Centre, Old Village School, Chestnut Grove, Burton Joyce, Nottingham NG14 5DZ   0602 313316

West Midlands: Conservation Centre, Firsby Road, Quinton, Birmingham B32 2QT   021 426 5588

Wales: The Conservation Centre, Forest Farm Road, Whitchurch, Cardiff CF4 7JH   0222 626660

East Anglia: Bayfordbury Estate, Hertford, Hertfordshire SG13 8LD   0992 583067

South West: The Old Estate Yard, Newton St Loe, Bath, Avon BA2 9BR   0225 872856

London: The London Ecology Centre, 80 York Way, London N1 9AG   01 278 4293

South: The Old Police Station, 3 London Road, Bagshot, Surrey GU19 5HW   0276 51186

Northern Ireland: The Pavilion, Cherryvale Playing Fields, Ravenshill Road, Belfast BT6 0BZ 0232 645169

British Trust for Ornithology
Beech Grove, Tring, Hertfordshire HP23 5NR 044 282 3461

Civic Trust
17 Carlton House Terrace, London SW1Y 5AW 01 930 0914

Community Service Volunteers
237 Pentonville Road, London N1 9NJ   01 278 6601

Conservation Society
12a Guildford Street, Chertsey, Surrey JT16 9BQ 09328 60975

Council for British Archaeology
112 Kennington Road, London SE11 6RE 01 582 0494

Council for Environmental Conservation (CoEnCo)
80 York Way, London N1 9AG   01 278 4736

Council for National Parks
45 Shelton Street, London WC2H 9HJ 01 240 3603/4

Council for the Protection of Rural England
4 Hobart Place, London SW1W 0HY   01 235 9481

Council for the Protection of Rural Wales
31 High Street, Welshpool, Powys SY21 7JP 0938 2525

Country Landowners' Association
16 Belgrave Square, London SW1X 8PQ 01 235 0511

Countryside Commission (England and Wales)
Headquarters: John Dower House, Crescent Place Cheltenham, Glos GL50 3RA   0242 21381

Countryside Commission for Scotland
Battleby, Redgorton, Perth PH1 3EW   0738 27921

Dartington Institute
Central Office, Shinners Bridge, Dartington, Totnes, Devon PQ9 6JE   0803 862271

Farming and Wildlife Advisory Group
National Agriculture Centre, Kenilworth, Warwickshire CV8 2RX   0203 696699

Field Studies Council
62 Wilson Street, London EC1V 2BU   01 247 4651

Friends of the Earth
377 City Road, London EC1   01 837 0731

The Game Conservancy
Burgate Manor, Fordingbridge, Hampshire SP6 1EF   0425 52381

Institute of Terrestrial Ecology
66 Hills Road, Cambridge CB2 1LA   0223 69745

Horticultural Trades Association
19 High Street, Theale, Reading   0734 303132

Landscape Institute
12 Carlton House Terrace, London SW1Y 5AH
01 839 4044

Mammal Society of the British Isles
Harvest House, 62 London Road, Reading
Berkshire 0734 861345

National Farmers' Union
Agriculture House, Knightsbridge, London
SW1X 7NJ 01 235 5077

National Farmers' Union of Scotland
17 Grosvenor Crescent, Edinburgh EH12 5EN
031 337 4333

The National Trust
36 Queen Anne's Gate, London SW1H 9AS
01 222 9251

National Trust for Scotland
5 Charlotte Square, Edinburgh EH2 4DU
031 225 5922

Nature Conservancy Council (Great Britain
headquarters and headquarters for England)
Northminster House, Peterborough PE1 1UA
0733 40345

Nature Conservancy Council (headquarters for
Scotland)
12 Hope Terrace, Edinburgh EH9 2AS
031 447 4784

Nature Conservancy Council (headquarters for
Wales)
Plas Penrhos, Penrhos Road, Bangor, Gwynedd
LL57 2LQ 0248 355141

The Open Spaces Society
25a Bell Street, Henley on Thames, Oxon
RG9 2BA 0491 573535

Ordnance Survey
Romsey Road, Maybush, Southampton SO9 4DH
0703 792000

The Ramblers' Association
1/5 Wandsworth Road, London SW8 2LJ
01 582 6826

Royal Society for Nature Conservation
The Green, Nettleham, Lincoln LN2 2NR
0522 752326

Royal Society for the Protection of Birds
The Lodge, Sandy, Beds SG19 2DL 0767 80551

Rural Development Commission (formerly
CoSIRA)
141 Castle Street, Salisbury, Wiltshire SP1 3TP
0722 336255

Scottish Civic Trust
24 George Square, Glasgow G2 1EF 041 221 1466

Scottish Conservation Projects Trust
Balallan House, 24 Allan Park, Stirling FK8 2QG
0786 79697

Scottish Landowners' Federation
18 Abercromby Place,
Edinburgh EH3 6TY 031 556 4466

Scottish Wildlife Trust
25 Johnston Terrace, Edinburgh EH1 2NH
031 226 4602

Town and Country Planning Association
17 Carlton House Terrace, London SW1Y 5AS
01 930 8903

Worldwide Fund for Nature
11-13 Ockford Road, Godalming, Surrey
04868 20551

Woodlands

Agricultural Training Board
Summit House, Glebe Way, West Wickham, Kent
BR4 0RF 01 777 9003

Arboricultural Association
Ampfield House, Ampfield, Romsey, Hants
0794 68717

Association of Professional Foresters
Brokerswood House, Brokerswood, near Westbury,
Wilts BA13 4EH 0373 822238

British Timber Merchants' Association (England and
Wales)
Ridgeway House, 6 Ridgeway Road, Long Ashton,
Bristol BS18 9EU 0272 394022

British Wood Preserving Association
150 Southampton Row, London WC1 01 837 8217

British Wood Pulp Association
Epworth House, 25 City Road, London EC1
01 628 5801

British Wood Turners Association
Secretary: R. Fraser, South Newton, Salisbury Wilts
SP2 0QL 0722 742211

Department of Agriculture for Northern Ireland:
Forest Service
Dundonald House, Upper Newtonards Road, Belfast BT4 3SB

Forestry Commission
Headquarters: 231 Corstorphine Road, Edinburgh
EH12 7AT 031 334 0303

Forest Research Station: Alice Holt Lodge,
Wrecclesham, Farnham, Surrey GU10 4LH
0420 22255

Northern Research Station: Roslin, Midlothian,
EH25 9SY 031 445 2176

Conservancy Offices:
North England: 1A Grosvenor Terrace, York
YO3 7BD   0904 20221

East England: Great Eastern House, Tenison Road,
Cambridge CB1 2DU   0223 314546

West England: 2nd Floor, Avon Fields House,
Somerdale, Keynsham BS18 2BD   02756 69481

North Scotland: 21 Church Street, Inverness
IV1 1EL   0463 232811

South Scotland: Greystone Park, 55/57 Moffat Road,
Dumfries, DG1 1NP   0387 69171

Mid Scotland: Portcullis House, 21 India Street,
Glasgow G2 4PL   041 248 3931

Wales: Victoria House, Victoria Terrace, Aber-
ystwyth, Dyfed SY23 2DQ   0970 612367

Forestry Commission Publications
Forest Research Station, Alice Holt Lodge (see
above) or Blair Adam Store, Clentry by Kelty, Fife
KY4 0JQ   0383 830311

Forestry Safety Council
231 Corstorphine Road, Edinburgh EH12 7AT

Forestry Training Council
231 Corstorphine Road, Edinburgh EH12 7AT
031 334 8083

Institute of Chartered Foresters
22 Walker   Street,   Edinburgh   EH3 7HR
031 225 2705

Royal Forestry Society of England, Wales and
Northern Ireland,
102 High Street, Tring, Hertfordshire HP23 4AH
0442 822028

Royal Scottish Forestry Society
10 Atholl   Crescent,   Edinburgh   EH3 8HA
031 229 8851

The Tree Council
Agriculture   House,   Knightsbridge,   London
SW1X 7NJ   01 235 2925

Timber Growers United Kingdom
Agriculture   House,   Knightsbridge,   London
SW1X 7NJ   01 235 2925

5 Dublin Street Lane South, Edinburgh EH1 3PX
031 557 0944

Woodland Trust
Autumn Park, Dysart Road, Grantham, Lincs
NG31 6LL   0476 74297

Specialist Suppliers

This is a brief list of suppliers and manufacturers of some items mentioned in the text. It is not a complete list, and these firms are not recommended in preference to any others.

General Forestry Equipment

Chieftain Forge Ltd
Burnside Road, Bathgate, West Lothian EH48 4PU
0506 52354
– machinery and hand tools, tree ties, guards and shelters

Honey Brothers Ltd
Peasmarsh, Guildford, Surrey GU3 1JR 0483 61362
– tree surgery and tree climbing equipment, chainsaws, protective clothing, tree ties and shelters, anti-transpirants, sundries

Hyett Adams Ltd
Oldends Lane, Stonehouse, Glos GL10 3SY
045382 2382
– hand tools, chainsaws and other machinery, protective clothing

Stanton Hope Ltd
11 Seax Court, Southfields, Laindon, Basildon, Essex SS15 6LY 0268 419141
– fencing and forestry hand tools, chainsaws, protective clothing, tree guards, ties and shelters, traps, chemicals and sundries

Chemical repellants

'AAprotect' – available from Stanton Hope Ltd (see above), and from ICI Plant Protection, Woolmead House West, Bear Lane, Farnham, Surrey GU9 7UB 0252 724525

'Dendrocol 17' – available from Berkshire Factors Ltd, Dale House, London Road, Sunningdale, Ascot, Berks SL5 0ER 0990 24101

Granular herbicide applicator

Stanton Hope Ltd (see above)

Red dye for liquid herbicides

Hortichem Ltd, 14 Edison Road, Churchfields Industrial Estate, Salisbury, Wiltshire SP2 7NU
0722 20133

Planting products

Acorn Planting Products Ltd
Church Lane, Surlingham, Norwich NR14 7DF
05088 279
– tree guards, shelters, mulching mats

A'dare Products Ltd
PO Box 1, Knighton, Powys LD7 1TN 0547 528908
– tree ties, guards, shelters, mulching mats

Corruplast Ltd
Correx House, Morelands Trading Estate, Bristol Rd, Gloucester GL1 5RZ 0452 301893
– tree shelters

Economic Forestry Group plc
Forestry House, Great Haseley, Oxfordshire OX9 7PG 08446 571
– tree ties, guards, shelters, loose mulches

English Woodlands Ltd
125 High Street, Uckfield, East Sussex TN22 1EG
0825 4235
– tree ties, guards, shelters, loose mulches

H S Jackson and Son (Fencing) Ltd
Stowting Common, Nr Ashford, Kent TN25 6BN
023 375 393
– tree ties, guards, shelters, loose mulches

J Toms Ltd
Wheeler Street, Headcorn, Ashford, Kent
0622 891111
– tree ties, guards, shelters, mulching mats

Tree Guards (Wire Netting) Bristol
Somersby Orchard, Greyfield, High Littleton, Bristol BS18 5YQ 0761 70489
– tree guards and shelters

Tubex Ltd
No 1, Tannery House, Tannery Lane, Send, Woking, Surrey 0483 225434
– tree ties, guards and shelters

Woodland Bark
The Old Coach House, Cuxwold, Caister, Lincoln LN7 6DA 0472 89 457
– loose mulches

Bibliography

Woodlands are the subject of a large volume of published source material. The list which follows includes those works to which reference has been made in the text, plus other useful sources.

Agate, E J (1983) *Footpaths* British Trust for Conservation Volunteers

Agate, E J (1986) *Fencing* British Trust for Conservation Volunteers

Agricultural Development and Advisory Service/Forestry Commission (1986) *Practical work in farm woods* Ministry of Agriculture, Fisheries and Food. Series of 8 leaflets

Agricultural Development and Advisory Service (1983) *Which Tree?* A farmers guide to tree selection. Ministry of Agriculture, Fisheries and Food

Aldhous, J R (1972) *Nursery Practice* HMSO Forestry Commission Bulletin 43

Allaby, M (1986) *The Woodland Trust book of British Woodlands* David and Charles

Anderson, M L (1961) *The Selection of Tree Species* Oliver and Boyd

Bean, W J (1970) *Trees and Shrubs Hardy in the British Isles* Butler and Tanner. Three volumes

Beckett, K and Beckett, G. (1979) *Planting Native Trees and Shrubs* Jarrold Colour Publications. Available from F & M Perring, B.S.B.I. Publications, 24 Glapthorn Road, Oundle, Peterborough PE8 4JQ.

Blatchford, O N (ed) 1978 *Forestry Practice* HMSO Forestry Commission Bulletin 14.

Blyth, J, Evans, J, Mutch, W E S and Sidwell, C (1987) *Farm Woodland Management* Farming Press Ltd

Brooks, A (revised 1983) *Hedging* British Trust for Conservation Volunteers

Brooks, A (revised 1981) *Waterways and Wetlands* British Trust for Conservation Volunteers

Bunce, R G H and Jeffers, J N R (1977) *Native Pinewoods of Scotland* Institute of Terrestrial Ecology, Proceedings of the Aviemore Symposium 1975

Bunce, R G H (1982) *A field key for classifying British woodland vegetation* Institute of Terrestrial Ecology

Caborn, J M (1965) *Shelterbelts and Windbreaks* Faber

Clouston, B (1977) *Landscape Design with Plants* Heinemann

Condry, W (1974) *Woodlands* Collins

Countryside Commission (1986) *Broadleaved Woodland* Countryside Commission Bibliography No 8

Crowe, S (1979) *The Landscape of Forests and Woods* HMSO Forestry Commission Booklet 44

Crowther, R E and Evans, J (1984) *Coppice* HMSO Forestry Commission Leaflet 83

Davies, R J (1987) *Trees and Weeds* Weed control for successful tree establishment HMSO Forestry Commission Handbook 2

Department of the Environment (1978) *Trees and Forestry* HMSO Joint Circular 36/78 from the Department of the Environment and 64/78 from the Welsh Office.

Edlin, H L (1970) *Trees, Woods and Man* Collins

Edlin, H L (1975) *Collins Guide to Tree Planting and Cultivation* Collins

Edlin, H L (1973) *Woodland Crafts of Britain* David and Charles

Evans, J (1984) *Silviculture of Broadleaved Woodland* HMSO Forestry Commission Bulletin 62

Edwards, P N (1983) *Timber Measurement A Field Guide* HMSO Forestry Commission Booklet 49

Forestry Commission *Catalogue of Publications* Published annually by the Forestry Commission. Includes details of all publications available from the Forestry Commission, Arboricultural Advisory and Information Service, and Forestry Safety Council. (Most titles which are included in the catalogue and referred to in this bibliography are listed here by author.)

Forestry Commission (1986) *Guidelines for the Management of Broadleaved Woodland* Forestry Commission

Forestry Commission (1986) *Control of Tree Felling* Forestry Commission

Forestry Safety Council *Forestry Industry Safety Guides* Forestry Safety Council. A series of leaflets on forestry hand tools, machinery and techniques, to be used as aids to practical training.

Game Conservancy *Woodlands for Pheasants* Game Conservancy Booklet 15

Gemmel, R P (1977) *Colonisation of Industrial Wasteland* Arnold

Godwin, H (1975) *The History of the British Flora* Cambridge University Press

Greig, J W and Strouts, R G (1983) *Honey Fungus* HMSO Arboricultural Leaflet 2 (available from the Forestry Commission)

Hart, C E (1987) *Private Woodlands: A Guide to British Timber Prices and Forestry Costings 1987* C E Hart, Chenies, Coleford, Gloucestershire GL16 8DT

Ivens, G W (ed) (1988) *UK Pesticide Guide 1988* CAB International and the British Crop Protection Council

Hillier, H G (1977) *Hillier's Manual of Trees and Shrubs* David and Charles

James, N D G (1966) *The Forester's Companion* Blackwell

James, N D G (1972) *The Arboriculturalist's Companion* Blackwell

Jobling, J and Pearce, M L (1977) *Free Growth of Oak* HMSO Forestry Commission Forest 113

Kirby, K J (1984) *Forestry operations and broadleaf woodland conservation* Nature Conservancy Council Focus on Nature Conservation No 8

Lambert, F (1957) *Tools and Devices for Coppice Crafts* Young Farmers' Club Booklet 31, republished 1977 by the Centre for Alternative Technology, Machynlleth, Powys

Leay, M J, Rowe, J and Young J D (1986) *Management Plans* A guide to their preparation and use. Countryside Commission

Liebscher, K (revised 1984) *Tree Nurseries* British Trust for Conservation Volunteers

Low, A J (1986) *Use of Broadleaved Species in Upland Forests* HMSO Forestry Commission Leaflet 88

McCullen and Webb (revised 1988) *A Manual on Urban Trees* An Foras Forbatha

Mathews, Russel (edit) (1987) *Conservation Monitoring and Management* Countryside Commission

Mercer, P C (1981) *The Treatment of Tree Wounds* HMSO Forestry Commission Arboriculture Research Note 28/81/PATH

Miles, R (1967) *Forestry in the English Landscape* Faber

Ministry of Agriculture, Fisheries and Food (1977) *Shelter Belts for Farmland* MAFF Leaflet 15

Ministry of Agriculture, Fisheries and Food (1988) *Revised Draft Code of Practice for the Agricultural and Commercial Horticultural Use of Pesticides* Ministry of Agriculture, Fisheries and Food

Mitchell, A F A (1974) *Field Guide to the Trees of Britain and Northern Europe* Collins

Morris, W G and Perring, F H (1974) *The British Oak, Its History and Natural History* Classey

Mummery, C and Tabor, R (1978) *Essex Woodlands in Trust* Essex Naturalists' Trust

Mummery, C, Tabor, R and Homewood, N (1976) *A Guide to the Techniques of Coppice Management* R Tabor and Essex Naturalists' Trust

Nature Conservancy Council (1981) *The conservation of butterflies* Nature Conservancy Council Booklet

Nature Conservancy Council (1982) *The conservation of lowland broadleaf woodland* Nature Conservancy Council Leaflet

Nature Conservancy Council (1982) *The conservation of semi-natural upland woodland* Nature Conservancy Council Leaflet

Nature Conservancy Council (1985) *Why plant native broadleaf trees?* Nature Conservancy Council

Neville Havins, P (1976) *The Forests of England* Robert Hale

Pepper, H W, Rowe, J J and Tee, L A (1985) *Individual Tree Protection* HMSO Arboricultural Leaflet 10 (available from the Forestry Commission)

Pepper, H W and Tee, L A (1986) *Forest Fencing* HMSO Forestry Commission Leaflet 87

Perring, F H and Walters, S M (1962) *Atlas of British Flora* Nelson

Peterken, G F (1974) 'A method for assessing woodland flora for conservation using indicator species' *Biological Conservation* 6: 4: 1974 239–45

Peterken, G F (1981) *Woodland Conservation and Management* Chapman and Hall

Pollard, E, Hooper, M D and Moore, N W (1974) *Hedges* Collins

Rackham, O (1975) *Hayley Wood – its history and ecology* Cambridgeshire and Isle of Ely Naturalists Trust Ltd

Rackham, O (1976) *Trees and woodland in the British landscape* Dent

Rackham, O (1980) *Ancient Woodland* Arnold

Ratcliffe, D (1977) *A Nature Conservation Review* Cambridge University Press

Rose, F and Harding, P T (1978) *Pasture-Woodlands in Lowland Britain and their Importance for the Conservation of the Epiphytes and Invertebrates Associated with Old Trees* Nature Conservancy Council and Institute of Terrestrial Ecology

Rowe, J J (1973) *Grey Squirrel Control* HMSO Forestry Commission Leaflet 56

Rowe, J J (1976) *Badger Gates* HMSO Forestry Commission Leaflet 68

Rushforth, Keith (1987) *Hillier Book of Tree Planting and Management* David and Charles

Sale, J S P, Tabbush, P M and Lane, P B (1986) *The Use of Herbicides in the Forest* Forestry Commission

Smart, N and Andrews, J (1985) *Birds and Broadleaves Handbook* Royal Society for Protection of Birds

Springthorpe, G D and Myhill, N G (ed) (1985) *Wildlife Rangers Handbook* Forestry Commission

Stebbings, Bob and Walshe, Sheila (1985) *Bat Boxes: A Guide to their History, Function, Construction and Use in the Conservation of Bats* Flora and Fauna Preservation Society

Steven, H M and Carlisle, A (1959) *The Native Pinewoods of Scotland* Oliver and Boyd

Stubbs, A E (1972) *Wildlife Conservation and Dead Wood* Devon Trust for Nature Conservation

Sussex Farming and Wildlife Advisory Group (1987) *East Sussex Demonstration Woodland* British Trust for Conservation Volunteers

Task Force Trees (1988) *Task Force Trees Action Pack* Countryside Commission

Tansley, A G (1939) *The British Isles and their Vegetation* Cambridge University Press

Warren, A and Goldsmith, F B (1974) *Conservation in Practice* John Wiley

Wilson, K W (1981) *Removal of Tree Stumps* HMSO Arboricultural Leaflet 7 (available from the Forestry Commission)

Woodland Trust (1986) *Community woodland resource pack* Woodland Trust

RELEVANT PERIODICALS

Arboricultural Journal
Forestry
Forestry and British Timber
Grower
Horticulture Week
Quarterly Journal of Forestry
Scottish Forestry
Timber Grower

Glossary

This is a list of specialist words that have been used in this handbook.

Afforestation The planting of trees on previously unwooded land.

Ancient woodland Woodland that has existed continuously on the site at least since 1600 AD.

Artificial woodland Woodland which is not semi-natural, eg a recent plantation.

Ball-rooted tree Tree transplanted with the earth around its roots intact.

Bare-rooted tree Tree lifted for transplanting without earth around its roots.

Bark Outer protective tissue of a woody stem.

Bast Thin layer of tissue between the bark and the cambium, which carries leaf-sap downwards to the roots.

Beating up Replacing failures after tree planting, also known as filling up.

Bole The stem or trunk of a tree.

Bolling The permanent trunk of a pollard.

Brash Small branches trimmed from the sides and top of a main stem. Also known as lop and top and as slash. (v) To cut away the side branches of conifers to about 6′ (2m) to improve access or for fire protection.

Bryophytes Mosses and liverworts.

Butt Bottom end (root end) of a log or pole.

Buttress Reinforcing projection near the base of the tree. Also known as a spur.

Callus Healing tissue formed by the cambium which grows out over a wound.

Cambium A layer of growth cells which form bast to the outside and wood on the inside.

Canopy The uppermost layer of woodland structure. Usually from 25′–100′ (8m–30m) above ground. Contains the standard, emergent and understorey trees.

Carr Fen scrub.

Chase A privately owned tract of land equivalent to a Forest.

Clone A tree or strain of trees propagated vegetatively from a single individual.

Collar The part of the stem around ground level where shoot meets root. Usually shown by a soil mark.

Coppice Broadleaved wood which is cut over at regular intervals to produce a number of shoots from each stool. Also known as copse. (v) To cut the shoots from a stool so that more will regrow.

Cord A volume of stacked logs, usually 8′ × 4′ × 4′ (2.4m × 1.2m × 1.2m), but varying in different districts. (v) To cut wood to cord lengths and to stack it in cords.

Coupe A coppice plot cut on a regular basis or a clear-felled area in a plantation. Also known as a panel.

Covert A small wood, usually in the midst of farmland, managed primarily for game.

Crown The spreading branches and foliage of a tree.

Crown lifting Removal of the lower branches of a tree, leaving the upper crown untouched.

Crown reduction Pruning back the crown to its main branches whilst maintaining its overall shape. Also known as drop-crotching.

Cutting A small section of young shoot or root used to propagate a new plant.

Danger zone The area within two tree lengths, in any direction, of a tree being felled.

Drift Cut coppice material or brash laid in rows for sorting or disposal.

Drip line The ground below the outermost branches of a tree's crown, where most of its feeding roots are concentrated.

Ecology The study of how living things relate to each other and to their environment.

Emergent tree A tree the crown of which overtops the standards in the woodlnd canopy.

Epiphyte A plant growing on another without being parasitic.

Feathered tree A young tree well furnished with branches to near ground level.

Felling cut The cut made from the back of the stem which fells the tree. Also known as the back cut.

Field layer That part of the woodland structure containing herbaceous plants and undershrubs. Usually several inches to several feet (about 100mm to a couple of metres) above ground level.

Flush An area of ground receiving nutrient-rich runoff. (v) The first spurt of growth after winter dormancy when the buds break.

Forest A tract of land, not necessarily wooded, controlled by the crown – originally for large game – and administered according to special rules. An area in which such rules once applied.

Ground layer That part of the woodland structure, up to several inches (about 100mm) above ground, containing bryophytes and the seedlings of plants of the higher layers.

Habitat The normal abode of a plant or animal, the recognisable area or environment in which an organism normally lives.

Hardwood Any broadleaved (deciduous) tree, irrespective of the actual hardness of its wood.

Heartwood The inner wood of larger branches and trunks which no longer carries sap. Heartwood is prone to decay in living trees but after felling it usually becomes more durable than sapwood.

High forest Woodland dominated by full-grown trees suitable for timber.

Hinge A portion of stem which is left uncut during felling to help control the timing and direction of fall. Also known as a hold.

Hoppus foot Obsolete unit of measurement for the cubic contents of round timber, equal to 0.036 cubic metre.

Kerf The cut made by a saw.

Layer A side shoot which roots to form a new but connected plant where it touches the ground. (v) To bend over and peg down a shoot so that it will take root.

Laying in Cutting away the buttresses of a tree before felling. Also known as rounding up.

Leader The main top shoot of a tree.

Node A swelling on a shoot which marks the position of a resting bud.

Park Originally, land enclosed for the keeping of semi-wild animals. Later, an area enclosed for amenity.

Pasture-woodland Woodland in which grazing or browsing has been the dominant influence.

Plantation An area of woodland where most of the trees have been planted for timber.

pH A measure of acidity and alkalinity on a scale from 0 to 14.0, pH 7 is neutral, less than 7 is acid and more than 7 is alkaline. In soils a pH of 4.5 and below is regarded as extremely acid, pH 6.6–7.3 is neutral and over 9 is very strongly alkaline.

Pole stage Stage in which the young tree resembles a pole – between the thicket stage and maturity.

Pollard A tree which is cut at 6'–12' (2m–4m) above ground level, then allowed to grow again to produce a crop of branches. (v) To cut the branches from such a tree so that they will regrow.

Primary woodland Woodland that has had a continuous cover of native trees throughout its history.

Prog A stout forked pole used for pushing and levering trees during felling and conversion.

Provenance The place of origin of a tree stock, which remains the same no matter where later generations of the tree are raised.

Pruning Cutting branches from a standing tree. Done to manage the crown shape of amenity trees, remove diseased branches or to produce knot-free wood in timber trees.

Recent woodland Woodland which has grown up since the year 1600.

Rotation Length of time between successive fellings of a plantation or cuttings of a coppice plot.

Sapwood Wood which carries sap. This may be all the wood in a young stem or the outermost layer in an older, larger tree or branch. Sapwood resists decay when alive, but is not very durable as timber.

Screefing Scraping away surface vegetation prior to planting to reduce competition from weeds.

Scrub In ecology, an area dominated by shrubs, possibly as a stage in succession to high forest. In forestry, an area of unproductive woodland.

Secondary woodland Woodland growing on a site that has been cleared at some time.

Semi-natural woodland On ancient sites, woods made up mainly of native species growing where their presence is apparently natural and which have not obviously been planted. On recent sites, all stands that have originated mainly by natural regeneration.

Sett A large unrooted cutting, usually of willow or poplar.

Shake Cracking of timber due to stresses of growth, impact of felling or drying.

Shredding A form of pollarding obsolete in the UK but common on the continent, in which the side branches are periodically cut off.

Shrub layer That part of the woodland structure, from about 6'–15' (2m–4.5m) above ground containing shrubs and young growth of canopy trees.

Singling Cutting out all but one stem on a coppice stool so that it will grow into a timber tree.

Sink A wedge shaped cut made in the front of a tree to control the direction of fall when felling. Also known as a bird's-mouth.

Snedding The removal of branches from a felled tree.

Softwood The timber of any coniferous tree, irrespective of the actual hardness of the wood.

Stag-heading Die-back of the crown of old trees, most commonly of oaks, leaving bare branches.

Standard A tree suitable for timber. A transplanted tree with 6' (1.8m) or more clear stem. In woodland structure a tree forming the dominant layer of the canopy.

Stem The living trunk of a shrub or tree.

Stool The stump or cut base of a shrub or tree from which new shoots grow.

Stooling A method of propagating coppice in which regrowth from stools is earthed over to root and later cut away for transplanting.

Structure The pattern of woodland habitat elements such as the height and density of crowns, position and size of glades and shape and orientation of margins.

Succession The process by which one community of plants gives way to another in a series from coloniser to climax.

Sucker A young tree arising from the roots of an older tree.

Thicket stage Stage after planting and before the pole stage when young trees have grown up enough to form a dense thicket.

Thinning Removal of selected trees from a crop to give the remainder more growing space. A tree so removed.

Timber Tree trunk suitable for making beams or sawing into planks; a tree with such a trunk; the use made of such a trunk.

Transplant Tree moved from one place to another to continue its growth.

Undercut Cut made in the front of a tree to reduce the chance of splitting when felling.

Understorey tree A tree the crown of which is below that of the dominant trees in the canopy.

Underwood Wood, whether growing or cut, of coppice poles, young suckers or (less often) pollard poles.

Whip A transplant under about 3' (1m) high. Also a weak spindly stem in a plantation.

Wolf A large, quick-growing but coarsely and poorly formed tree of low timber quality.

Wood The part of the stem, inside the cambium, which supports the tree, carries water to the crown and stores reserves of food over the winter. Also poles and branches of smaller diameter than timber.

Index